CULTURE AND THERAPY

CULTURE AND THERAPY
An Integrative Approach

Jefferson M. Fish

JASON ARONSON INC.
Northvale, New Jersey
London

Production Editor: Judith D. Cohen

This book was set in 10 point Garamond by TechType of Upper Saddle River, New Jersey, and printed and bound by Book-mart Press of North Bergen, New Jersey.

Library of Congress Cataloging-in-Publication Data

Fish, Jefferson M.
    Culture and therapy : an integrative approach / Jefferson M. Fish.
      p. cm.
    Includes bibliographical references and index.
    ISBN 1-56821-545-2 (alk. paper)
    1. Eclectic psychotherapy. 2. Psychotherapy—Philosophy.
  3. Psychotherapy—Social aspects. I. Title.
RC489.E24F57 1996
616.89'14—dc20   95-41695

Manufactured in the United States of America. Jason Aronson Inc. offers books and cassettes. For information and catalog write to Jason Aronson Inc., 230 Livingston Street, Northvale, New Jersey 07647.

To Dolores and Krekamey, my microculture

Contents

Contents

Preface and Acknowledgments

This book attempts to understand therapy in its sociocultural context and offers encouragement to therapists in evolving their own theoretical orientation and personal direction. It suggests that in doing so it is useful to adopt an outlook of pragmatic iconoclasm.

Throughout the country, therapists (and everyone else) are confronted by a baffling cultural diversity. *Culture and Therapy* aims at helping clinicians develop a sociocultural perspective so they can detect their own inappropriate assumptions, learn from their clients, and thus make their skills and knowledge useful to people from unfamiliar backgrounds. In particular, this book views social and cultural factors, including the interactionally magnified effects of unexpected events, as important influences on behavior. It attempts to integrate a discussion of these influences with relevant principles of anthropology and sociology.

The perspective of the book is the binocular vision of the therapist as subject and object, viewing oneself both as an individual and as a representative of one's culture (or profession or other social group), as both an insider in one's culture and an outsider in another culture, as both the recipient of environmental influences and an influencer of the environment, as both the therapist and client of one's own self-therapy, and as both teacher and student, supervisor and therapist, in evolving one's own theoretical orientation.

What happens when a therapist adopts this binocular perspective? One sees things differently, challenges assumptions, and develops in unexpected ways both individually and professionally.

In offering a vision of the therapist as a pragmatic iconoclast, this book suggests that it is useful to challenge ideas and assumptions to see what works, try out new approaches and evaluate their effects, and continually evolve—dropping even new ideas for newer ones if they work better. Some therapists have always developed in this way; the rewards of personal growth and professional competence have often outweighed the penalties for independent thinking. But as American society has become more conformist, so have American therapists. This book offers guidance in moving in a different direction.

The problem I confronted was how to communicate this message. My solution was to use myself as both subject and object—an example of a therapist whose theoretical evolution could be discussed over a period of more than three decades. This discussion is both subjective (Part I consists of a theoretical autobiography, along with a summary of relevant principles) and objective (Parts II, III, and IV integrate unpublished and published writings about culture and therapy from the past two decades).

Organizing the book in this way also allows me not only to

present ideas about therapy and perspectives on alternative approaches, but to do so in such a way that subjective elements from the theoretical autobiography (how certain experiences led to certain ideas) can be juxtaposed with their objective counterparts (the presentation of specific ideas about theory and practice) in Parts II, III, and IV. In addition, within the theoretical autobiography it is possible to turn around theoretical concepts to see how they can explain the evolution of an orientation. This reversal of perspective also offers an opportunity to look at the effects of applying an evolving approach to changing one's own behavior (self-therapy).

This organization of the book promotes the view of a theoretical orientation as a process in evolution rather than as a crystalline structure frozen in time. For this reason, events in the theoretical autobiography are presented in chronological order. I have usually hesitated to label my orientation because I haven't wanted to be committed to the implications of that label as my thinking continues to evolve. For example, in teaching therapy courses I have told my students, "I am going to present what I believe now, and the theoretical and empirical justification for those beliefs. But I have believed other things in the past with equal conviction; and if the best predictor of future behavior is past behavior, I am likely to believe something different—which I cannot now anticipate—in the near or distant future." Nevertheless, when pushed to label my evolving orientation, I have settled for describing it as "sociocultural interactional cognitive environmental determinism"—or, more briefly, "sociocultural."

Being specific about content goes against the grain of viewing an orientation as an evolving process, but even with these reservations I offer the following thoughts in the hope that they may be of use to some readers. In terms of the current jargon, some therapists might view the approach in this book as a "limited eclecticism" that integrates the following elements:

1. Individual behavior is understood in terms of concepts from social learning theory and general psychology, especially social psychology.
2. At the interactional level, behavior is understood in terms of concepts from systems theory, anthropology, and sociology.
3. Therapeutic interventions are designed for rapid change and are mainly strategic, systemic, behavioral, and cognitive—technical eclecticism is advocated.

In many ways, *Culture and Therapy* is the product of my own evolution. I have devoted my career to training clinical psychologists and have been acutely aware of the tension between training graduate students as researchers and academicians—challenging assumptions and synthesizing disparate ideas—and as professionals—accepting the mental health establishment's official version of reality and sticking to conventional practice (as medicine has done, from leeches to lobotomies). As the profession of therapy has become increasingly bureaucratized, there are more accrediting agencies, subspecializations, third-party payers, codes of conduct, laws, and lawsuits, all encouraging conformity in thought and deed. While the history of therapy is one of considerable imagination and inventiveness, a participant nowadays sees creative intellectual activity being squeezed out of clinical practice. Therapists tell clients to take risks for their personal growth, while avoiding risks for their own professional growth. It is bizarre.

This book is an invitation for therapists to join me on an intellectual journey. I hope that the book will give aid and comfort to those therapists who want to resist the social and cultural pressures to conform while opening themselves to a larger sociocultural reality, and who want to undertake their own intellectual journey—to learn and grow and change throughout their careers, to retain intellectual rigor while fostering their own creativity, and to do so while promoting the welfare of their clients.

In writing this book I have minimized the use of jargon and tried to explain complex concepts clearly, so as to make the ideas accessible to people with a variety of backgrounds. In addition, since the concepts in the book are drawn from a wide range of sources in the social sciences, I could not have expected readers to be familiar with all of them and therefore have chosen to explain things as I go along. The result is, however, that variations in subject matter occasionally produce variability in diction.

I should also mention the way I've handled race, gender, and nationality terminology. There is no single correct solution at the present moment, and since culture changes over time even the present choices may look less desirable in the future. Nevertheless, for what it's worth, this is why I've done what I've done.

Since races as conceived by Americans do not exist, I have refused to use terms like *Negro* and *Caucasian,* so as to avoid perpetuating misconceptions. I have similarly decided not to capitalize *black* or *white* to avoid the possible implication that they refer to biological entities. (I am aware that we use words like *unicorn* to refer to nonexistent species, but the potential for misunderstanding is not so great because Americans know they are imaginary.) When referring to social groups, as opposed to purported races, I have generally used terms like *African American, European American,* or others with cultural rather than biological content. In a similar manner, I have attempted to update gender usage in parts written when the cultural norms for personal pronouns were different. Finally, despite misgivings, I have used the word *American* to refer to people from the United States of America, since that is its customary meaning here—although inhabitants of other parts of the New World also regard themselves as Americans.

From a sociocultural perspective, the influences that contributed to this book are more numerous than I can mention or am even aware of. A number of people and organizations contributed in diverse and important ways that I am particularly grateful for, and I would like to acknowledge them explicitly. Since such a list can never be complete, I also want to thank those friends and colleagues whose names do not appear.

A research leave from St. John's University provided me with the necessary writing time; and the university's Word Processing Center and Faculty Support Center were of significant assistance at several points along the way.

Among those who were most helpful, I particularly want to thank Wandajune Bishop, Michael Engber, Robert Ghiradella, Theodore D. Kemper, Christopher Monte, Dolores Newton, and Michael Rohrbaugh. I am grateful for their time and suggestions; the book is a better one for their help; its shortcomings remain my responsibility.

I owe a special debt of gratitude to my wife, Dolores Newton, who has been the most important intellectual (as well as emotional) influence on my adult life, and without whom I might never have become immersed in social and cultural issues.

Finally, I would like to thank my Brazilian friends and colleagues for the opportunity to become a part of their world. I have tried several times to make a list of their names, but it rapidly grows to absurd proportions. Instead of making such a list, I will personally give them each an *abraço* the next time I go to Brazil. I will limit myself here to acknowledging Saulo Monte Serrat, who more than anyone else made my experience as a visiting professor a success, and who remains my model of a good citizen.

PART I

THE EVOLUTION OF AN ORIENTATION

Introduction

The development of a therapist's orientation can be seen as a case study of the social influence process. The same principles that explain the acquisition and change of behavior in general should be exemplified in the evolution of a therapist's theoretical orientation and behavior with clients.

In addition to social learning processes, this book emphasizes the role of unexpected events, the unpredictable evolution of behavior in complex systems, and the importance of sociocultural influences. These elements point the way to an integration of sociological and anthropological perspectives into a therapeutic orientation. They also provide encouragement for therapists to view their own orientation as a process in evolution and to take advantage of their unique experiences so as to develop in unexpected ways.

The first four chapters of Part I take the form of a theoretical autobiography—a look at the influences leading to the evolution of a sociocultural orientation. Chapter 5 then calls attention to some of the most important points presented along the way. It abstracts five key therapeutic principles and discusses the therapeutic relationship, the context of therapy, and the process of learning to learn.

Part I also paves the way for the theoretical and clinical contributions of Parts II, III, and IV by clarifying the social context within which these ideas developed. Thus, Chapter 3, "The Influence of Anthropology," foreshadows Part II, "Social and Cultural Issues"; Chapter 2, "The Behavior Therapy Movement," is linked to Part III, "Behavioral and Cognitive Therapies"; and Chapter 4, "The Systems Movement," is related to Part IV, "Strategic and Systemic Therapies."

In this therapist's theoretical odyssey, then, Part I emphasizes its chronology, and Parts II, III, and IV deal with its content.

1

Becoming a Therapist

Early in my career I married an African American anthropologist who studies Brazilian Indians. Soon we had a daughter and moved to Brazil for a couple of years. My experiences there—as a psychologist in a large city and a visitor with the Krikati tribe in the remote interior—led me to develop in unexpected ways and eventually to rethink the question of what a therapist's theoretical orientation is and how it evolves.

Over the years, I have come increasingly to understand therapy in its social and cultural context. Doing so has involved challenging a number of deeply held beliefs and values. It has suggested to me that if therapists want to, they can develop a distinctive orientation by seeking out new knowledge and experiences and by adopting a stance of pragmatic iconoclasm.

Encounters with culturally different people and ideas lead to
unpredictable change in unexpected directions.

I began graduate study, in 1964, as a Freudian. My goal was
to get a Ph.D. in clinical psychology, attend an analytic institute,
and, like the character in Tom Lehrer's satirical song, "The Old
Dope Peddler," "do well by doing good." I don't think I
appreciated the extent to which, for lack of other inspiring role
models, I wanted to be what my therapist seemed to me—a
benevolent man, earning both gratitude and a good income by
helping troubled but not troublesome members of the middle
class.

At the same time, I really was interested in weird behavior
and the process of change. Clinical psychology students did field
work one day a week at the psychiatric ward of Harlem Hospital. We each got to choose a patient to spend the afternoon with,
and I asked for the most deviant person I could find—a 27-year-
old man who had long since been labeled a chronic schizophrenic, having spent the previous twelve years in mental
hospitals. In his medicated state, he seemed a frightened and sad
person, and he spent his time either lying on his bed or pacing
the hall. When he spoke, which was not often, much of what he
said was confused or delusional.

I became his once-a-week companion, sitting at his side
when he was lying down and pacing the hall with him. While I
was with him, I reflected the feelings that he expressed or that I
intuited, because this was something I knew how to do. I didn't
make interpretations, because that would have been considered
therapy. We were told not to do therapy because we hadn't been
trained to do it and weren't receiving supervision.

It was a strange message, seemingly reifying ways of talking
and infringing on First Amendment Rights—"this kind of talk is
okay, that kind of talk isn't." In any event, no one else was

doing therapy with him, though he did see a psychiatrist for occasional brief visits, mainly to monitor his medication.

Because I was with him all the time I noticed that, during his slow pacing of the hall, each return was a few steps short of the previous one, tracing an elongated coil until at some point when his path was short he began all over. No one else had noticed that he was doing this.

The importance of observing behavior was a theme that would become important to me. When you observe behavior, patterns emerge. When you focus exclusively on understanding the inner world, you do not see those patterns.

Gradually, the man improved. He began to care for himself more, his speech became more coherent, and his psychiatrist was considering encouraging him to look for work. I had let him know from our first contact that when the semester ended I would be transferred to another field work placement, and I reminded him of that fact periodically. Eventually, my transfer took place, and reports from students who replaced me indicated that the man's behavior deteriorated to its previous level. It appeared that my reflecting his feelings, and/or my companionship, had had some effect, though not enough to continue in my absence. A few years later, I discovered that these results were about what one could expect from client-centered therapy with similar people (Rogers et al. 1967).

Another thing about Harlem Hospital. The staff and patients of the psychiatric unit were all black, except for the psychologist, and the graduate students from Columbia were all white. In 1964 the civil rights movement was under way, with Martin Luther King and Malcolm X as the most prominent voices. People of good will wanted to, as Spike Lee later put it, "do the right thing."

(As a child in Manhattan, I had had a close friend who was

from Puerto Rico. But from the fourth grade on, when my parents moved to the Bronx, all my friends had been white, and my closest friends had been Jewish, like me. Similarly, all my girlfriends had been white, and my two long-term relationships had been with Jewish women.)

Over the semester at Harlem Hospital, I noticed that the staff and patients stopped looking black. They just looked like any other people, which is to say white people, with darker skins and different facial features, rather than black people. It was an interesting experience. Familiarity had led to a change in visual perception.

I have had this experience in three other areas; and the passage of time allowed for an A-B-A reversal in two of them. In one case, I worked for three months alongside a man with cerebral palsy. At first, his spastic movements were disconcerting and his speech was almost impossible to understand. Over time, I grew accustomed to his speech and movements, and they faded into the background like an accent and gestures, as his ironic wit and other characteristic behavior formed the figure. I didn't see him for a couple of years, and when I ran into him by accident I was startled to rediscover the degree to which his behavior was compromised, and how different he seemed from my memory of him.

Another example comes from my long-term involvement with Brazil (which I will discuss more fully when I reach it in chronological order). Every time I arrive in Brazil, I am shocked by the poverty. Initially it took months, but now, within a few weeks, I no longer notice it. So it would appear that this kind of perceptual habituation does not have a moral dimension.

One final example has to do with the strange kind of talk referred to as loose associations. I tend to feel a bit confused when I first hear it, and then suddenly recognize that it's not my comprehension that is at fault but that the speaker isn't making sense. My experience has been that when I get to know someone who talks this way, I gradually get to understand what he or she means. Some psychologists would label this habituation a loss of diagnostic acuity, an inability to recognize that I am talking to a schizophrenic. (On the other hand, written evidence of thought disorder seems to be common in the essays of normal college students who are trying to bluff their way through, but don't know what they're talking about.)

There is an extensive literature on perception in the fields of experimental psychology and social psychology. Perhaps if my coursework and interests had led me in this direction I might have become involved with the idea of therapy as a process of changing clients' perceptions—a view advocated by Gestalt therapists, among others. After all, therapy is just a word. It didn't exist before Freud, and it has come to denote an ever-expanding variety of phenomena simply because someone says, "This is therapy." Psychological knowledge about perception, like all science, is in the public domain. If therapists attempt to apply it for the benefit of others it would seem that they should be encouraged, rather than discouraged on the grounds that they are exceeding their training.

Another cross-cultural experience I had during my first year of graduate school was the development of close friendships with two classmates of British-American ancestry from Ohio and California. This was hardly an enormous cultural gulf to bridge. They were American and male and middle class and white, like me, though they were neither New Yorkers nor Jewish. I remember a discussion with my California friend over whether a certain situation would lead one to experience shame or guilt. Almost simultaneously, I asked him, "What is shame?" and he asked me, "What is guilt?" This struck both of us as a cultural difference.

During my second year, we did field work at Roosevelt Hospital. At the end of work one day the three of us were standing around telling jokes and laughing as we waited for the elevator. A nurse came over and chastised us.

"Ssh!" she said. "Don't you know there are some very depressed patients here?"

The distorting effects of the ideology of mental illness (Szasz 1961) have never ceased to amaze me. Presumably, because the people on the ward were called patients, they were like other patients recovering from surgery or in pain from an undiagnosed ailment and needed to rest. Instead of the disease of appendicitis, they were suffering from the disease of depression. The nurse really seemed to believe that it would be bad for depressed people to laugh.

In the same way, since one person is labeled a therapist and the other a client, it is assumed that therapy is something that the former does to the latter. It is not uncommon for a session to begin with the therapist feeling fine and the client feeling depressed. By the end of the session both people are depressed. It is clear that change has taken place, and that the client has been the more effective influencer of behavior.

During my second year, I took Allen Bergin's course in research in psychotherapy, and it was an eye-opener. Our clinical director was Sol Garfield, and the subsequent collaboration of the two on a series of *Handbooks of Psychotherapy and Behavior Change* (Bergin and Garfield 1971, 1994, Garfield and Bergin 1978, 1986) has provided a major service to clinicians with these critical syntheses and evaluations of therapy research.

At the time, I was still a believer in psychoanalysis, but my faith was being tested. Nothing qualitatively different from it seemed to exist then, and the mildly different alternatives, such as client-centered therapy, paled by intellectual comparison. It took me a number of years to see that being deep wasn't the same as being right, and that intellectual fascination could as easily lead down a blind alley as to the truth. Someone once said, "When a beautiful theory is contradicted by some ugly facts, so much the worse for the facts." Unfortunately, since people's welfare is at stake in therapy, we sometimes have to give up the *bon mot* for the *mot juste*.

In 1965, Eysenck's assertion (1952) that two thirds of clients get better with or without therapy still seemed the most reasonable evaluation of the field. (It was only six years later that Bergin's laborious reanalysis [1971] of Eysenck's paper showed that it asked the wrong questions, used inappropriate data, and drew flawed inferences from the studies it reviewed.) In fact, there was an otherworldly quality to the split between our applied clinical courses and our clinical research courses. In the former we would learn what to do in assessment or therapy, and in the latter we learned that research revealed that what we were supposed to do was invalid or didn't work.

Different students handled the dissonance in different ways. Some decided that the negative results simply meant that the subtlety of clinical work was too ineffable to be detected by coarse research procedures ("so much the worse for the facts"). One student, who had received the only A in a course on assessment research, was fond of asking professors questions such as, "If there's no evidence that what you do works, how can you justify accepting money for it?" He was dropped from the program for having "authority problems."

Around this time, I made a slip of the tongue and referred to our "cynical psychology program." Not only was training characterized by glaring contradictions, but we couldn't do anything about them. One professor said, "To be a clinical psychologist you need a great tolerance for ambiguity." We were fifteen graduate students who had been selected from several hundred applicants; but by the end of the second year seven of us had flunked out, dropped out, or been thrown out. Another professor said, "Clinical psychology training is a natural stress experiment. If you can survive it, you have what it takes to be a clinical psychologist." This was good advice; it helped to get me through the program. I have offered it to my students, and some of them have thanked me.

It is too bad that I hadn't become familiar with—and enamored of—Brazilian culture back then. I might have saved myself some *angst* (or, more properly, *angústia*) if I had realized that the need for consistency is a peculiarly American preoccupation. A decade later, I would be upset at Brazilian students' blandness in the face of apparent contradictions. They, in contrast, saw my reaction as yet another example of American rigidity. But I digress.

Bergin's course suggested that some things actually did work (which was reassuring), though not especially the brand of therapy I was committed to (which was not). More importantly, it raised the possibility of an empirically based therapy, or of a theoretically based therapy that was open to corrective empirical feedback. I had already become a doubter, so I recognized that there might well be an upper limit to how much therapy could help (which might vary according to the type of problem or other variable), and that this upper limit might even be rather low. Nevertheless, it might be possible to determine this limit, and then at least we would know something.

There were two things that seemed to work. One was the Rogerian trinity of empathy, warmth, and genuineness. I don't want to diminish the importance of the discovery that if you act nice to people who are upset, and convince them that you understand them, they will feel better. I actually did an empathy study for my doctoral dissertation (Fish 1970), so at one point I was quite involved in the client-centered literature. It's just that this is a path that I did not ultimately pursue in developing my understanding of problem behavior and therapy.

The other thing that seemed to work—and in fact seemed to work better than anything else, though results were preliminary and scattered—was something entirely new, that I had never heard of before. It was called behavior therapy.

Unlike the variations on a theme that most therapies seemed to be, behavior therapy was qualitatively different. First, while other approaches positively reveled in the proliferation of unverifiable concepts, behavior therapy was at least ideologically committed to the importance of observation and the corrective feedback provided by verification. Second, it attempted to change behavior directly, rather than by indirect effects on people's hypothesized personalities—for example, modifying their defensive structures or encouraging self-actualization. This seemed plausible, since we had learned in our assessment courses that the more distant (temporally or conceptually) a measured behavior was from a predicted behavior, the lower the correlation between the two. Third, a clearly specified technique had actually been invented—systematic desensitization (Wolpe 1958)—for a specific neurosis (phobias); and there was both clinical evidence (e.g., Wolpe's case studies) and experimental evidence (e.g., Lang and Lazovik 1963) that it was effective in a high percentage of cases, and usually in a small number of sessions. In addition, the Introduction to Ullmann and Krasner's book *Case Studies in Behavior Modification* (1965) hinted at an approach to clinical theory that was different from anything I had encountered and raised the possibility of merging the theoretical base of therapy with the theoretical base of the rest of psychology.

Finally, since behavior therapy was brief, it appeared socially responsible. The community mental health movement was well under way by then, and it was generally understood that only prevention could have a major impact on psychological problems. (Unfortunately, little was known then, and not much more now, about how to do prevention, and little of that has been implemented.) At least brief therapy offered the potential of reaching much larger numbers of people. Even at that time, the trickle-down rationale (or rationalization) of psychoanalysis, that treating the elite could make the world a better place, seemed self-serving and socially irresponsible.

So behavior therapy was exciting, but I was still intellectually committed to psychoanalysis. Since we had all studied learning theory, it was not difficult to see that Wolpe's theoretical explanation for systematic desensitization did not bear a close resemblance to Hullian or other theory (cf. Breger and McGaugh 1965). Furthermore, there were so many interpretations of learning that to claim that behavior therapy was based on "modern learning theory" was really empty rhetoric. It was like saying that some pill that worked for unclear reasons did so because of "modern medical theory."

My view of psychological theory by then had become less credulous, as was to be expected from a "cynical psychology" student. Sigmund Koch once said, "In physics we have rigid concepts and flexible minds, and in psychology we have flexible concepts and rigid minds." It seemed to me that theories of therapy and the therapies themselves were related more for historical than logical reasons. That is, since a single person, say Freud or Rogers, came up with both a theory and a therapy, everyone appeared to believe that the therapy implemented the theory. It seemed entirely plausible that, in a different world, Rogers might have claimed that silence would allow the client to experience himself more fully, or that Freud might have claimed that reflection of feeling would open the defenses from the conscious side of the ego, so that id impulses could more easily be partially expressed in awareness.

I wanted to use behavior therapy techniques because they worked (or at least to see first hand if they really did work); but I felt no need to commit myself to Wolpe's "flexible" learning theory explanation—I could just as easily give my own "flexible" psychoanalytic explanation.

During 1966–1967 I did my internship at the Langley Porter Neuropsychiatric Institute in San Francisco. That year was the height of the hippie epoch, and San Francisco was the place to be. My internship ended during the Summer of Love and I returned to New York not too long after the Hippie Funeral in Golden Gate Park marked the symbolic end of the era. Even with all its excesses, it is easy to be nostalgic for a time when people who were against war would put a flower in the barrel of a gun, and when posters urged one to "Help save water. Bathe with friends!"

One incident typifies what was best about that special time. A small, aging, out-of-shape psychiatrist, dressed in a business suit and driving a new Cadillac, ran a red light in the Haight Ashbury. A hippie in a pickup truck, who had had the right of way, screeched to a halt, narrowly averting an accident. He stormed out of his truck, a massive, angry, long-haired, bearded young man wearing colorful clothes and beads. The psychiatrist got out of his car, smiled at him, and said, "Love!" The hippie was instantly transformed. He too smiled and said, "Love!"; and the two men embraced and returned peacefully to their vehicles.

During my internship I was disabused of the illusion that, unlike the uptight world of academia, the clinical world would have a freewheeling sharing of feelings and clinical open-mindedness, curiosity, and experimentation. It has long been a commonplace that the median number of publications of Ph.D.'s in clinical psychology is zero. An academic colleague, concerned about the behavior of psychologists devoted to full-time clinical work, once suggested ironically that zero is actually the median number of publications read after completing the doctorate. Unfortunately, therapists in clinical settings—because of time commitments or whatever other reasons—are even less involved in new developments than are therapists in academia, though there are significant exceptions to this generalization in both groups. I had hoped to be taught something more about behavior therapy on my internship, but discovered that I would have to rely on my own reading.

The internship experience contained a number of contradictory elements. The peripheral experiences—which were available, but not required, if our schedules permitted—were stimulating. There were Jungian seminars with Joe Wheelwright, Transactional Analysis seminars with Eric Berne, and Gestalt Therapy workshops with Fritz Perls. Joe Kamiya was doing his early research on alpha conditioning and Paul Ekman was in the early stages of his work on nonverbal behavior. Arnold Lazarus even came across the bay from Sausalito to speak on behavior therapy. But the core training focused on the same analytically oriented therapy and standard testing batteries that I had been immersed in 3,000 miles away. The overall experience was one of "here are some new ideas—don't try them out in your own work."

Away from the internship, I participated in the Synanon square games (Yablonsky 1967), an emotional roller coaster of leaderless group therapy used by addicts in a self-help program. These were "square games," since most of the group members (players) were nonaddicts (squares), while a minority were ex-addicts who used the experience as part of their transition back to the outside world. A laudable aspect of the square games (and of Synanon) was the inclusion of people from diverse social, cultural, economic, and racial backgrounds—though the squares tended to be more educated and from a higher social class than the addicts.

Since this was a game rather than therapy, and since I was a participant rather than a therapist (though in truth everyone functioned as both therapist and client), this activity posed no danger. If it had been called therapy and I had been called a therapist, my standing as a graduate student might have been jeopardized for practicing psychology without a license. These days, participation might additionally be punishable as unprofessional conduct for cooperating with unlicensed practitioners.

Synanon ultimately went bad. A psychiatrist friend said, "What do you expect from a bunch of sociopaths?" There are two problems with this reaction. First, there was real idealism in the organization, at least at the beginning, and some people really were helped. More importantly, the attempt to explain organizational breakdown in terms of individual personalities is partial at best. My own view is that Synanon's difficulty stemmed from what Watzlawick and colleagues (1974) called "The Utopia Syndrome." That is, when people try to achieve the unattainable, and escalate their attempts in the face of failure, they can make a much worse mess than they started out with. A small example of this is a marriage that breaks up because it fails to achieve the unrealizable expectations of one or both parties, who make matters worse by trying to force each other to act the way they're supposed to. A large example is the breakdown of Communism, which demonstrated that forcible attempts to do away with social inequality are doomed. It is a difficult but important lesson that much more can be accomplished by trying to make a marriage a little bit better, or by trying to promote somewhat greater social equality.

It is hard for many therapists to believe—I wouldn't have believed it myself back then—that one of the reasons that change seems so slow and hard won is that they are trying to reach an unattainable goal of major changes in personality. Unfortunately, Freud's (1963b) title *Analysis Terminable and Interminable* was quite appropriate. The idea that analysis (or therapy) could actually prolong suffering and make matters worse by trying to achieve the unachievable, and that aiming for a small but realizable change might set off a spiral of unexpected positive results, had not been considered at the time. Whatever the problem, more therapy was the solution.

In the case of Synanon, by creating a powerful institution

with a powerful ideology, well-meaning people learned once again that power corrupts.

At the internship, one of my yearlong cases was a timid man whose activities were greatly constricted, partially for psychological reasons and partially from pain that had achieved chronicity through a series of "utopian" surgical interventions. While the surgery may actually have made his pain worse, the equally persistent application of therapy seemed merely to be having no effect. Each year he received the same kind of psychodynamically oriented therapy from another clinical psychology intern—I was his sixth or seventh therapist—and each year he stayed pretty much the same. After a couple of months, it seemed to me that I was doing more or less what the other therapists had been doing, and was observing the same nonresults.

This is usually referred to as "making progress." Therapists typically point to this new client insight or that new emotional experience, shake their head knowingly about how slow the change process is, and pat each other on the back for their persistence. I have come to view the delusion, that no change is really "making progress," as a strange subcultural phenomenon. Even when I was most committed to psychoanalysis, I viewed no change as no change and tried to figure out what I could do differently. In fact, viewing therapy as a process of hypothesis testing is something that has always characterized my work, and I have refined it over the years as my orientation has gone through numerous twists and turns. Whatever my theory at the time, I try to figure out what is going on, formulate a theory-based intervention that should cause change, predict explicitly to myself what I expect to happen, and then compare my prediction to what actually happens. Based on the results and previous evidence, I then stick to, revise, or completely reformulate the hypothesis.

Some therapists act as if a recognition that no change is

taking place constitutes an admission of incompetence, and therefore insist that the client is "making progress." From my point of view, "no change" is seen as useful disconfirming evidence, which helps me to formulate a better hypothesis. Perhaps this positive view of "no change" can be useful to long-term therapists who would like to see quicker results.

Note that whether one calls it "no change" or "making progress," and views it as negative or positive, is a question of labeling. Some labels promote change more than others and are therefore more useful. Thus, in a way, relabeling can be seen as a counterpart to insight. Therapists who believe in insight want to help their clients discover the Truth. This assumes there is a Truth to discover, rather than different ways of construing reality. This point of view antedates behavior therapy (e.g., Kelly 1955), and is common in sociology and anthropology, which study the ways in which reality is socially constructed. Therapists who use relabeling are interested in the pragmatic consequences of thinking in different ways and help clients shift to thoughts that achieve the change they desire.

In the case of my client, "no change" meant that if I kept doing what hadn't worked for me, and hadn't worked for a series of therapists before me, it would most likely continue not to work. Every session seemed to confirm this interpretation of events. So I decided to do something different. Since he was so timid, I thought of turning the hypothesis around. For years, the view of his therapists had been that once he developed enough insight, or had enough of therapy's ineffable interpersonal magic, he would gain the confidence to partake more of life. I entertained the hypothesis (privately, to myself, because I knew it was a therapeutic heresy) that if I could get him to act less timid he might find that he liked it and so become less timid. I did "assertive training," as it was called then, right out of Chapter 4 of the recently published *Behavior Therapy Techniques* (Wolpe and Lazarus 1966).

I couldn't very well tell my supervisor that I was doing behavior therapy, so I told her I was trying to help him express his feelings; she accepted this.

What is the ethical status of what I told my supervisor? In terms of moral reasoning (e.g., Kohlberg 1963), it seems to me I did the right thing, since I acted in the interest of my client's welfare. In terms of professional ethics, at least as the field exists today, it could be argued that I was in no position to do what I did because responsibility for his welfare belonged to the institution and through it to my supervisor, a licensed professional; my job as an unlicensed intern was to carry out her instructions.

I believe the situation is murkier. The problem arises from the "flexible" nature of psychological concepts. My supervisor went along with the rationale of encouraging my client to express his feelings because she believed that his timidity was the result of an overly strong defensive structure, and that expressing his feelings would allow for some weakening of his defenses and a corresponding strengthening of his ego. If she had been a classical analyst, she might have objected that I was really encouraging acting out—the expression of feelings in everyday behavior—which is deemed undesirable because it might lessen the likelihood of his expressing them verbally in therapy.

I just wanted to do something different. My supervisor would have been opposed to my doing conditioning, but at the time I didn't particularly believe that assertiveness training worked because of conditioning. Wolpe and Lazarus were claiming that assertiveness training worked because it counter-conditioned the client's anxiety in social situations, but there are not many behavior therapists today who would accept that explanation. To me, the psychodynamic explanation seemed as reasonable or unreasonable as the conditioning explanation.

So the problem was not with what I did, but with what I

believed. My supervisor knew and approved of what I was doing as long as it was labeled "expressing feelings," but would have disapproved of it if it had been labeled "assertive training," or, even worse, "counterconditioning." It is in this sense that therapeutic approaches are like religions: they require of therapists conformity not just in deed but in thought as well, along with continual reaffirmations of faith.

My client improved dramatically. At the end of the internship, my supervisor singled this case out for special praise. Her worldview was confirmed—if the therapist hangs in there long enough, therapy will eventually work. My worldview was also confirmed—when there is no change, try something different. I also decided to learn more about behavior therapy.

I returned to New York for a year's therapy practicum, along with some final coursework. At the same time, I spent one day a week in Philadelphia for a behavior therapy course with Joseph Wolpe. Arnold Lazarus had by then moved to Philadelphia to work with Wolpe, and he also taught some of the classes.

My practicum supervisor at Columbia was Rosalea Schonbar, a Sullivanian analyst. She was particularly good at helping therapists to "be themselves." Being oneself as a therapist is not the same as being oneself among friends—one remains always within the therapist role. Nevertheless, except for classical psychoanalysis (which has become much less common, at least in the United States, since I was a graduate student), most approaches to therapy allow for considerable individual variation in the way in which theory is implemented. It seems to me that therapists do better to capitalize on their strengths and compensate for their weaknesses, rather than attempt to imitate an ideal form or famous therapist associated with their approach. For example, I am more extroverted and talkative than most therapists, so I tend to engage with clients socially, while more introverted colleagues communicate more of a quiet sensitivity. Neither is better, and both can be used effectively in encouraging therapeutic change.

In my current work as a supervisor, I try to give explicit feedback to encourage therapists to be themselves more effectively. One therapist had a talent for apt metaphor. For example, she was doing marital therapy, and the wife said, "You can't get him to open up. He's like a rock." She replied, "He's not a rock, he's a rosebud. If you try to force him open you may hurt him, but if you give him enough light and air and water him patiently, he'll blossom into a beautiful rose." So I told the therapist I thought this was a strength of hers and encouraged her to use more metaphors in her work.

Toward the end of the year I was speaking with a graduate of the program who had entered analytic training. He said, "Rosalea taught me to be myself as a therapist. I've since discovered that that was very destructive."

There was a deli across the street from the university where many of us would buy sandwiches to eat in the lounge. One particular time during the winter several of us walked there together, and since it was so close we didn't bother to wear coats. As we crossed the street, I thought to myself, "I feel cold." Suddenly I had a realization: "That's because it is cold!" With my years of personal therapy and training as a therapist, I had become so attuned to every nuance of my inner world that I had become blind to the most obvious elements of my environment and their powerful determining effect on my experience. This epiphany contributed significantly to my decision to get postdoctoral training in behavior therapy.

I was still concerned that if I became a behavior therapist I would lose my humanity and treat clients mechanically. That was the antibehavioral propaganda at the time, and there are still circles where it is essentially unchanged. At its core, it is an

ethnocentric stereotype that members of some therapeutic subcultures spread about another one, and like all such stereotypes
it is based largely on fear of the unknown. Arnold Lazarus had a
tape satirizing it at the time, which began with the therapist
saying to a new client, "Don't bother telling me your problems.
Just sit over there in the chair with the wires."

I decided to enter behavior therapy to see what it was like.
In truth, I didn't really have a problem; this was one of the best
periods of my life. I was working on a promising dissertation
proposal, and it looked as if I was actually going to get my
doctorate. In addition, it had been nearly two years since I had
successfully terminated my seemingly interminable analytically
oriented therapy. (I now view my therapist as having acted
essentially as an auxiliary parent, offering well-intentioned advice amidst considerable silence, so as to help keep me out of
adolescent excesses during the transition to young adulthood.
While I did have some real problems, and I do believe that the
overall effect was positive, therapy involved an extraordinary
amount of money and professional time to achieve results that
probably could have been obtained by a benevolent adult with
parental experience.[1])

I wasn't going with anyone at the time—maybe I was a bit

---

1. Unfortunately, such people are hard to find. As we have gone
from extended kin networks to the nuclear family, and from the social
contacts in towns and neighborhoods to urban anonymity, fewer
informal sources are available to help troubled individuals and families.
Community psychologists have long proposed identifying and paying
local change agents to play a helping role, but it does not look as if
funds for this purpose will be available in the foreseeable future. In this
way, the American system—using highly trained therapists to provide
expensive solutions for the psychological problems of the few—mir-
rors the waste, inequities, and inefficiencies of the provision of medical
care.

lonely. I really can't remember what I decided to call a problem
to justify my consulting a behavior therapist. Anyway, my
hidden agenda was to see if the therapist would be a decent and
sensitive human being or a cold, mechanical technician.

In truth, I could have terminated successfully in five minutes. The therapist was a pleasant, older woman with an agreeable, informal manner. She had been a Sullivanian analyst who,
like me, had been impressed with the literature on behavior
therapy. She had read everything she could about it, which was
easy enough to do in those early days, and had paid for
supervision. I remember being impressed by her casual dress and
sandals—signs of informality that were not permitted graduate
students, who had to "appear professional."

She dutifully desensitized whatever I claimed I had, and we
terminated in under ten sessions. One side benefit of the therapy
was that I learned the process of systematic desensitization, and
over the next few months, whenever anything bothered me, I
would construct a hierarchy and desensitize myself. Eventually,
the novelty of desensitization wore off (extinguished, in my new
vocabulary) and I found better ways to spend my solitary time.

Back then, I was still naive about how much damage
therapy can do, though Allen Bergin (1966) had already identified the deterioration effect and there was some talk about
"psycho-noxious" therapists. These were individual rather than
interactional explanations, however. They recognized merely
that therapy might be bad for some people or conditions, or that
some therapists might be destructive. The field had not yet
advanced to a recognition that the process of therapy itself
could create problems where none existed.

One can easily imagine a marriage between two therapists
who are sitting around quietly, as often happens, when one of
them happens to notice that they are not communicating. If he
or she calls attention to this, as by saying "I guess we have
nothing to say to each other right now," a dangerous cycle

could easily be initiated. They might try to understand why they're not communicating or, even worse, take unilateral or joint action to do something about it. These acts in turn would have consequences, and pretty soon the chain of action and reaction could create a real problem. The same kind of cycle can take place between therapist and client (Watzlawick et al. 1974). In other words, trying to solve a nonexistent problem can really make a mess out of things.

Medicine says *nihil nocere* (freely translated as "don't make matters worse"), and we all know the expression "If it ain't broke, don't fix it," but many therapists still believe that therapy is good for everyone. I first believed it as well, then came to view it as self-serving but benign, and now see it as self-serving and harmful. So I am grateful to my behavior therapist for the brevity of the treatment. She not only helped me to decide to get further training, but she didn't create problems where none existed.

In short, during the year 1967 to 1968 I was being trained in behavior therapy in Philadelphia, was a behavior therapy client myself, worked on a Rogerian dissertation, and did psychodynamic therapy under Sullivanian supervision.

That was also the year of the Columbia riots. I had one client, a middle-aged, conservative man who believed that the disruptions on American campuses, as well as those in Europe, were evidence of an international Communist plot. Trying out my Rogerian genuineness, I shared with him my belief that this was not the case and managed to create an awkwardness between us that took a while to get over. Apparently the therapeutic value of authenticity of expression does not apply to political disagreements.

Therapists' belief in the value of openness is based in part on the ethnocentric notion that we are all basically alike. While it is true that openness can sometimes reveal unexpected commonalities among people, it can also reveal irreconcilable differences, so a therapist's decision about whether and when to be open is best made based on its likely consequences in a given situation, rather than on general principles.

Meanwhile, in contrast to my conservative client, I received a call from another client of a different political persuasion, who said, "I can't come for therapy today because I'm occupying the Mathematics building."

2

The Behavior Therapy Movement

I spent the following year in the postdoctoral program in behavior modification at the State University of New York at Stony Brook, though I was still putting the finishing touches on my dissertation during the first semester. The decision to use the term *behavior modification* rather than *behavior therapy* was an ideological one, and in my view praiseworthy. The notion was that abnormal or undesired behavior was not qualitatively different from any other behavior, was explainable by the same psychological principles, and could be changed by applying those principles. Since there was no illness, there was no therapy—just the modification of behavior.

In the semantic wars that followed, the term *behavior modification* was demolished by nonbehavioral opponents applying it inappropriately to all sorts of unpleasant activities, such as calling lobotomies "behavior modification surgery," until a retreat had to be made to the earlier "behavior therapy." Leonard Krasner (1976), who had been my supervisor at the time, eventually published an epitaph for behavior modification.

I attended the program because I was interested in learning the new techniques, even though I was unimpressed by their theoretical rationales. However, from early in the program, a prepublication draft of Ullmann and Krasner's forthcoming abnormal psychology text (1969) was available. It contained what I viewed as the field's first reasonable theoretical explanation of both abnormal behavior and behavior therapy. It called its explanation *social learning theory.*

The best known clinical application of learning theory at the time was Dollard and Miller's translation (1950) of Freud into Hull. In a sense, Ullmann and Krasner's most distinctive contribution could be said to be a translation of sociology, especially role theory and the theory of deviance, into Skinner. Their presentation had three features that particularly appealed to me. First, it based its descriptions and explanations as much as possible on observable behavior; second, it indicated a theoretical continuity between clinical psychology and the rest of psychology; and third, it viewed human behavior as part of a larger interactive social context, rather than as coming from individual organisms each acting alone.

The term *social learning theory* has been used to encompass a number of differing and overlapping conceptualizations (e.g., Bandura 1977b, Rotter 1954). What they have in common is a view of human behavior as arising from and continually evolving through distinctively human social interactions. This is a view with a significantly different perspective from that of biological determinism with its emphasis on inherited predispositions, psychoanalysis with its emphasis on early childhood experiences and unconscious processes, and Rogerian and related approaches with their culturally American emphasis on individualism (masquerading under theoretical labels like self-actualization).

Among psychologists who view behavior from a social learning perspective, some emphasize the *learning* while others emphasize the *social*. What attracted me to Ullmann and Krasner's formulation was its social emphasis, showing the continuity of clinical theory not just with psychology, but with sociology as well, and by implication with the other social sciences. (Leonard Krasner is particularly interested in history, while over the years my interests were to evolve in the direction of anthropology.)

Already, by the time of my postdoc, there were two differing views of what behavior therapy was. (That is, there was intellectual conflict over what the new field should consist of, how it should define itself, and, by implication, what it should exclude.) One view was that behavior therapy consisted of an ever-growing series of experimentally validated techniques for the treatment of an ever-expanding range of human problems. Everyone was in favor of the development of such techniques, but such a definition seemed to limit the field to a bag of tricks. Furthermore, it seemed to promote the idea of sorting people into functionally equivalent groups, which went against the grain of the learning theory notion that each individual is unique as the result of a unique learning history.

The other view was that behavior therapy consisted of the application of principles of general psychology to the changing of human behavior. Within general psychology, the psychology of learning was the field that was most significantly applied, though I would soon come to see most behavior therapy (that is, verbal therapy with nonpsychotic, non-brain-damaged, nonchildren) as resembling applied social psychology more than applied learning theory. Nowadays, I would want to expand the definition of behavior therapy to include the application of principles and knowledge from all the social and behavioral sciences to the changing of human behavior.

The view of behavior therapy as the application of empirically supported principles, instead of merely the application of empirically validated techniques, was clinically liberating. It meant that, at the very least, if the client should show up with a unique problem for which no technique existed, the clinician was free to improvise an intervention. The two constraints on innovation were that it had to be based on empirically supported principles, and its usefulness had to be evaluated by its effects on the client's behavior.

Skinner's concept of a functional analysis of behavior was most helpful. While it referred to understanding a given behavior in terms of discriminative and reinforcing stimuli, the concept could easily be expanded to include anything that could be explicitly specified, of which the behavior was a function. Krasner and Ullmann (1973) ultimately settled on the term *behavior influence,* which nicely recognized that various elements might influence (or partially determine) a given behavior.

In addition, both views of behavior therapy shifted the focus of work from a psychoanalytic emphasis on the past (understanding how the behavior came about, often going back as far as childhood) to the present and future (understanding the current determinants of the behavior and using this knowledge to change it in a desired direction).

I didn't realize at the time that the excitement, creativity, openness to new ideas, and innovativeness of the behavior therapy movement were due not so much to behavior therapy itself as to the youth of a new social movement (and, secondarily, to the greater acceptance of unconventionality during the sixties). Watching the movement mature (or grow stodgy), and then participating in the same process a decade later as the youthful systems movement followed on the path from creativity to conventionality, has had a sobering effect. If one wants to be an innovative therapist, one has to be willing to detach from institutionalized authority; a creative bureaucracy is an oxymoron.

At any rate, those were heady times, as behavior therapy challenged in practice one after another psychoanalytic assumption about therapy. It is hard to realize that Carl Rogers's decision to tape therapy sessions, so that one could study what was actually happening, was initially greeted with shock. My own dissertation involved listening carefully to randomly selected segments of therapy tapes of forty-three (nonbehavior) therapists. The overall impression I got was of how boring most therapy is, though I made no quantitative ratings of boredom at the time. (The joke is that the therapist dreams that he's fallen asleep during a session, and then awakes to find out that it's true.)

If Rogers had breached the sanctity of the therapy session by taping, then behavior therapists marched in through the gap. Supervisors might observe through a one-way mirror, and even make suggestions via a "bug-in-the-ear." (This turned out to be a bad idea, as the therapist's expression would change strangely when receiving transmissions, and, if the volume was loud enough, the client might even have the sensation of hearing voices. Eventually, telephonic communication between the two rooms was found to work better, since it was a culturally understood form of exclusive contact, which third parties— clients—were already socialized to accept.) A supervisor might sit in on a session, to get a firsthand view of a client, and might even demonstrate a particular technique. A supervisee might sit in on a supervisor's case to observe the latter's work or offer another opinion. A therapist might make a home visit, or a school visit, or go to some other setting to observe behavior in its natural context and possibly even intervene on the spot.

Third parties might be brought into a therapy session. For

example, in the university clinic, if a male client was com-
plaining about feelings of inadequacy with and unattractiveness
to women, a female graduate student in clinical psychology
might be invited to sit in for a few sessions and offer candid and
specific observations about the client's behavior and suggestions
for change. Naturally, clients' permission for such participation
was requested, but there was rarely difficulty in obtaining it
because of the collaborative, problem-solving relationships that
were being developed in therapy. Walking by the postdocs'
offices, one might well hear animated exclamations or
laughter—a far cry from what I had been listening to on my
dissertation tapes.

Years later, I rented the office of an analytically oriented
therapist one day a week. The first thing I would do was hide the
box of tissues that was prominently displayed at the side of the
client's chair. The demand characteristics—"this is a place
where you should cry"—were quite different from "this is a
place to solve problems." If someone did cry, I could always
make the tissues available when needed.

This is also a reasonable point to mention the use of humor,
surprise, and the absurd in therapy. Some therapists seem to feel
that it is disrespectful to treat a person's problems lightly, even
if a gloomy outlook is a key part of the difficulty. To the
contrary, it is often helpful to make a client's situation seem
amusing, so that his or her own laughter can derail thoughts that
are chugging along the track to misery (Belson 1988).

As an example of the creativity of early behavior therapists,
I can mention a case presented by one speaker (I don't remember
his name) from his work in the counseling center at a geograph-
ically isolated liberal arts college. A female student sought help
because she felt lonely and isolated, no male students had shown
interest in her, and the only potential male companions were
other students. What the therapist did, which worked, was to
spread a rumor on campus, without her knowledge, that she had

once had a brief affair with Marlon Brando. The rumor included the information that she didn't like to discuss the affair and would deny that it had ever happened if asked about it. Apparently, the male students' curiosity was piqued to find out what Marlon Brando had seen in her, so "therapy" was successful.

Even with the openness of 1968, I had ethical reservations about spreading rumors about clients without their consent. (These included issues of confidentiality, the implicitly agreed-upon nature of the therapeutic relationship, and the lack of client knowledge of a potentially embarrassing intervention.) But the case does illustrate the creative thinking and innovative work that was going on at the time. In addition, it emphasizes the way in which both behavioral problems and their solution were seen as existing in the client's social world, away from the consulting room. This was very different from the view that the problems existed in the client's head and that their solution took place during the therapy session.

There was an inclusiveness as well to the speakers invited to the postdoctoral program. Albert Ellis and Aaron Beck spoke about their cognitive approaches, and Jay Haley spoke about what has come to be called strategic therapy. We learned about token economies and community-based programs. We were familiar with Milton Erickson's brilliant clinical work with paradox and hypnosis, as well as with Theodore Barber's more plausible theoretical explanation for how hypnotic behavior worked. As far as we and the program were concerned, it was all behavior therapy. The term *technical eclecticism* (Lazarus 1967) wasn't yet in use, but its spirit was pervasive.

It is disappointing, more than twenty-five years later, to see that the field has become overwhelmingly the office practice of verbal therapy and that practitioners distinguish among themselves as behavior therapists, cognitive behavior therapists, and cognitive therapists. They even make microsubdistinctions, such as cognitive therapists intellectually descended from Beck versus cognitive therapists intellectually descended from Ellis. Meanwhile, as therapy has gotten more cognitive, therapists have found more things to talk about; and as therapy has gotten longer, at least some cognitive therapists are looking for a rapprochement with psychoanalysis. It is an ironic development that Skinner might well have predicted (the more sessions, the more money).[1]

It was somewhere in the middle of the postdoc that my theoretical orientation—the way I explain behavior to myself— shifted from psychoanalytic to social learning. I sometimes tell my students that I haven't had an ego since 1968. The point of this assertion is that the ego (or reinforcement, for that matter) has no independent material existence. It is a concept used to organize observations in a useful manner. When I ceased to use the concept ego to explain my own—or others'—behavior, I ceased to have an ego.

Let me explain how my orientation shifted. In one case after another I used social learning principles and behavior therapy techniques, and obtained good results. My experience of the work was that change was taking place one step at a time, more or less the way it had when I was doing psychodynamically oriented therapy, except that it was much more rapid. In each case, however, I was able after the fact to give a "flexible" psychodynamic explanation for why the change had taken

---

1. This is not to imply that economic contingencies are the only element affecting such therapists' behavior. Many psycho-analysts and other long-term therapists see clients at reduced fees. However, from the point of view of an environmentally oriented brief therapist, long-term therapy is less desirable than brief therapy because it interferes with and postpones clients' learning to deal with the naturally occurring contingencies in their environment. Furthermore, therapists' orientations offer them no more exemption from the effects of environmental contingencies than they do from other forces of nature.

place. At some point it dawned on me, though, that I couldn't reverse the process. That is, I couldn't use analytic theory to generate the novel interventions, or even routine techniques, that were producing the results. So I abandoned psychoanalysis on pragmatic grounds.

I should mention that there have been many innovations in analytic theory, which I have not kept up with, since I changed my orientation. I view these more as resembling innovations in literary criticism (literary "theory") than in psychological theory. One psychologist (Scott 1991) even predicts that the future of psychoanalysis lies in English departments rather than psychology departments. These "theoretical" innovations seem to be new ways of thinking about the same old therapy, rather than part of an inductive endeavor, in which theory leads to predictions, which lead to empirical tests, which lead to changes in therapy.

I would like to point out two lessons regarding my shift in orientation. The first is that it exemplifies behavior change leading to cognitive change rather than the reverse. It was only after I changed my behavior as a therapist, and was exposed to the real-life consequences of this change for my clients, that I revised my thinking to fit my new behavior. In fact, this is one of the main reasons I have been advocating that therapists try out new ways of responding. By exposing their work to the natural contingencies of the environment, their therapeutic repertoire can grow while becoming increasingly adaptive/effective.

There is no doubt that cognitive change sometimes leads to behavior change, as well as vice versa; and the two are often intertwined in a feedback process with one kind of change leading to the other leading to more change of the first kind, and so on. Nevertheless, since one experiences actual consequences, many of which cannot be anticipated, as the result of behavior change, and only fantasied consequences as a result of cognitive change, my general tendency is to view behavior change as the more potent of the two.

The second lesson has to do with a utilitarian attitude toward theory. Some people view theory as an object of beauty and grow attached to theories as they might to a favorite painting or work of music. I am sympathetic to this aesthetic impulse, and when all other things are equal (which they never are) I would choose the more pleasing of two theories. Even here, Occam's razor is relevant, and the beauty of simplicity is to be preferred to baroque complexity. Nevertheless, people who are looking for beautiful theories would do better to try mathematics—or, if they insist on relevance to the real world, physics—rather than the messy, "flexible" world of psychology.

For most therapists, theory functions as a kind of secular religion. It not only has instrumental value in helping them to assist their clients, but it explains their own behavior and place in the world, is a shared symbolic system that organizes communication within their professional reference group, and gives meaning to their lives. Where would they be without it? Personal ads in intellectual publications, like *The New York Review of Books*, often specify that the potential partner should have been psychoanalyzed, much as they might specify his or her religion.

My own view is that theories are more or less useful ways of organizing observations. If the history of science shows anything, it is that all theories eventually get discarded—or superseded—and that as the number of scientists increases, the longevity of theories decreases. So given that our theories aren't exactly on the level of quantum mechanics, or even Newtonian mechanics, and aren't likely to be around for long anyway, there's no reason to be particularly attached to them.

Fascination with psychological phenomena, especially the change process, and a concern for the welfare of others have drawn me to therapy, not a quasi-religious commitment to a particular theory. And so I found it relatively easy to make a major theoretical shift from psychoanalysis to social learning theory once I was convinced that thinking in the latter way would produce better therapy results. But in a similar manner my commitment to social learning theory was not made with religious intensity.

Theoretical openness is not the same as theoretical eclecticism. Once one has a theoretical viewpoint, there are some concepts that are coherent with it and others that don't fit. This doesn't mean that theories have proprietary rights over observations, data, or subject matter. Some psychoanalysts seem to believe that behavior therapists cannot remain theoretically consistent in their work if they pay attention to slips of the tongue, or consider the clinical relevance of a boy's relationship to his mother in understanding and changing his behavior. Doing so, they seem to assert, would imply an acceptance of psychoanalytic theory. However, all behavior is fair game for all theories; and the relevant question is which theory is supported by more evidence or leads to more effective interventions. It may be that nonanalysts owe Freud a historical debt for having called attention to certain behavior and having made interesting comments on it at the time. But a historical debt is not a theoretical debt; and other theories are free to consider, explain, or otherwise deal with the behavior in any way they choose.

In contrast to theoretical eclecticism, there is no problem with technical eclecticism. If a technique used by practitioners of a different orientation can be understood theoretically in terms of one's own orientation, one is free to make use of it. What all this means is that when one shifts orientations, one has to do a kind of clinical inventory and rethink a whole series of technical issues.

Here are some examples from my shift. While I no longer had any special interest in dreams, I had no problem dealing with them if a client particularly wanted to do so. If I was doing assertiveness training, I would simply point out an element in the dream where the client was being assertive, or could be interpreted to be showing a desire to become more assertive, or something of the kind. Dreams are so complex and ambiguous that there's always plenty of material available to pursue any conceivable therapeutic strategy.

Similarly with unconscious motivation. Since, by definition, there is no way that a person can be aware of something that is unconscious, and since clients often expect interpretations in terms of unconscious content, they are an excellent vehicle for indirect suggestions. For example, "Perhaps that's an indication that, unconsciously, you're getting ready to do X."

I remember one case in which I had successfully desensitized a client's fear, and in which he expressed concern that, since therapy hadn't resolved his Oedipus complex, the change in his behavior might be temporary. So I desensitized his Oedipus complex. I used an elaborate rationale, and hypnosis (so that I could desensitize his unconscious); but the point of the whole exercise was to change his expectancy that the effects of therapy would be temporary. That is, the "oedipal desensitization" made sense in terms of technical eclecticism. The effects of expectancies on behavior are an important part of social learning theory and the central concept of placebo therapy (Fish 1973). But "oedipal desensitization" is absurd theoretically—conditioning concepts are absent from psychoanalysis, and the Oedipus complex plays no role in social learning theory.

In fact, the more therapy I did, the more central the concept of expectancy seemed to be. I don't remember when I first read Jerome Frank's *Persuasion and Healing* (1961, 1973, Frank and Frank 1991), but the openmindedness and imagination that led him to compare therapy to the placebo effect, religious revivalism, and brainwashing were laudable, and the common elements he saw seemed reasonable. In fact, I came to believe that the differing expectancies set up by the ways in which psychoanalysts and behavior therapists arrived at goals, defined the therapeutic process, and arranged the therapeutic contract played a key role in the different rates of change in the two kinds of therapy.

When analysts told clients that their problems were merely surface manifestations of deeper difficulties with their entire personality, that it would take a long time to restructure their personality, and that no promises could be made that therapy would work, they were essentially setting up an expectancy of no change. In contrast, when behavior therapists told clients that their problems consisted merely of a short list of behavioral difficulties, and that research has shown specific techniques to be effective in resolving those difficulties within a relatively brief time, they were setting up an expectancy of change. In terms of Abramson and colleagues' reformulated theory of learned helplessness (1978)—which I view as merely specifying some of the ways in which self-fulfilling expectancies can be positive or negative—psychoanalysts can be seen as telling clients that their problems are stable and global, while behavior therapists label them temporary and specific.

This discussion of relabeling and expectancies provides a contrast to the psychoanalytic emphasis on meaning. Analysts seem to believe that meaning is an attribute of behavior more or less in the way that color or shape is an attribute of a physical object, and that through therapeutic dialog it is possible to discover true meanings (which may lie behind surface appearances). While this belief, like other articles of faith, is not open to empirical verification, there is good reason for asserting that it is not a useful stance. (I actually believe it to be false; but my view is similarly untestable.) An alternative view is that meaning is socially constructed—by societies, cultures, and smaller groups—primarily through language. Thus, instead of viewing therapeutic interaction as a process of discovering meanings, it may more fruitfully be seen as a process of negotiating, constructing, and otherwise changing meanings. From this point of view, the analyst's attempt to discover the meaning of an unusual behavior (a "symptom") is misguided, since meaning isn't something a behavior "has." Instead, the therapist may attempt to label behavior differently or alter expectancies about its occurrence because the effects of doing so may be regarded by the client as more desirable than the effects of current labels or expectancies. In "insight," analysts believe that their clients discover the true meaning of their behavior, which differs from their previous understanding (and which usually conforms to the analyst's theory; Jungian insights are different from Freudian ones, for example). In relabeling, the therapist does not believe that the new label is any truer than the old one, since labels do not possess truth; it is just more useful.

Perhaps, before continuing, this would be a good place to indicate my current view of psychoanalysis. Certainly, it is an important theory in the history of psychology. Nevertheless, in light of where the field is today, I believe that it is fatally flawed.

The most serious theoretical shortcoming of psychoanalysis is that it is not verifiable. While it is evident that much behavior takes place without awareness (e.g., many conditioned responses), the attribution of multiple and contradictory motives, processes, and defenses to "the unconscious" creates an unverifiable theory. By taking "flexibility" of explanation to an extreme, a given set of circumstances that should predict a specific behavior can always be "shown" after the fact to have predicted its opposite (e.g., by reaction formation), or something else (e.g., by displacement), or nothing at all (e.g., by repression). Assertions about what goes on in the minds of nonverbal infants, whose brains are not fully developed, is another example of constructing a theory from unverifiable propositions.[2]

A second major theoretical shortcoming of psychoanalysis is its conception of causality, known as psychic determinism. This view, which asserts that all mental events are completely determined (or "overdetermined"), was a reasonable one given the mechanistic Newtonian view of causality when Freud developed his theory. However, since mental events are related to neuronal events at the molecular level, psychic determinism is inconsistent with the probabilistic causation of quantum mechanics. For this reason, it is fair to say that the psychoanalytic view of causality is simply wrong.

A third major theoretical error of psychoanalysis was to attempt to explore universal content rather than universal processes. Psychology has made significant progress by following the opposite strategy. That is, psychologists have studied processes such as perception or learning, and assumed that people's individual and shared experiences (life histories and culture) fill in the content. On the face of it, the notion that Freud could discover human universals by listening to the fantasies of neurotic upper middle class women in turn-of-the-century Vienna is absurd. It is no surprise that changes in Western culture, such as in the role of women, have subjected psychoanalysis to charges of ethnocentrism.

Beyond this, the mistaken strategy of looking for universal content led to the question of how that content could have gotten into everyone's psyche. The answer that Freud came up

---

2. There has, of course, been research stimulated by psychoanalytic conceptualizations—though its findings remain open to alternative explanations. The objection is not that there are no testable psychoanalytic propositions, but rather that major elements of the theory are in principle untestable. For a theory to pass scientific muster it must not have such gaps.

with, which was scientifically respectable at the time but has been known to be false for decades, was the Lamarckian theory of the inheritance of acquired characteristics. This was the fourth major error in psychoanalytic theory. Freud was committed to a then popular formulation known as recapitulation theory, in which the stages of psychological development were thought to correspond to the stages of human history (Gould 1981, 1987). But the specifics of his Lamarckian commitment, while interesting, don't really matter. The point is that, given our current knowledge of genetics, no matter how many generations of men may—contrary to anthropological knowledge— be supposed to have risen up and killed their fathers, there is no way that such an "oedipal" tendency could have gotten into the genetic material of subsequent generations. While psychoanalysts today may not consider recapitulation theory to be as important as Freud did, the objection remains concerning the origin of the Oedipus complex, dream symbols, and all other purportedly universal content.

A fifth theoretical shortcoming is that psychoanalysis bases its explanation of adult behavior largely on the events of early childhood. Unfortunately, it is by now a psychological commonplace that the more temporally distant a behavioral measurement, the less good it is as a predictor. (For example, college grades are predicted better by high school grades than by elementary school grades.) So basing predictions on early childhood is a poor strategy. Not only does it give disproportionate weight to poor predictors, but it slights the ongoing formative importance of experiences throughout the life span. This is not to say that, if things go very wrong in childhood (e.g., early trauma or deprivation), they can't mess up the rest of a person's life. Rather, it is to recognize that, if they go well enough, subsequent events will be more important—and that, even if they go quite well, later traumas can still have lifelong negative consequences.

There are other problems with psychoanalytic theory. (For example, it could be argued that the theory reifies different ways of viewing experience into "structures." Thus, one's desires get called the id, rational reactions get called the ego, and moral reactions get called the superego. But why stop there? Why not call reactions along the beauty–ugliness dimension the aesthego? Without strong empirical evidence, there is no reason to believe that human mental processes are actually organized into an id, ego, and superego.) But, to my mind, the above five theoretical criticisms are sufficiently devastating. Hence, I view psychoanalysis as an important theory in psychology's past but one that has been superseded by present knowledge.

To return to my postdoc, the hypnosis training I received further contributed to my viewing therapy largely as a process of expectancy modification. In one case, a client whom I had been seeing for problems other than the following, and who was an excellent hypnotic subject, scheduled an emergency session. He was to appear in a play the next day and had developed an immobilizing stage fright that both made him forget his lines and endangered the entire production. After briefly assessing the dimensions of his anxiety, I used a hypnotic relaxation induction and began desensitizing him with an improvised hierarchy. The only problem was that desensitization was going too slowly for us to complete the process within the session. So I began including indirect suggestions during some of the intervals between hierarchy items, such as "Now that we've completed *this* scene, desensitization should move along more rapidly," or "Good. We're three quarters of the way through the hierarchy." It appeared that my client's belief in the treatment and the fact that he had to go on stage the next day combined to accelerate the desensitization process considerably, and we were able to complete the hierarchy during the session. Two days later, he called to say that his performance had been a success, and that he hadn't been distracted by anxiety during the play.

From my reading about the history of hypnosis, I had been struck by the way in which the behavior of hypnotized subjects has conformed to contemporaneous theories of hypnosis, instead of the reverse. So I tried inventing new "hypnotic" phenomena; and sure enough, my subjects displayed them. In one instance, prior to beginning hypnosis with a good subject, I said, "You know how we've already tried posthypnotic suggestions. Today we'll do a prehypnotic suggestion. That's a suggestion I tell you before you're hypnotized, but that takes effect after you come out of hypnosis. The prehypnotic suggestion is that after you come out of hypnosis, you won't be able to see the wastepaper basket in the corner, or remember that I told you this, until I say 'Now you can see it!' Okay?"

The man readily agreed—as was to be expected from a good hypnotic subject—and we proceeded with a hypnotic induction followed by numerous suggestions. At the end of the session, after responding to suggestions to awaken and that he was no longer hypnotized, he displayed the called-for negative hallucination; and he was appropriately amazed when the basket reappeared after the signal. It seemed as if the reason that posthypnotic suggestions were a classical hypnotic phenomenon, and prehypnotic suggestions were nonexistent before I improvised the label, was merely a historical curiosity. If different theories of hypnosis had evolved, then hypnotic subjects would generously have confirmed them instead, and different behaviors would have been considered classical.

In other words, in both my work as a therapist and in my training as a hypnotist, the power of expectancy seemed to be enormous. I wanted to do what worked; and what worked was the placebo effect. After my "cynical psychology" graduate training, in which it had appeared that nothing worked, I was delighted that something really did seem to work rather well, after all. It has come as something of a disappointment to me, if not a surprise, that most behavior therapists, like other therapists, have regarded placebo/expectancy effects as something distasteful and "nonspecific," which ought to be controlled for in experimental studies. I still see them as agreeable and specific main effects that form the core of the behavioral and cognitive therapies.

While the view of placebo/expectancy effects as central to therapy, which I elaborated in *Placebo Therapy* (Fish 1973), has not yet become a dominant one, it has continued to grow and influence the field. For example, Patrick Pentony's book *Models of Influence in Psychotherapy* (1981) discussed it in detail as one of three principal models. (Interestingly, Pentony wrote most approvingly about the contextual or systemic model, at a time when I had already moved in that direction. This suggests that similar environmental influences were leading our thinking to evolve in similar directions at the same time, though we had no contact with each other.) More recently, Irving Kirsch summarized his ongoing research program along with a discussion of new theoretical ideas and clinical approaches in his book *Changing Expectations* (1990). In particular, the term *response expectancy,* which he coined, has proved quite useful. As a theoretical term, it is more precise than *placebo* and highlights the finding that, when one expects oneself to make a nonvolitional response, that response becomes more probable. The concept is relevant both to understanding the development of much involuntary behavior referred to as abnormal or symptomatic, and to changing such behavior. In addition, *response expectancy* has the semantic advantage of sounding scientific. Behavioral and cognitive therapists may be more willing to think of themselves as modifiers of response expectancies than as dispensers of placebos, and thus the term may have a persuasive advantage among practitioners. Finally, the centrality of the placebo effect to medicine, including psychiatry, is a virtual guarantee that the effects of expectancy will not be ignored despite the preference of many practitioners for their "beautiful" theories over "ugly" facts. (Even here, beauty is in the eye of the beholder. Therapists with a sense of irony, who can accept themselves and their clients with warmth, as participants in the human comedy, may find aesthetic satisfaction in the powerful effects of humble expectancies. Other therapists— whose breathless, wide-eyed view of themselves and others as miraculous manifestations of perfection, or whose profound vision falls on sufferers of existential Weltschmerz, or whose analytic insight beholds repressed cauldrons of sexual and aggressive impulses—may have a different aesthetic sensibility.)

In one sense, the contrast between my views and those of most behavioral and cognitive therapists regarding the centrality of placebo/expectancy effects can be seen as a difference of emphasis. To me, Ellis's rational-emotive therapy and Beck's cognitive therapy, along with systematic desensitization and other cognitive and behavioral techniques, are primarily means for changing clients' expectations of their own behavior, which leads in turn to the behavior actually changing. In addition, the techniques may possess some additional validity above and beyond placebo/expectancy effects, which is all to the good. In contrast, most cognitive and behavior therapists seem to be so committed to asserting the validity of their chosen techniques that they find it distressing to view them primarily as vehicles for expectancy effects. So, instead, they focus on the validity of the techniques and attempt to encourage positive expectancies as a kind of add-on.

There are, however, some differences in clinical practice that result from this difference in theoretical emphasis. A commitment to particular techniques limits a therapist to those techniques, while a commitment to the application of principles (such as changing clients' expectancies about their own behavior) leaves a therapist free to innovate. The feedback from the actual changes in the client's behavior—or lack thereof—is the corrective that pulls the therapist back from innovation for its own sake.

This raises the issue of whether a therapist doing therapy is acting like a scientist (or an applied scientist, or engineer). Among many behavior therapists this was a popular point of view. They argued that, unlike psychoanalysis, behavior therapy was empirically based, and that the relationship between therapist and client could be compared to that between experimenter and subject. At the time, and for many years thereafter, I disagreed with the comparison. I argued that the scientist's highest value is truth, while a therapist's highest value is the client's welfare. A scientist uses control groups and other kinds of logical checks to elucidate what leads to what. A therapist uses multiple interventions, some of which may not work, or may even partially cancel each other out, with the ultimate goal that the overall effect of hopelessly intermingled treatments is the desired behavioral change.

I now think that I was wrong; the therapist-as-scientist simile is a good one. While it may carry some undesirable semantic baggage—a therapist does not maintain the stance of detached observer vis-à-vis a client—it has one outstanding advantage. That is the image of the therapist as a hypothesis tester. A scientist's hypotheses may be logically deduced from theory, or may originate as vague hunches or even dream images (e.g., the benzene ring as a snake with its tail in its mouth), but the scientist formulates them so they can be empirically tested. In the same way, a therapist's hypotheses may come from logical deduction or intuition; but therapy progresses by refining them into interventions and comparing the actual outcome with predictions.

Perhaps this is an appropriate point to comment on the therapeutic relationship. My own view is that a collaborative relationship is all that is really necessary or desirable in order to solve problems. The relationship has to be at least somewhat positive, so that the client will cooperate, but if it gets extremely intense, that can make termination and the client's return to a life-without-therapy quite difficult. A cooperative problem-solving relationship does not generally encourage such intensity, so it is usually not a complication. When the client does express feelings about the therapist, they are not dwelt on unless they become disruptive to treatment, since they are not relevant to the problem at hand. This way of working seems natural when therapy is problem focused—it is analogous to a worker complimenting a colleague or boss without the task orientation of the two being disrupted for an extensive exploration of their feelings about each other.

Those feelings that clients do have about their therapist I regard as generally understandable in the context of the therapeutic situation (just as I regard behavior in general as understandable in the context of the situation in which it occurs). When a female client meets with a male therapist, for example, she enters a relationship where she knows that she can trust him, even with secrets she may have told no one else, where he is an intelligent and understanding man who shows interest in her thoughts and feelings and concern for her welfare, and where she can discuss intimate matters including her sexual feelings and experiences. If one compares this description to kinds of relationships she has been in before, or has known of or fantasized about, it sounds a lot like a romantic involvement. So it isn't surprising if she should experience the kinds of feelings she experiences in romantic relationships. (This is an example of what Skinnerians refer to as stimulus control.) There is no need for a concept of transference, or to assert that her feelings for the therapist are really the remnants of a childhood oedipal

desire for her father. Occam's razor—the principle of parsimony—declares that we should opt for the simpler explanation.

Of course, therapy isn't exactly like a romantic involvement; for example, it occurs at regularly scheduled times, and
she has to pay for it. The more therapy focuses on dissimilar
elements—problem-solving talk, "homework assignments,"
and the like—the less likely she is to "fall in love" with her
therapist.[3] The more therapy focuses on similar elements—like
talk about the relationship itself—the more it encourages such
feelings.

In some cases, the client's feelings for the therapist are
clearly related to events that are going on elsewhere in the
client's life. In such situations, the psychoanalytic focus on the
client's inner world serves to blind the therapist to interpersonal
determinants of the client's feelings. Consider the fairly
common situation of a woman whose husband has an affair,
which she is only partially aware of, and who enters therapy
with a male therapist. In such a situation, entering therapy can
be seen as a symmetrical move on her part, and her "transference love" for her therapist can be seen as matching her
husband's feelings for his lover. Just as her husband can't talk
with her about the affair because it is secret, she can't talk about
therapy with him because it is confidential. Such a relationship
is clearly second best; and it is easy to see that feminist therapists
might feel ungenerous toward the therapist. They might accuse
him of making the wife pay for his sympathy and for her
unrequited fantasies while the husband gets a real sexual rela-

---

3. Naturally, some students fall in love with their teachers, just as
some people fall in love with their boss or a colleague at work. Thus,
the problem is best conceptualized as a statistical one (not encouraging
clients to romanticize the therapeutic relationship more than they do
any other), rather than by making reference to universal and unverifiable concepts like transference.

tionship for free (though he might ultimately wind up paying in other ways). One wonders whether the therapist's credulous assertion that the wife's feelings are provoked by her childhood father rather than her actual husband, and that she needs to gain insight into their early origin, would satisfy such critics.

So, if the concept of transference is unnecessary, how can one make sense of the behavior that occurs in the psychoanalytic relationship? It is similar to another well-known kind of relationship—seduction.

In a romantic relationship a man says "I love you" because he means it; a seducer says it to get the woman to sleep with him. In a romantic relationship, he communicates concerned understanding and encourages her to love him because he means it; in psychoanalytic therapy, he does so to persuade her to commit to therapy. While the lover shows outer sensitivity to her thoughts and feelings, inwardly he does care; while the analytic therapist shows such outer sensitivity, inwardly he regards her thoughts and feelings as having other meanings. When the woman finds out that the seducer doesn't love her, she gets angry; when the analytic client finds out that her therapist doesn't love her, she has "negative transference" (feelings that seem to me appropriate to the situation she finds herself in).

It is easy to understand why termination is such a problem for psychoanalysts. They have created such an interpersonal tangle that it takes a long time to extricate themselves from it. Termination in psychoanalytic therapy usually takes much longer than the entire course of problem-focused therapy. When the problem is solved, problem-focused therapy ends naturally—the collaboration has achieved its goal. When the problem is not solved, or is only partially solved, this is openly acknowledged. Even though some things in life don't work out, one can still tell when they are over. The end of a collaborative, problem-focused relationship is, at least, identifiable. The combination of ill-defined goals (e.g., personality growth; "Where id was, there shall ego be") with a deliberately sticky relationship makes the end of psychoanalytic therapy difficult to define. No wonder Freud (1963b) wrote *Analysis Terminable and Interminable!*[4]

In a similar way, I would also advocate a collaborative, problem-focused relationship for therapy supervision. Both participants know what they're doing, and the emphasis is on solving the client's problems rather than on the therapist-supervisor relationship.

My own experience is that therapists tend to be rather open about their feelings about clients when these are treated pragmatically, as occasionally relevant sources of leads about what is going on in a perplexing interaction. Supervisors who characteristically ask, "How did you feel about that?" and explore the therapist's feelings about the client, significant others in the therapist's life, or even the supervisor, tend to provoke defensiveness and diminished self-disclosure. Those who characteristically ask, "What did you do about that?" and explore the consequences of the therapist's intervention, in a problem-solving quest for what to do next, tend to engage cooperation. Thus, even though—or, more accurately, because—therapist self-disclosure is not seen as especially important, more of it

---

4. I fear that this brief discussion may seem exaggerated—even to the point of parody—by those who view the therapeutic relationship in intrapsychic terms. Unfortunately, to those who understand the relationship in terms of sociocultural interaction, that is how it looks. To psychoanalysts, this discussion may provoke the unavoidable kind of discomfort that one feels when encountering someone from another culture. For those who are intrigued rather than offended, Haley's *The Art of Psychoanalysis* (1958), which also appears as the Epilogue to his *Strategies of Psychotherapy* (1963), *is* intended as a satire; but it also provides an interesting view of the therapeutic relationship in terms of one-upmanship.

tends to occur. It shows up as part of the problem-solving process in interactions like the following:

Therapist: I was getting annoyed at him for always giving some lame excuse for not doing the task he'd agreed to.

Supervisor: Maybe we should come up with a task, the point of which would be for him not to do it.

Therapist: No. I think this last one really would have worked if I could have gotten him to do it. I'm just wondering whether he might be giving me a hard time in response to my annoyance.

If, instead, the supervisor had asked, "Does that feeling of annoyance remind you of your feelings about anyone else?" or, worse, "I wonder if you're also feeling annoyed at me?" the therapist would likely become more cautious at being put on the spot, in addition to being deflected from a consideration of the client's behavior.

During my postdoc, there was still considerable turmoil in the country and on the campuses. One of the invited speakers at Stony Brook, around the time that I defended my dissertation and was formally launched on my career, was Sigmund Koch, and he drew a large crowd. As he surveyed the sea of faces, he said, "I bet you're upset at the compromises you have to make as graduate students." The agreement was widespread and audible. "Well," he continued, "they're nothing compared to the compromises you're going to have to make after you get your doctorates."

Something else important happened toward the end of my postdoc. I met my wife-to-be. Since, in terms of the subject matter of this chapter, my wife has had a considerable impact on my orientation, I will attempt to discuss certain aspects of this impact. At the same time, I will try both to contain my impulse to play the proud husband and limit my self-disclosure to what is relevant.

Since I did not begin my postdoc with either the intent or expectancy of meeting my wife, this is an appropriate place for a pause to consider the role of chance events on the development of behavior. In chronological order, this discussion belongs with my later involvement with the systems movement; but it is such a striking example that I am bringing it up now.

The way most behavior therapists think about change in general—perhaps because conditioning takes place gradually (though cognitive change often does not)—is that it occurs in small steps in the direction of chosen goals. For example, if a shy man comes for assertiveness training, gradually overcomes his shyness, meets a woman, and gets married, he would be seen as exemplifying this view of change. After identifying his social skills deficits, the therapist might use role-playing, role reversal, and homework assignments, beginning with the simplest social behaviors and gradually moving up through ever more challenging forms of heterosexual involvement. The success of this gradual, planful approach would seem to confirm the therapist's view of change.

Thinking in terms of a longer time span challenges this view. Once the man is married, his life goes off in a particular direction. If he had consulted the behavior therapist a year earlier, or a year later, and had achieved the same desired result, he most likely would have met and married a different woman, and his life would have gone off in a very different direction. Hence, five or ten years after successfully completing therapy, his life might be in a quite different place, depending significantly simply on the date of having started therapy.

Another way of putting this is that there are multiple interacting and unforeseeable influences on behavior, so that, even within the context of a deterministic theory, long-term outcomes are difficult to predict. This is the case even when we are sure that certain events do have a significant impact on subsequent behavior.

3

The Influence of Anthropology

I met my wife, Dolores Newton, in the spring of 1969. She is an anthropologist who had returned at mid-year from her second stint of field work with the Krikati Indians in central Brazil to join the anthropology department at the State University of New York at Stony Brook.

I was impressed by the adventurousness of a woman who had gone with another graduate student to Brazil to do field work with the most primitive tribe she could find. ("Primitive" is a technical term, referring only to a society's level of technological development. Similarly, "civilized" means only that a society has cities.) The two had driven a jeep along unpaved roads deep into the interior, looking for a tribe that was supposed to have been killed off by ranchers in the 1930s but that recent reports had said still existed. They had entered the village and declared, "We'd like to live with you for a year."

Her desire to work with the most primitive group she could find was in some ways reminiscent of my initial impulse to work with the most psychotic person on the ward—we both wanted to understand behavior that was as different as possible from our own. In addition, behavior that violates norms is of particular interest because it helps to identify what those norms are. Getting to know Americans who behave abnormally, or members of another culture whose normal behavior violates American assumptions, helps one to understand oneself and American culture. For example, when a friend of mine asked her, "Did you really eat anteater? What did it taste like?" she said, "It tasted a lot like monkey." This interaction was useful in revealing American food taboos.

Marrying an anthropologist meant that I was in for a number of unanticipated changes. I had assumed that I would return to New York City, or to some other metropolis, after my postdoc; suburban living was not for me. However, since Stony Brook was so far from the city, my wife's job meant that I was to become a suburbanite. Even more significant, from the time that we knew we were going to get married it was clear that we were going to spend some time living in Brazil.

Since psychology and anthropology are subcultures in their own right, I was to get an opportunity to see anthropology from the inside, and to be able to compare and contrast its worldview with the psychological one that I had been acculturating myself to over the previous five years. While I will return to this subject below, the basic difference between the two is that psychology looks at the behavior of individuals, but a society is the unit of anthropological study—individuals are of interest only insofar as they illuminate something about the group. Since American society is individualistic, the psychological perspective is easier for Americans to grasp. In contrast, the anthropological perspective goes against the grain of individualism and could easily be seen as subversive were it not for the additional view of America as a melting pot or salad bowl. These images recognize that the country is made up of diverse groups whose norms and behavior are exemplified by their members, but also view the groups as jointly constituting a superordinate unity to which each individual is supposed to owe primary loyalty.

And there was something else. Dolores is black. Being married to a black anthropologist has a number of advantages. First, there is the opportunity for exposure to the African American subculture that is not ordinarily available to most whites. Then, since she is an anthropologist, there is the opportunity to make intellectual sense of the cross-cultural experience. I got quite interested in questions of race and culture; it was as if I had my own personal research institute. She could answer questions, help me to ask better questions, suggest readings, look things up, or consult colleagues. (I also provided her some exposure to psychology. Unfortunately, she shared the anthropological view of the "human" areas of psychology [e.g., social, personality, developmental, and clinical] as American ethnocentrism masquerading as science; and this limited her interest.)

Becoming intellectual companions was a process of crossing disciplinary subcultures as well as American subcultures. One early discussion about race became heated as each of us grew frustrated with the other's lack of logic in attempting to conclude things about certain populations. It turned out that, as a psychologist, I was using the term *population* to mean statistical population, while as an anthropologist she was using it to mean breeding population.

There were other differences between our two disciplinary worlds. For all its "flexibility," psychological theory is a model of rigor compared to its counterpart in social and cultural anthropology. Early on in our relationship I asked, in all naïveté, if she could recommend to me the equivalent of a theories of personality text. "You know, a book that summarizes the different anthropological theories—where you plug in information about some variables in a society and get information about others as output." It took a while for her to understand what I was asking, and even longer for me to understand—let alone believe—that there are no such theories. That isn't what anthropology is about. The closest approximation to such a theory—quite fascinating in its own right, though leaving out much of the content of the field—is Marvin Harris's cultural materialism (1980).

From my point of view, clinically relevant psychology is scientific—albeit in a preparadigmatic stage—while anthropology can't even decide on its subject matter. There is actually debate among cultural anthropologists over whether the field belongs in the humanities or the social sciences.

In methodological terms as well, psychologists can take heart. While anthropologists have developed clever qualitative methods (e.g., Spradley 1979, 1980), they tend to be quantitatively naïve. For example, there seems to be an unwritten custom of one anthropologist to a tribe, or at least of a new researcher getting a previous researcher's permission before studying "his" or "her" people. Similarly, anthropologists are very protective of their data and field notes. To an outsider this looks like insecurity (if another researcher wrote something different, that might throw doubt on one's own conclusions). In contrast, psychologists learn early about reliability and validity. If two psychologists give the same test to the same person and get different results, that shows something about the reliability of the test, not (ordinarily) about the honesty or competence of the psychologists. I now have cross-cultural experience and can personally attest to how difficult it is to understand another culture. Not only do cultures often change with breathtaking rapidity, but they are so complex that even differing contemporaneous accounts can be extremely useful, serving as binocular perspectives that offer a more rounded understanding.

What anthropology has going for it is the fascination of its material. Cultural variation is so amazingly broad that learning about it is a continual source of personal and theoretical growth. Counterexamples from another culture expose both one's own ethnocentric assumptions and the ethnocentric assumptions in psychological theory. (A psychologist from India, for example, complained to me about the lack of a role for the grandparents in the Oedipus complex. This is a very embarrassing omission— hundreds of millions of counterexamples—for a supposedly universal phenomenon.)

On the other hand, for all the relative theoretical and methodological strength of psychology, most psychologists are blind to culture. I recently interviewed an experienced clinical psychologist and, among other things, asked him about his cultural background. He said that he didn't have any! (He was a midwesterner of British-American ancestry.) As best I could understand his thinking, he viewed himself as a normal, or regular, or garden variety human being. Without in any way labeling himself as superior or disparaging others, he seemed to believe that culture was something that members of non-standard groups had—people like white ethnics, Jews, Asians, Hispanics, or blacks.

While a cultural perspective may go against the grain of American individualism, it fits in well with social learning theory. People learn their language, food preferences, aesthetic taste in music and the arts, religion, preferences for clothing and body decoration, and numerous other cultural traits through social interaction. (*Cultural trait* is a vague anthropological term and doesn't have the specific meaning of *psychological trait*.) People do, of course, change their behavior over time; and there is considerable—though not unlimited—variation within a given culture. While it may seem unfair, perhaps even un-American, to say that you cannot choose your culture, unfortunately that's the way it is. Your culture chooses you.

I might like to speak Chinese instead of English, but the choice of language was made for me before I knew what was going on. I cannot come up with apt Chinese metaphors, expressions, or cultural references, because I haven't been exposed to them, and most of them, if translated into English, would have to be explained to me. Even if I devoted the rest of my life to becoming Chinese, and my physical appearance were not an issue, I would still be recognizable to a member of the culture as an American, trying—as anthropologists say—to "go native."

I witnessed an interesting example of this principle—that your culture chooses you—in Brazil. An American anthropologist was called in by a community of Japanese immigrants who had been having difficulties with their children. They guessed that the problem might be cultural in nature and asked him for an opinion. After spending a reasonable amount of time observing the children, their families, and the community, he gave the parents his verdict. Their sons and daughters were normal Brazilian children!

To return to the point about the role of chance events in the development of behavior: by going on my postdoc I met my wife. And meeting her led to many unanticipated changes. I got interested in anthropology, especially the areas of race and culture, developed cross-cultural interests, was exposed to the subcultures of American anthropologists, suburban Americans, African Americans and to Brazilian culture (later, on my own, to French culture and to other Latin American cultures), learned Portuguese (and later French and Spanish), and generally developed intellectually in entirely unanticipated directions. I made sense of these experiences in terms of my new social learning orientation and in this way deepened my understanding of the theory—another example of cognitive change following behavioral change. In addition, my understanding of social learning theory increasingly emphasized its articulation with the other social sciences as well as the social content of what is learned, while the trend in psychology was for the theory to increasingly emphasize the learning process itself, and cognitive elements within that process.

Here is an example of anthropological thinking that is useful to a social learning perspective, but that most psychologists are unaware of—the etic versus emic distinction. The terms were invented by the linguist Kenneth Pike (1954), who used the endings of the words phon*etic* and phon*emic* to generalize the categories beyond their linguistic context.

Consider the vowel sounds in the spoken words *bit* versus *beat* (or *beet*). Why is it that people who speak English with a French accent always say the former when they mean the latter and vice versa? It would seem to take a perverse attention to detail to always use the wrong sound. Interestingly, the French speaker is quite consistent and can be described as following a simple rule; the perversity is in the ear of the English-speaking beholder. Where English has two vowels—each with its own range of sound—French has only one, with a range of sound falling between those of the other two. This is the only vowel the French speaker uses. Since the pronunciation of the English vowel is never correct, it is always heard by an English speaker as the wrong alternative.

To deal with such issues, linguists have invented the distinction between the phonetic and phonemic domains. Phonetics refers to the actual physical range of speech sounds as produced by the vocal apparatus and measurable objectively by physical instruments. Phonemics refers to the units of meaning that a given language associates with a particular range of sound vibrations. Phonetics deals with sounds in the physical world; phonemics deals with sounds in the world of meaning. Along the physical range of vowel sounds from one end of *bit* to the other end of *beat*, French has one meaning unit, and English has two.

By extension, for therapists, etics could be defined as the domain of objectively observable behavior, and emics as the domain of subjective meaning. For this reason, etic comparisons can be made cross-culturally (e.g., the protein content of a group's diet), while emics is limited to social description (e.g., the meaning of food in social interaction).[1] Naturally, one has to take care that the categories or units of "objectively observable behavior" do not reflect cultural biases. Anthropologists, whose scope is rather broader, have correspondingly more complex definitions of the terms (cf. Harris 1968, Chapter 20, 1980, Part I).

These definitions accept emics within the world of empirical investigation. Meanings, from a social science perspective, do not exist in a numinous world of Platonic ideals but are invented and shared by ongoing groups of interacting people. On the other hand, it is clear that there are etic limitations on emic variation—just as the sounds that the human speech apparatus can produce, or auditory apparatus can detect, set limitations on the phonemes that can be found in human languages. While there is not a one-to-one correspondence between behavioral and etic approaches, or cognitive and emic approaches, their considerable overlap is suggestive of the theoretical limi-

---

1. Much of the heat in the recent controversy over social constructivism results from confounding the etic versus emic distinction. This is done by comparing emic categories as if they were physical entities rather than social constructions, or by insisting that all reality is socially constructed (denying etics). Social reality is socially constructed, and the understanding of physical reality is in part socially constructed, though constrained by physical limits, but physical reality itself is not socially constructed.

tations of cognitive explanatory strategies. Similarly, the psychoanalytic attempt to "discover" the "real meaning" of behavior can be seen as a confusion of the etic and emic domains.

The etic versus emic example allows for combining the themes about the effects of unpredictable events and of the relationship between cognitive and behavioral change. It is fair to say that if I had never met my wife (an unpredicted etic/behavioral event), I would probably never have heard of the etic versus emic distinction, and my thinking would not have been influenced by it (an emic/cognitive consequence). A similar point could be made about much of the content of Part II of this book.

During the summer after my postdoc, I traveled in Europe. In a minor accident early in the vacation, I bruised my leg. No damage had been done, but it made walking painful and I was doing a lot of walking. I spent about a half hour in my hotel room doing my best to hypnotize myself. (At the time, my training had been only in hypnotizing others, but I understood the basic principles and my motivation was high.) I gave myself all kinds of suggestions for not feeling pain, or being bothered by pain, or attending to pain, along with various qualifications saying that if I had done any real damage I would become aware of it and get medical attention.

About two weeks later, the thought crossed my mind: I wonder how my leg is. I immediately became aware of a slight ache. So it had worked!

One can test therapeutic principles and gain experience with techniques not only by applying them to others but by trying them out on oneself. In this way, a therapist can learn from both perspectives—as subject and object, observer and observed—and can be both the influencer and the one influenced. If self-therapy has no effect or makes matters worse, and the issue is important enough, one can always consult a therapist (though I at least have not yet managed to be less than ineffective in changing my own behavior). Meanwhile, self-therapy can be seen as a reasonable alternative to a training analysis for therapists who are interested in behavior change. At the minimum, it is much less expensive; and since it is aimed at affecting specific behavior, it avoids the complications that can arise from trying to solve problems that don't exist.

The effects of unanticipated events are a major theme of this book, and the next two years were full of them. A professor at Stony Brook went on sabbatical, allowing me to stay on for a year and get married. Staying in New York made it possible to take courses in hypnosis at Columbia University's medical school; and these in turn were a partial stimulus to begin writing *Placebo Therapy*[2] (Fish 1973).

During that time, there was an aged couple living in the apartment beneath us who were both extremely senile. Their son would come to visit them every day, but they didn't know who he was; and they would complain crazily about having been robbed when they couldn't find things they had misplaced. I was perplexed by them, and one day asked an experienced social work colleague how such severely limited people were able to survive on their own. "I've seen it many times," he said; "two halves make a whole!" Sure enough, as I observed them more closely, I saw that the husband could lead his wife to and from the supermarket, and that she could buy food and cook.

The memory of this couple stayed with me; and it was to fall into place a number of years later when I got involved with the systems movement (an involvement I will discuss in detail below).

---

2. Along with discussing ways of using expectancies in therapy, this book, in its cross-cultural allusions and examples, reflected the beginnings of an involvement with culture.

For the next three years I returned to academia (Hunter College, City University of New York) where I completed writing *Placebo Therapy* and got it published, while we pursued various leads trying to find university positions in Brazil.

During this time our daughter was born, and we named her for two Krikati women (Krekamey Ropkui). Consistent with subcultural naming practices, American blacks were generally accepting of and curious about her names (I was once even asked if they were Hebrew), while American whites were generally silently—or sometimes not so silently—disapproving (one candid little girl in a supermarket said, "Why didn't you call her Mary?"). It was interesting to discover later that the variation in naming practices of Portuguese speakers is much greater than that of Americans. In addition to the most common religious and Portuguese sources, Brazilians use names from the classics (I had a student named Hippolytus; Julius Caesar is a well-known anthropologist), from more recent history, including American presidents (Wilson and Lincoln are common; a woman behind me in a bus station said, "Shut up, Jefferson!" to her 3-year-old son), from native, or as they say, indigenous Brazilians (I had a student named Avany), and from other countries. They also just make up names because they like the sound. In contrast, in Portugal under the Salazar dictatorship all names had to be chosen from the government's official list.

Eventually, through anthropologist contacts, we landed visiting professorships at two universities in a large city in the interior of the state of São Paulo.

The final process of packing, putting belongings in storage, and arranging for the appropriate work permits, visas, and airline tickets was exhausting. We got virtually no sleep during the forty-eight hours prior to departure, or on the night flight with our 22-month-old daughter. When we arrived in Brazil, officials kept us at the airport for twelve hours, raising a variety of incomprehensible objections to our documentation (in retro-spect, they were probably looking for a payoff). During the first week's scurrying around to get the additional documents they had demanded, I fell and broke my knee. So our arrival in Brazil was not auspicious.

I am detailing these misadventures because I want to make clear that—with the possible exception of being detained at the airport—*they do not constitute culture shock*. There are two kinds of problems that confront one on entering another cul-ture. One is physical hardship, including deprivation of the customary comforts of home; and the other is the psychological stress of finding oneself in a new social world where the rules are different.

Only the latter is properly termed culture shock. One doesn't know what the rules are, and doesn't know what to ask. Well-meaning natives aren't much help, even if they can communicate across the language barrier, because they have no idea how the rules of your alien culture might be different from their own.

I had thought that my wife would ease my entry into Brazilian culture, and she was of real help. Still, I came to realize that her experience with Brazil had been more like that of a tourist; her cultural immersion, and culture shock, had been mainly with the Krikati.

In any event, physical hardship and culture shock get mixed together to make for a doubly difficult adaptation. One way in which they can be made to interact is if you seek solace from your hosts for your physical hardship—not a good idea. Since Brazilians do not expect tap water to be drinkable or buildings to be heated (when it is 50° outdoors in a tropical winter, it is 50° indoors), complaints will get no sympathy. A better approach is to observe the normal behavior all around you and then ask for clarification. ("It seems that people wear more layers of clothing in the morning when it's cold, take them off as the day warms up, and then put them on again as it gets cold at night. Is that right?'')

I had had only one semester's Portuguese prior to arriving, but I had been told there would be simultaneous translators in my classes. It turned out that the translators could read English but didn't know what it sounded like. (A Brazilian in New York was distressed at not being able to get a taxi driver to stop by saying "High cheer!" She was doing her best to pronounce "Right here!" So the differences are significant.)

Things were looking pretty grim. I could have gotten angry: "You told me I'd have a simultaneous translator; you broke your promise, so I'm going home." In fact, two American professors I subsequently helped to hire for the program did just that; one left after a semester, and the other turned around and headed home after a couple of weeks when Brazil didn't meet his expectations. However, a key reason we were in Brazil was for us to live with the Krikati during intersession. I wanted the experience, and felt I owed it to my wife. In addition, our daughter was doing fine, picking up Portuguese effortlessly, once she figured out that it was a different language from English. I needed help, and the only English-speaking therapist in town was me.

So I reframed my situation. (Reframing tends to refer to a broader change of context than relabeling, though the usages of the two terms overlap.) I now do this routinely, in getting clients or supervisees to break out of modes of thought that perpetuate the no-win situation they're in. Just turn everything upside down (applied iconoclasm): bad is good and good is bad; advantages are disadvantages, and vice versa; and so on until something useful emerges. Back then, I had only the concept of relabeling, without the reversal strategy; and it's always harder to get sufficient distance to change oneself than to figure out a way to change someone else. Anyway, this is what I came up with, and it saved the day:

> I am not an underpaid, mistreated psychology professor, attempting to teach under impossible conditions, I told myself. I am a lucky American who managed to get Brazilians to actually *pay* me to participate in a language immersion program. Such programs usually cost thousands of dollars, have a few students and one teacher. In my case, I'm the sole student, I have dozens of teachers, and I'm being paid thousands of dollars to learn Portuguese!

In my next class, I took a vote. How many people want me to try to teach in Portuguese? Everyone! How many people want me to keep teaching in English with simultaneous translation? No one. All right then, I said—or communicated in my broken Portuguese—you'll have to help me out.

So I turned my psychology lectures into Portuguese lessons. I did my homework, writing out the lectures practically word for word in English and looking up key vocabulary beforehand. Classes were spent using my students to help me put sentences together (Brazilians—even illiterate ones—use all the compound tenses and subjunctives of classical Latin). In this way, I was fluent—if only minimally so—in Portuguese by the end of the first semester.

This example, of reframing my classes as Portuguese lessons, once again illustrates the comparison between relabeling and insight. I had the same "Aha!" experience from my reframe that people claim to have when achieving insight into what purports to be reality. Was I really a teacher of psychology or a student in a language immersion? Changing the way I thought about the situation transformed me from a wretched sufferer of injustice to a motivated participant in a challenging enterprise. Without wanting to overdo it, I could say that it resembled the kind of experience claimed by people who have been saved by religion or therapy.

In addition to lecturing, I did group supervision of therapy practica. All students in the graduate program were licensed psychologists, some with years of experience, and many were professors in undergraduate programs as well. (In Brazil, professional education in psychology, medicine, law, and other fields begins right after high school, in self-contained institutes. The system is quite different from the American one, leading to a more rapid formation of professionals. Neither the country nor the students are economically prepared to sustain America's longer and more expensive training.) Nearly all therapists were young, single, and purportedly virginal women; the program was at a Catholic university.

The program was so new that there was as yet no clinic; so we began by discussing ongoing cases from my supervisees' private practices. Progress was slow because of my minimal Portuguese; but the therapists participated in good spirit. The first case one of them brought up was of a couple in marital therapy. The husband wanted to have oral sex, but the wife thought that was perverted. What did I think?

Welcome to the cross-cultural mine field! I didn't want to shock or offend them, but therapy was therapy, and we had to do what was right. On the other hand, I had no idea of what would be functionally "right" for Brazilians. Eventually, after getting more information, I responded cheerfully that most American therapists thought that whatever a couple felt like doing was okay, as long as it didn't land them in the hospital. They seemed satisfied by this answer, and we went on to form a good working alliance.

In retrospect, now that I am familiar with Brazilian culture, I can appreciate their sly humor in throwing me such a curve at the outset. They doubtless recognized the awkward position I was in and were curious to see how I would react. (In addition, they may have been testing me to see how much they could confide about their private lives.) Someone once said that an anthropologist doing field work is like a sunflower in a field of daisies. It is easy when learning another culture to forget that you are an object of interest yourself. Rather than neutrally observing usual behavior, you may well be observing rare behavior that is provoked by your unusual presence.

This is an important parallel between the roles of therapist and anthropologist. Both are participant observers. By then I had long since rejected the Freudian notion of the therapist as a blank screen. I remember hearing of a classical analyst who, once sessions on the couch began, would hide behind the door while the analysand entered and left the office, so as not to give even visual cues about himself. He thought he was being a blank screen, offering no information about himself. Amazing! As anyone could see, he was engaging in bizarre social behavior; and his extensive training had blinded him to this self-recognition.

When I arrived in Brazil, I thought I was a citizen of the world—a characteristically American form of egalitarian naïveté. It was obvious to Brazilians that I was American: I couldn't even speak Portuguese. The process of learning Brazilian culture was simultaneously a process of discovering what it meant to be American. Whenever something apparently impossible happened, I would try to understand it, and in this way I would come to recognize my own culturally based assumptions. Here is a common example, concerning the use of time.

> "Professor, I'd like to meet with you Thursday from 3:00 to 4:00 P.M."
>
> "Unfortunately, I have an appointment from 2:30 to 3:30."
>
> "Fine. I'll see you at 3:00."

The first time something like this happened, I thought that there might have been a problem with my Portuguese or with the student's hearing. Or perhaps she was just trying to bulldoze me into changing my schedule. Nothing of the sort! Once I was able to communicate that such behavior actually required an explanation, I would get something like the following.

"You Americans are so rigid. I'll come a little late, and when the people you're with see that I'm waiting they'll leave a little early. It will all work out."

In fact, my strong emotional reaction after arriving in the country, when things weren't the way they were supposed to be, was very much an American reaction. Americans see life as predictable, insist on playing by the rules, and treat unexpected rule changes as unfair rather than normal. They're more likely to pick up their marbles and go home than try to figure out how to play by the new rules. For Brazilians, in contrast, life is unpredictable and consists of one impossible situation after another. Thus, the ability to adapt to unexpected rule changes is both necessary and highly valued. Americans' behavior to the contrary therefore seems rigid to Brazilians—and, after having lived there, to me as well, though I recognize that I could never achieve Brazilian flexibility. (These and other cultural generalizations should be understood as illustrative, with the implicit recognition of substantial individual and subcultural variation within each culture.)

In fact, Brazilians' openness to fundamental change was one of the things that made my work there so rewarding. I had had experience in two American psychology departments, which made decisions such as "We need to hire a social psychologist specializing in attribution theory." Even with a Ph.D., a professor is a cog in a wheel. In contrast, when I met with the director of the psychology institute and asked him what courses he needed me to teach, he said, "What do they need to learn?" I was in charge of the concentration in behavior modification, and I had free rein, as long as what I did was academically substantive. As a result, I contributed much more in time and enthusiasm than professors do in the United States (though there was little support available for research).

Since the program was new, students varied from those who had recently completed their training to those with years of experience. In group supervision, it was easy to identify thera-pists who were already able to function as independent profes-sionals. As a result, I set up a practicum in supervision, offering them a kind of training they hadn't had. American university bureaucracies rarely make it possible to create, change, and eliminate courses on the spur of the moment, based on the current constellation of faculty and of student interests and competencies. In addition, by doing group supervision of sub-stantial numbers of therapists and supervisors, I was to come into contact with a large number of cases, thereby getting an opportunity to observe indirectly the intimate lives of many Brazilians.

The graduate clinic was soon set up in a large house. Some therapists expressed concern that, since we were a Catholic university, the requisite crucifix might have an inhibiting effect on clients' candor. A characteristically Brazilian decision was made to display the crucifix prominently in the front entryway. Since clients entered the waiting room through a side entrance, there was no difficulty. The ability to come up with this kind of solution is one of the most fascinating aspects of the Brazilian way of thinking; and Brazilian Portuguese may have as many terms for this kind of innovative behavior (e.g., *dar um jeitinho*, or *quebrar o galho*) as Eskimoan languages have words for snow.

Americans tend to view such solutions as immoral, for finessing the implicit conflict over principle. We put an end to slavery, for example, through the Civil War, a bloodbath un-equaled on the planet until World War I. Brazil, in contrast, simply passed a law saying that after a certain date anyone born to a slave would be free. For all my admiration of Brazilian flexibility, the gradual phasing out of slavery is a hard notion for me to swallow. Still, I wonder whether a dose of Brazilian thinking might not occasionally be helpful to Americans in resolving intractable policy problems that reflect deep social divisions. In the therapy domain, it is easy to see how such thinking can be an asset in helping clients to solve their problems. One need only put some theoretical and ethical constraints on its most enthusiastic application.

I was consulted about how to spend the discretionary part of the budget for furnishing the clinic. Since I was concerned that sounds from the consulting rooms could be heard in the waiting room, I suggested we invest in rugs, better sound insulation for the doors, white noise generators or radios, and other means for preserving confidentiality. After thanking me for my helpful input, the people in charge spent the money on fancy furniture for the waiting room. Even in therapy, social status seemed a more important value in Brazil than privacy. I remember a therapist in a group I was supervising saying, "I want to ask you about a private case of mine; but confidentiality is very important. I'm seeing a depressed woman who's having an affair with a very prominent man." Another therapist chimed in, "I know who it is!" That this very private affair was actually public suggested that even basic therapeutic values like confidentiality have to be understood as culturally relative.

In addition, the decisions about the display of the crucifix and the purchase of furniture illustrate the way in which material culture (the product of the intentional modification of the physical world) is intertwined with therapy. The furnishing of a consulting room—let alone the fact that such a specialized type of room exists—actualizes implicit cultural norms for a physical environment conducive to psychological change. Furthermore, material culture is another area where anthropology has an interface with psychology. In this case, environmental psychology, especially environmental design (Krasner 1980) is the relevant counterpart.

Once the graduate clinic was functioning, the university made my services available to the public, since I was the only English-speaking therapist in the city. In addition, once my Portuguese was good enough, I was also the therapist for a small number of Brazilians. These two experiences provided an illuminating contrast.

There were three kinds of Americans living with their families in the area, and I worked with all three. The first were academicians—either university professors like my wife and me, or teachers at the American school; the second were executives of multinational corporations; and the third were missionaries, mainly Protestant fundamentalists and Mormons. While the academicians' strategy was primarily to adapt to Brazilian culture, the other two groups tried more to maintain American cultural enclaves.

The businessmen (they were all men) sent their children to the American school, attended American churches, had their own golf club, and imported films of the week's football games (this was before the advent of VCRs). They and their children sometimes learned a reasonable amount of Portuguese, because of their contact with Brazilians, though their wives rarely did. A typical businessman grew up in a small town in the south or midwest, attended an obscure college majoring in beer and women, took a job with a multinational corporation, started a family, and went to Brazil to manage a factory so as to accelerate his corporate climb. While in Brazil, where the cost of living was lower than in the states, he received extra hardship pay, enjoyed a prestigious and challenging job, lived in a large house with servants and a chauffeur, hobnobbed with the mayor and other government officials, and often got his picture in the newspaper. His wife, in contrast, lived in isolated splendor, sometimes got depressed or drank too much, and sometimes was kept occupied by troublesome children or adolescents. Some of these marriages went through stormy times or even fell apart.

In contrast, while coming from a geographical and social class background similar to that of the businessmen, the missionaries did learn Portuguese and had considerable contact with poor Brazilians. However, neither they nor the Brazilians were particularly good at distinguishing their American religions from the rest of American culture they brought with them. They were offering a package deal of social-educational-medical services, American customs, and religion to people they were trying to save. (One missionary told me he believed that the devil was a person who literally walked the streets and tempted people.) They did not view their charges as people they could learn from, but as sinners who needed their teaching; thus they attempted to protect themselves from Brazilian culture rather than learn from it.

Even though I was living in Brazil, when I was doing therapy in English with Americans I found myself temporarily in an American world. While clients from academicians' families seemed more similar to me, and those from the other two groups seemed different from me and similar to each other, all of this similarity and difference was within an American context. In therapy, even though we were in Brazil, we were all Americans communicating in a shared dialect (American English, not British or Australian or some other variety) with an implicit universe of discourse regarding social class, age, gender, race, religion, politics, and other social categories. This does not mean that we shared positions or perspectives on particular issues; we knew that we did not. But we shared assumptions about the dimensions of discourse and range of possibilities. If, for example, I had had another appointment from 2:30 to 3:30, no American client would have thought of asking for a 3:00 to 4:00 appointment, or would have considered it a possibility consistent with my schedule.

When I was doing therapy in Portuguese with a Brazilian client I was on my own in Brazilian culture. The mode of expression, dimensions of social reality, nature of problems, and possible solutions all existed in Brazilian terms. This is what makes therapy in another language and another culture so fascinating. Nevertheless, one has to know one's limits where specific knowledge is involved. For example, as part of one case, my client was considering a choice between two careers. I was inclined to option A but recognized that I knew nothing about the Brazilian job market, salaries, or prestige hierarchy for work, and that my preference was based on how the two possibilities would function in the states. So I invited one of my supervisees to sit in on the therapy for a few sessions. It turned out that option B was a much better choice, and we counseled the client accordingly.

Sometimes, when I saw an American and a Brazilian client in succession, I had the sensation of shifting cultural perspectives: now I'm thinking in an American way, trying to help other Americans living in Brazil; now I'm trying to think in a Brazilian way to help Brazilians. (I have subsequently had the experience of doing therapy in Portuguese with Brazilians in the United States. In some ways it is the mirror image of doing therapy in Brazil with Americans. There is a mental shifting of gears, and then I'm seeing things from a Brazilian perspective, viewing American culture and the problems it creates for Brazilian immigrants as best I can through Brazilian eyes.)

While being a foreigner has obvious disadvantages as a therapist, it also has some advantages. For example, Brazilians place a high value on foreign authorities. My flawed Portuguese, American accent, and imperfect understanding of Brazilian culture actually served to enhance my prestige as a foreign visiting professor. Unfortunately, as I became more acculturated I seemed more like an immigrant; and as a result my professional prestige began to decline. Thus, the greater my competence, the lower my placebo value—an ironic state of affairs for a therapist.

A foreigner can also pretend not to understand (and often actually does not understand). For example, if I wanted a Brazilian client to give more information about an embarrassing subject, I could excuse my limited Portuguese or foreignness and probe for greater explicitness based on my linguistic or cultural handicap. It is harder for clients to turn down a request for information when they think you don't understand than when they think you're being nosy.

After we had been in Brazil a year it came time for our trip to the Krikati. If Brazil is about as different a Western culture from ours as exists, the Krikati are about as different as it is possible to find anywhere in the world. In 1975 they were approximately 300 hunter-gatherer-horticulturalists, living about 300 miles south of Belém, the city at the mouth of the Amazon river, and about 50 miles east of Imperatriz, a boom town on the Tocantíns river (a major tributary of the Amazon). The interior of the north of Brazil is a world apart from the industrialized south. For example, the last leg of our trip involved finding someone in a small town to drive us by jeep to the Krikati village. Before we left, we had lunch at the local inn. The sleeping facilities were a large room with hooks on opposing walls for travelers to hang their hammocks. There was no electricity or running water; food was served in a sheltered outdoor area after being cooked on an open hearth; and the "restrooms" were the banana patch.

The physical appearance of the Krikati was distinctive— short, dark, muscular, barefoot people, wearing few clothes (the women were topless, and children were naked), with designs painted on some bodies. Their faces were particularly revealing of a non-Western aesthetic—plucked eyebrows and eyelashes, front teeth filed to points, distinctive hairstyles, designs painted on some faces, earlobes of older men distended to leave holes for earplugs ranging from one to three inches in diameter. The village consisted of extended families living in thatched-roofed, wood-framed huts arranged in a large circle around a central ceremonial area.

Living for a month in an extremely different culture is a challenging experience. People like me, not used to camping in the wilderness, would find the physical hardship to be great—getting water from and bathing in the river, eating a limited diet (mainly manioc, rice, beans, and some fruits; no meat or other vegetables on most days), and learning to sleep in a hammock. There was also no privacy. For example, one morning we awoke to see about fifteen people sitting around us, watching silently. (This incident once again illustrates how interesting participant-observers are to the observed.)

In cultural terms, the Krikati were so different that it was hard for me to make heads or tails of them. My wife, who had lived with them twice before for extended periods of time, felt that so much was going on she could barely keep track of it. My experience, not being able to read the cultural cues, was that nothing was happening—a bit like sitting in the dayroom of a psychiatric hospital with everyone staring off into space.

I decided to do something psychological. We were friendly with a particular family who had a daughter about the same age as ours. So I asked the father if I could make a tape recording of his life history. I explained in some detail that I wanted to know about what his life had been like, beginning with his earliest childhood recollections and continuing with anything he wanted to tell me, including where he had lived, and what he had done, thought, and felt, as he grew up. He agreed, and said secretively that he would make the recording at night, when others were asleep. I understood this as a request for confidentiality in light of his anticipated self-revelation, and hastened to cooperate with him.

Since I am recounting our conversations in everyday English, I should describe their actual linguistic form. My Portuguese was that of an English-speaking American professor who had learned the language from the college-educated urban elite of São Paulo, Brazil's richest and most developed state. His Portuguese was that of a Krikati-speaking, nonliterate, native Brazilian who had learned the local dialect from impoverished illiterate peasants in one of the poorest and least developed rural areas of the country. Even without the immense Krikati-American cultural gulf, there were real linguistic impediments to our communication. My wife, who had mainly learned her Portuguese from the Krikati, was a great help in making the process work.

He, my wife, and I made the recording at night, by the light of a kerosene lamp, in low voices, while our daughter slept in a nearby hammock. I began once again with an excessively detailed explanation of what I was asking him to say and briefly recounted my own life history to serve as a model. When I turned on the tape recorder, he began speaking dramatically in Krikati. I waited respectfully for about ten minutes; but when it was clear that this was all that was forthcoming, I broke in to ask that he speak Portuguese. He responded, in essence, that his Portuguese wasn't fully adequate to the task, and besides, too much would be lost in translation. I accepted this for the moment and waited patiently as he went on in Krikati for more than half an hour.

When he had finished, I thanked him but explained that I wouldn't be able to understand the tape because I didn't speak Krikati. He repeated his objection that too much would be lost in translation and added, "Anyway, you could write it down." It turned out that he knew that writing could reproduce the

sounds of spoken words. However, he wasn't aware that, even
though one could say written words aloud by reading them, one
didn't necessarily understand the meaning of the sounds. This
gave him pause, and eventually he consented to repeat in
Portuguese what he had just recorded.

He proceeded to tell one of the most bizarre, elaborate, and
incomprehensible stories I had ever heard, involving lice, and
people, and animals in jumbled action. Before coming to the
Krikati, I had entertained the possibility that they would seem
psychotic to my American eyes; and to my horrified fascination
this life history was appearing to confirm my guess.

I had reasoned from social learning theory that no behavior
is intrinsically normal or crazy; it is the social setting in which it
occurs—the discriminative and reinforcing stimuli that accompany it—that determine its sanity. Thus, it is normal to brush
one's teeth in the bathroom at 7:00 A.M., but it is abnormal to
brush them at noon in Times Square. It might follow that, in a
very different culture, the alterations in the settings for behavior
similar to our own, or the similarity of settings for behavior
different from our own, might be so great as to make its people
appear psychotic. I already knew that some Krikati sometimes
acted crazy in the tribe's own terms. For example, one man who
was considered crazy had chewed some cheese (not necessarily
recognized as food by the tribe) and used it to smear over his
body and shoes. His deviant behavior was considered to have
resulted from having eaten vulture meat (a diagnosis similar in
some ways to our toxic psychosis). But such examples didn't
negate the possibility that all Krikati might seem crazy to
someone from a culture as distant as my own.

Fortunately, I asked the right question. I say fortunately
because, when the cultural and linguistic gulf is this wide, luck
plays a greater role than skill. For example, they didn't seem to
understand either/or questions. "Which do you like better,
hunting or working in the garden?" "I like to hunt; I like to

work in the garden." So even a good question asked in the wrong way might not get a useful answer. What I asked was, "And all this happened to you?"

He was surprised by my question. "No, of course not." It took a while to straighten out what had happened, but eventually we came to understand that he had been telling a tribal myth. His behavior constituted a good faith effort to respond to his understanding of my request. His secretive manner stemmed from the presumptuousness of the act—only the elders had the prerogative to pass on such information to outsiders. The Krikati did not seem psychotic after all, just very different and easily misunderstood. When you are dealing with people who have no concept of a life history or of an interview, the culture-bound nature of clinical interactions is vividly revealed. In a sense, the Krikati could be said to be beyond the reach of therapy because the concept of therapy is not a part of their culture (though they have their own ways of explaining and dealing with what we would consider personal and social difficulties).

The return to the southern urban Brazil that had become my reference culture was in some ways a jarring experience. There was a sense of "Did my experience with the Krikati really happen?" Within a few days of leaving the village, I was sitting at a meeting of the psychology graduate faculty. Something about the meeting felt strange, and I was midway through it before I realized what it was. We were a group of men sitting in a circle and talking together, but we were all wearing clothes and none of us was painted.

While my own cases and those I supervised in Brazil generally went quite well, there were a few where the results were disappointing despite extensive clinical efforts. For the most part, these were cases where the person exhibiting problem behavior was a child or adolescent, but where the

parents somehow couldn't be mobilized to change their behavior—for example, by ignoring their child's undesired behavior and rewarding more appropriate alternatives. (These are
generally called "resistant" cases, and many behavior therapists
use the term to describe passively or actively uncooperative
behavior, without accepting the psychoanalytic assertion that
the behavior expresses a defense against unconscious impulses.)

One particularly interesting case was that of an adolescent
only daughter who lived with her parents and wouldn't leave
her bed except to go to the bathroom. She wasn't physically ill,
she wasn't psychotic, she wasn't particularly depressed, and
while there was some anxiety about leaving the house, she
wasn't really agoraphobic. It was clear that her parents' sympathy for her, and dancing attendance on her, were reinforcing
her bedridden behavior. We tried all sorts of things including
home visits by the therapist, but the parents wouldn't shift their
"caretaking" behavior significantly. Other than increasing her
time out of bed, but still in the house, therapy did relatively
little.

It was this kind of case that made me consider learning more
about family therapy after my return to the United States. I had
initially dismissed the field when I read Nathan Ackerman's *The
Psychodynamics of Family Life* (1958) as more-of-the-same
psychodynamic therapy, this time done with families, much as
psychodynamic group therapy was more-of-the-same therapy
done with unrelated people. I had long since read Jay Haley's
Strategies of Psychotherapy (1963), but my interest in the book
at the time had mainly been in paradox and Milton Erickson's
work. Now I was thinking of learning more about what Haley or
other intellectual descendants of Gregory Bateson's double-bind
theory of schizophrenia project (Bateson et al. 1956, Watzlawick et al. 1967) had to say concerning family therapy.

A few years later, for example, I would have approached
therapy with the young woman rather differently, wondering

whether her remaining in bed was in some way linked to her parents' marriage, and considering her opposite-of-leaving-home behavior in terms of the family life cycle. (While it was normative at the time for Brazilians to live with their parents until they got married, there were other Brazilian ways of adolescents becoming more independent that she was clearly not manifesting.) In addition, while I still thought a therapist should be willing to go to great lengths to achieve change, I had become sensitive to the counterproductive danger of the therapist working harder for change than the clients. So while I might subsequently have encouraged the therapist to make a couple of home visits to see the whole family together and observe the problem in its context, I would have been cautious about a too-active therapist reinforcing the parents' helpless behavior much as they were reinforcing their daughter's.

After getting a sense of what was going on, I would probably have had the therapist shift the focus to the parents, point out how wonderful they were at taking care of their daughter, imply that they wouldn't have known what to do with themselves if they hadn't had her to occupy them, and praise the daughter for sacrificing her current comfort and future existence—including potential contacts with the opposite sex—to ensure her parents' well-being. My guess is that such an approach would have led to all three protesting that they had better things to do with their lives and acting more appropriately. However, even when such an intervention doesn't work, it often stirs things up enough so that new information becomes available that can form the basis for a more effective intervention. But I'm getting ahead of the story.

As we prepared to leave for the United States, I was aware that I no longer would see my culture through the same eyes. For example, I came to Brazil with the implicit American view of North America, Latin America, and Europe as three differing

Western regions. After a while, I had come to understand that Brazilians saw only two regions—North America + Northern Europe and Latin America + Latin Europe—and grew to accept their perspective as more useful. In a sense I had become more interested in American culture while I was in Brazil, now that I could sometimes see it from the outside, rather than merely have it serve as my natural frame of reference. A book that I found particularly useful in developing this new interest once I got back was Edward Stewart's *American Cultural Patterns* (1972, Stewart and Bennett 1991).

When we returned to the United States after twenty-six months, we had to deal with re-entry shock, the returnees' counterpart to culture shock. Once again, a distinction has to be made between the physical discomfort associated with resuming one's existence within one's culture of origin and re-entry shock itself, which refers to the behavioral shifting of gears to a largely unchanged but by now somewhat alien set of cultural rules. There are two parts to this experience. One is the loss of the other culture's way of life. (I particularly missed Brazilians' warmth, informality, sense of humor, flexibility, and commingling of work and sociability.) The other is readjusting to a strangely familiar way of life that no longer seems normal, but only like an alternative way of doing things. The combination gives one the feeling of being a Martian in human disguise— being different while appearing normal. There is also a degree of frustration about the inability to communicate to relatives, friends, and colleagues what one has gone through, and how the everyday world now seems transformed by one's cross-cultural perspective.

In general, biculturalism is a great asset. Like binocular vision it allows one a depth of perspective that emerges from combining different points of view. But re-entry shock also illustrates the downside of biculturalism—the feeling of being different that others, in both cultures, cannot understand. Even under these circumstances, although feeling like an outsider may be uncomfortable, it is still useful in helping a therapist to take the stance of participant observer.

During the process of readaptation to American social contingencies, it rapidly became evident how much cultural learning had gone on at least partially independent from conscious control. I will give three examples. When Brazilian men shake hands, they not only clasp and shake each other's right hand but also pat each other's right flank with their left hand. This kind of greeting is unfamiliar to American men and they react to it in American terms with the discomfort associated with a possible homosexual intimacy—the smile of greeting disappears and the flank patting is not reciprocated. Since the handshake consists of straightforward motor behavior, I didn't have to shake very many hands before I returned to the American pattern.

The next example has to do with punctuality and the use of time. Shortly after returning to the states, I went to a meeting of the American Psychological Association. There was a lecture I wanted to attend, and I made a point of reminding myself that I had to be there when it started. When I arrived at the appointed hour, I was startled to see that the hall was filled. Then it struck me—in the United States you don't arrive at the indicated time, you arrive early and the scheduled time is when the event actually begins.

During my stay in Brazil I had been more punctual than Brazilians and had even irritated students with my intolerance for behavior such as coming an hour late for class. Nevertheless, my own sense of what constituted on-time behavior, and of how important it was, had gradually eroded; and it has never been fully restored. It is the difference between knowing that it is important to be on time and knowing that it is supposed to be important to be on time. New Englanders who move to southern California (or Brazil) and spend a couple of years with mild winters sometimes never fully reaccustom themselves to winter harshness. In the same way, my internal punctuality regulator somehow got slightly shifted without my conscious involvement, and it hasn't shifted all the way back despite my subsequent awareness.

The third example is something that happened while our daughter, who was 4 years old at the time, lost her ability to speak Portuguese. She became a monolingual speaker of English over a period of six months, although my wife and I spoke Portuguese to her, read her bedtime stories in Portuguese, and played Brazilian children's records. She also lost her Brazilian gestures and other cultural traits, miraculously transforming herself before our eyes from a Brazilian child into an American child. While parents do play an important role in children's development, the effect of the surrounding culture is clearly more important. Most psychological theories, not just psychoanalysis, give disproportionate weight to the family because they implicitly assume culture to be a constant. We had a natural—and literal—A-B-A design in our family. Our daughter was American, then Brazilian, then American, while we pretty much looked on, unable to do more than slightly damp the rate of change.

There was a period during which she could neither speak nor understand Portuguese. Nevertheless, if one of us said "Fecha a porta" ("Close the door"), she would close the door. It was behavior that looked something like a response to a posthypnotic suggestion. For example, if we asked, "Why did you close the door?" she'd say, "I don't know." My understanding of her behavior was that her response to language was not only mediated by meaning, but was also direct—somewhat like the way a dog might be able to respond appropriately to "Fetch the paper," without speaking English. It seemed to me that her strange behavior suggested that there are at least two types of associations between language and action, and that they need not decay at the same rate.

The point I am making, however, is not so much a linguistic one as one about awareness. Just as living in Brazil had demonstrated that my family and I were American in many ways that we had been unaware of, returning to the United States revealed that we had also become Brazilian in many ways without realizing it. This suggests that much cultural learning (and extinction) is nonverbal and even nonconscious, and that much of the cross-cultural experience simply cannot be communicated in words.

Recognizing that much that is cultural is not conscious does not imply that it is unconscious in the psychoanalytic sense (motivatedly out of awareness or repressed). Rather, such behavior is nonconscious either because it is nonverbal (and perhaps even nonimaginal) or because it was learned or is performed largely without awareness.

4

The Systems
Movement

When I returned to the United States, I continued my interest in cross-cultural issues and also did some reading in the field of environmental psychology. I sat in on Leonard Krasner's Environmental Design seminar at the State University of New York at Stony Brook (Krasner 1980); and while I found the field an important one, and was an intellectual adherent of its ideas, somehow it didn't excite me enough personally to pursue it. Like community psychology, it was removed just enough from the arena of interpersonal interaction to diminish my enthusiasm. No doubt, well-designed interventions at the level of public policy, urban planning, architecture, and so forth, have an important impact on the behavior of millions of people (as does the lack of thoughtful interventions). Nevertheless, my own personal interest seemed to be more at the level of understanding and changing behavior that I could see with my own eyes.

As a result, and as I had intended anyway, I began to delve into the small but growing literature on brief family therapy. The works I came across seemed to be associated with the imprecise but suggestive labels "structural," "strategic," and "systemic"; and I also made contacts with practitioners and authors in the field. While there was a variety of other kinds of people who called themselves family therapists, they were associated with already established orientations (e.g., Freudians or Rogerians). They seemed simply to be plying their trade with nuclear families rather than with individuals, offering little in the way of innovative theory or practice. So the subgroup that I got involved with, which I will refer to as the "systems movement" (and which has since become the dominant force in the field of family therapy), was the one where the action was.

My personal interests—as opposed to unpredicted events— were clearly an important determinant of this move. Nevertheless, the fact that I got involved in the systems movement, rather than the environmental psychology movement, can be seen as another of those turning points in the development of an orientation that all therapists go through.

Since I was involved fairly early with both the behavior therapy and systems movements, this might be a good point to make a brief comparison of their strengths and weaknesses. Both movements in their early stages were characterized by intellectual ferment and excitement, openness to new ideas, iconoclasm concerning the medical model and associated traditions of diagnosis and treatment, a commitment to brief therapy, and interdisciplinary participation based on intellectual outlook (behaviorism or systems) rather than location in the mental health prestige hierarchy (nursing–social work–psychology–psychiatry).

Nevertheless, there were also marked differences from the beginning. Psychology was clearly the dominant profession in behavior therapy, and this put a particular stamp on the movement's evolution. It meant that the center of the movement's development was in universities (mainly in psychology departments, and principally within clinical psychology programs), and that a high value was placed on empirical research. In general, this has been a great advantage; and behavior therapy has continually evolved as ideas are tested and revised or discarded based on experimental evidence rather than mere anecdote or persuasive rationale. More importantly, the movement shares an ideology of openness—behavior therapists readily share their theories, data, methods, and techniques, so that points of view and information can be readily exchanged and compared. (There have been some recent limitations on the spread of techniques, analogous to but more limited than the difficulties described below regarding the systems movement.)

There are also some disadvantages, since science can easily become scientism (sometimes referred to as "physics envy"). Often clinical subtleties are downplayed or overlooked in case descriptions, which focus instead on theoretical or methodological issues. Also, the most celebrated behavior therapists tend to be the best known researchers—who are not always the best clinicians—so that there is a paucity of impressive clinical role models. In addition, as with all movements, there are some purists who are more concerned with determining what is and is not behavioral (presumably one should do only the former) than with doing what works. Thus, a movement that was inclusive in its beginning is showing signs of divisiveness, mutual exclusion, and the creation of subcamps and even subsubcamps. This tendency is a particular annoyance to me, as an advocate of dialog between and even partial merger of the behavior therapy and systems movements.

Finally, behavior therapy is preponderantly a white,

middle-class, American movement. While behavior therapists, like other mental health professionals, are generally well intentioned as regards foreigners, the poor, and members of minority groups, they are not *of* them; and the field lacks prominent cross-cultural concerns or role models. This is by no means a theoretically necessary aspect of behavior therapy, but it is a culturally unfortunate fact.

In contrast, social work has been the dominant profession in the systems movement. To begin with, this has meant that there has been a concern with the poor and minority groups from the outset (e.g., Minuchin et al. 1967). Furthermore, not only was problem behavior viewed from the context of the network of familial interaction of which it was a part, but the family itself was viewed as part of a larger interrelated social fabric.

In part, this perspective was theoretical. Arthur Koestler's concept (1972) of the holon illustrates the point of view. A holon is an entity that is a whole when considered in relation to its constituent parts, but a part when viewed from a higher organizational perspective. For example, a cell is a whole in relation to its nucleus, cell membrane, and cytoplasm, but is a part of an organ (which itself is a holon, as a part of an organism). In the same way, a family is a whole in relation to its members, but a part of an extended family, neighborhood, and society.

However, beyond the theoretical perspective of systems theory, there was also the historical commitment of social work to the poor, immigrants, and minority groups, the emphasis on social responsibility in training, and the everyday experience of working under difficult circumstances with disadvantaged groups. These all contributed to facilitating a view of problem behavior as being part of a larger social context rather than an expression of individual pathology. Furthermore, since the profession is situated relatively low in the mental health status hierarchy, while providing the bulk of services for the most difficult cases at the lowest pay, social workers can feel in a small way the effects of condescension toward a struggle under difficult circumstances that pervade the lives of their clients.

Beyond this, while the systems movement is now centered in the United States, because of the sheer numbers of practitioners, journals, training centers, and other resources, its founding members are an international group. Although it is true that Joseph Wolpe and Arnold Lazarus left South Africa's apartheid to come to the United States, there is nothing particularly South African about their contributions to behavior therapy. In contrast, Salvador Minuchin's sensitivity to family hierarchies, and Mara Selvini Palazzoli's perceptiveness regarding complex multigenerational interactional patterns, are clearly related to Latin American and Italian patterns of familial interaction. Both of these differ from American middle-class patterns; and so the systems movement has incorporated useful perspectives from other cultures and been sensitive to cross-cultural differences from its inception.

Unfortunately, the scientific tradition and an empirically oriented skepticism are not particularly central to social work, and the systems movement has suffered from a lack of sufficient corrective feedback provided by empirical investigation. It is one thing to say "I haven't been trained in research, I have no interest in doing research, and studying the behavior over time of interacting networks of people is very difficult." That seems an easily defensible position. The field needs both practitioners and researchers; both make socially useful contributions; there is no need to choose between them.

It is something else again to say "Research is based on a linear epistemology, and systems theory is based on a circular epistemology, so nothing useful could possibly come out of research." This is the same "so much the worse for the facts" attitude that has plagued so many other therapeutic approaches.

Granted that much research will be poorly done, misleading, or irrelevant, it is still likely that the entire corpus of research will shed more light on the field than would its absence, and so it should be encouraged even while recognizing that it is no panacea. After all, nothing is. So negative attitudes toward research, while not universal, are a real liability in the systems movement.

While behavior therapy is centered in universities, family therapy is centered in private training institutes. Such institutes must survive economically on their own, and so the theoretical formulations and clinical skills they offer tend to be regarded as salable items rather than part of the free exchange of ideas. This has several unfortunate consequences. First of all, economic incentives accelerate the movement toward differentiation, leading each institute to highlight the distinctiveness of its approach, to view others as rivals, and to claim its trainees as allies in the intellectual and clinical struggle. As a result, therapists who are interested in comparing theoretical formulations and practicing technical eclecticism run into resistance. Beyond this, the institute outlook makes it difficult to generate intellectually satisfying debate. I have, at meetings, more than once approached well-known figures in the movement with specific questions about their writings or presentations and received the response, "You should enroll in our training program, where all of this is spelled out in great detail." This response comes from a hierarchy of values where money is above truth; it is something I simply haven't encountered among behavior therapists.[1] In fairness, it has to be recognized that tenured professors don't sell their ideas for a living in the same sense as those working in

---

1. The only exception to this generalization, and one that is still being hotly debated by behavior therapists, is Eye Movement Desensitization and Reprocessing (EMDR) (Baer et al. 1992, Fish 1992, Shapiro 1992).

private training institutes, and that institutes and individuals vary in their openness to theoretical discourse. Still, the centrality of training institutes and economic influences on them constitute a particular impediment to the intellectual development of the systems movement.

The systems movement has an impressive roster of so-called master therapists, whose work has been taped and is intellectually and aesthetically stimulating in addition to being clinically informative. The value placed on clinical subtlety and creativity, and the extent to which efforts have been made to explicate well-chosen clinical examples, is a clinical highlight of the movement. At the same time, there is a tendency toward what might be called a cult of great therapists. That is, rather than emphasize the principles of change that are skillfully or insightfully applied by a particular clinician, there is a tendency to glorify particular individuals and imply that other therapists are hopeless mediocrities. In partial compensation, the use (especially in training) of a consultation team behind the one-way mirror, when it is well handled, creates a mutually supportive atmosphere of problem solving that—unlike hero worship—is clinically helpful. This atmosphere is similar to the one I experienced during my postdoctoral behavioral training.

Finally, the cult of great therapists also extends to a cult of great thinkers. Gregory Bateson and Milton Erickson are undoubtedly the seminal theoretical and clinical innovators of the movement, and they have made admirable contributions. Unfortunately, both had flawed expository styles, and these styles, as widely imitated models, have had undesirable consequences for the movement.

Jay Haley, whose lucid writing communicates his ideas clearly, once said that "Bateson sometimes seemed to give the impression that if you understood him, he wasn't being profound enough" ("The new epistemology," 1982, p. 27). A brief example of Bateson's style is his devising the term "schismogenisis'' (1972) to refer to the process by which sequences of positive (i.e., deviation amplifying) feedback can lead to systemic reorganization or breakup. His work was important despite, rather than because of, such neologenesis, which was also pedantogenic since it exacerbated therapists' feelings of intellectual inferiority. Writers like Coyne (1982) have sometimes tried to debunk such stylistic tendencies, citing George Orwell's classic essay "Politics and the English Language" (1954) in arguing for clarity of expression. Nevertheless, an obscurantist strain persists in systemic writing, emphasizing big words, complex syntax, and unclear meaning; and its aim seems more to be intellectual intimidation than theoretical illumination.

As a therapist, I have to admit to being dazzled by Milton Erickson. When I recognize how little was known forty to sixty years ago, and what he knew, I am amazed by his clinical creativity. Still, he was not an impressive theoretician. Many of his ideas about how hypnosis works (as opposed to his imaginative clinical use of hypnosis) were either wrong or uninterpretable. As a master of confusion and indirect suggestion he was unequaled in his ability to use words to get people to change their behavior. Nevertheless, it is the opposite use of language—clarity and explicit drawing of inferences—that is needed to delineate clinical strategies and techniques so that they may be critically evaluated. Finally, as something of a clinical showman, he often left his audiences with an admiring sense of "How did he do that?"—not an explicit form of communication that lends itself to critical evaluation. As a result, there is a clinical strain in the systems movement that seeks to amaze rather than explicate.

In contrast, given the scientific ideology of the behavior therapy movement, theoretical and clinical writings tend to make their points explicitly. While there is no scarcity of bad behavioral writing, its shortcomings tend to be those of lifeless journal prose, rather than impenetrable theoretical pseudoprofundity or magical clinical razzle-dazzle.

Systems theory itself, as I see it, isn't really a theory at all. It is best thought of as a level of analysis—interactional rather than individual—or even a point of view. Like ecology, systems theory declares, "Consider context."

How much context? There are no real guidelines. Practitioners at the Mental Research Institute of Palo Alto look at the immediate interactions around problem behavior, while those in Milan, Italy, look at an interactional panorama extending over generations. Clinically, my own preference is to opt for parsimony. I tend to start small, and add more context when I can't find a way to solve the problem at a given level of organization. Still, the level of organization at which I start seems to be intuitive, which I regard as unfortunate. Rather than have advocates of different degrees of context argue over who is right, it would be helpful if someone would come up with a theoretical schema suggesting what information about a problem and the interactions around it is necessary to determine the level of organization at which to address it. Unfortunately, this kind of thinking is discouraged by the differentiation in the field, just as it is even more difficult to get those in the behavior therapy movement and the systems movement to learn from and work with each other.

In addition to being a science, ecology serves for some people as a kind of religion, much the way a therapeutic orientation does for others. This is also the case in the systems movement. That is, there are those like me who find systemic thinking useful in changing problem behavior. Others go beyond this into making systems into a way of life—seemingly reifying the system (an abstraction) while denying the reality of the individual. As therapists, they say things like "I always treat the entire system," though, given the concept of the holon, the sentence seems meaningless or false. They appear to mean that they try to get at least the entire nuclear family to attend all sessions, though this seems to me to compromise the therapist's flexibility. (My practice has been to decide in each session whom I want to see the next time, and sometimes have individuals or groups leave or enter during the session as events evolve.) Some therapists insist on including all nuclear family members in each intervention or in other ways adhere to a rigid format for working with all cases.

It should also be mentioned that most people in the systems movement are primarily committed to the change process and find systems thinking useful in provoking change. There are, however, some therapists who are primarily committed to the family as a social institution and who use systems thinking in the service of this end. To draw the distinction broadly, the former group are interested in solving behavioral problems, while the latter are interested in saving the family. Unfortunately, since there is a field known as family therapy, the perception of outsiders is that the systems movement is about families rather than about the social organization of behavior. Thus, nonsystemic therapists would tend to see a conceptual similarity between family therapy and group therapy (i.e., therapy with several people at once), while the systemic view would be that a greater similarity exists between family therapy and organizational psychology (i.e., understanding and changing the pattern of behavior of people in a social system).

Systems thinking offered two things that were absent from social learning theory. These were not ideas that were inconsistent with it—rather, they simply weren't part of the way behavior therapists thought, and thus didn't inform their clinical behavior. The first is the difference between understanding behavior among three or more people, and understanding the behavior of an individual or of two people. The second is the concept of hierarchy.

Many psychological orientations understand human behavior as the behavior of individuals. Systematic desensitization is used to countercondition an individual's anxiety that is viewed as having been conditioned to a specifiable class of situations. Psychoanalysis views neurotic behavior as stemming from personality deficits arising in childhood and attempts to bring about changes by gradually strengthening the personality through a healing relationship. In these approaches and others—especially where the concept of personality is prominent—it is the individual who has the problem and who is treated individually to solve it.

Social learning theory innovated by considering the interrelated behavior of two people. Consider a child with temper tantrums. Instead of viewing the problem behavior as that of the individual child, and treating it with play therapy or a variant of systematic desensitization (e.g., using emotive imagery [Lazarus and Abramovitz 1962] instead of relaxation), a therapist might look at the mother–child interaction. From this perspective, the mother's attention when the child has a tantrum reinforces it (makes it more probable in the future), and the cessation of the tantrum when the mother attends reinforces the mother (makes it more likely that she will attend to tantrums in the future).

There are two important differences inherent in this perspective. The first is that behavior is now viewed as interactional—part of a process between two people—rather than individual. The second is that the persistence of behavior is viewed as the result of its ongoing maintenance by present circumstances, rather than as part of an enduring individual disposition. This means that the behavior can be changed *by changing the interaction that is currently maintaining it*. Furthermore, it also means that an individual's problem can be solved *by changing someone else's behavior*.

The interactional perspective of social learning theory—looking at the interrelated behavior of two people instead of just one—was something really different. Behavior therapists were well aware that there are more than two people in the world, and social learning theory had no conceptual impediments to dealing with larger numbers, but for some reason the question never seems to have arisen. It was as if there was an implicit assumption that larger groups of ongoing relationships could be adequately described as a series of two-person relationships.

The systems movement called this assumption into question, though since participants in the two movements don't particularly communicate with one another, word didn't get out for quite a while. A common systemic example, also of temper tantrums, can serve to illustrate the point. (It also illustrates that systemic considerations tend to cover a longer time span than events immediately preceding and following the behavior in question.) In this case, let us bring a father into the picture and look at a complete cycle of behavior over time, including that of the marital couple as well as the child:

1. The more the parents fight, the more the child has tantrums.
2. The more the child has tantrums, the less the parents fight.
3. The less the parents fight, the less the child has tantrums.
4. The less the child has tantrums, the more the parents fight.
5(=1). The more the parents fight, the more the child has tantrums.

This sequence lends itself to a social learning analysis, depending on a more detailed description of what is going on. The following is one possible example:

1. The fights are a discriminative stimulus for the child's tantrums.

2. The tantrums are an aversive stimulus that suppresses the fights.
3. The removal of the discriminative stimulus diminishes the tantrums.
4. The removal of the aversive stimulus increases the frequency of the fights, and so on.

Another possibility is that the cessation of a fight (rather than, or in addition to, the mother's attention) reinforces a tantrum. Yet another possibility is that one or both parents may, by their fighting, be serving as models for tantrum behavior and/or for the consequences it receives.

Whatever the case, the point is that understanding behavior as part of a complex interaction among three or more people both changes one's understanding of that behavior and offers the possibility of many different strategies for change. For example, this perspective allows one to view the tantrums as related to the interaction between the parents, rather than as an expression of the child's personality, or as part of a reciprocal relationship between mother and child. This implies a new strategy of changing the tantrums by changing the interaction between the parents. That is, an individual's problem can be solved *by changing the interaction between two other people*.

In addition, by viewing problem behavior in its context, one can see that it is merely one part of a much longer repetitive cycle of interaction among several people, consisting of a sequence of behavior, such as A does X, then B does Y, then C does Z, and so forth until we get back to A does X. This kind of understanding of behavior in its context allows for changing the behavior by disrupting the cycle at any point (e.g., between X and Y, or between Y and Z). One might prevent some link of the chain from occurring, or add different links (e.g., "Dad, just for this week, let's have you deal with Johnny when he blows up, and you, mom, can leave the room"), or change the sequence of events (e.g., "The next time Johnny has a tantrum, I'd like the two of you to pretend to have an argument, even if you don't feel like it"). There are many additional strategies available, and they can be found in the systems literature. My point is simply to illustrate that thinking in terms of three or more people greatly increases the possibility for therapeutic action.

The other concept that was missing from social learning theory was hierarchy. Once again, it is not inconsistent with anything in the theory; rather, behavior therapists just didn't think that way. The example of the mother reinforcing the child and the child reinforcing the mother, while a useful one, does overlook the power differential between the two. One could, of course, point out specific differences in the reinforcers at the disposal of each, differences in their respective behavioral repertoires, and even—by describing in minute detail who does what to whom and with what effect—show how the power differential operates in practice.

Still, social learning theory in its essence is a theory of the behavior of individuals, explained by their interactions with others. It is not a theory of the patterned behavior of interacting groups. The difference in perspective is much like the difference in outlook between psychology and anthropology that I described earlier. When one starts with the group (or "system"), one thinks in terms of inherently relational concepts. Describing a hierarchical relationship in terms of individuals reinforcing each other is a bit like describing the way a word processing program works in terms of the binary code of machine language. Even Ullmann and Krasner's formulation of social learning theory (1969), while containing individual concepts like social role, omitted relational concepts like hierarchy.

The advantage of systemic thinking is that it allows for conceptualization at the relational level. Not only the concept of hierarchy, but related ones like alliances (people acting in concert), coalitions (joint action against one or more people), coalitions across hierarchical boundaries (e.g., mother and son against father), denied or secret coalitions, and a variety of others become available for the conceptualization of the relations among individuals. It becomes possible, for example, to view problem behavior as a part of the overall field of power politics within a family, and to develop ways of changing it by realigning the constellation of forces.

Systems thinking also allows one to view relationships in terms of whether the behavior repetitively exchanged between participants is similar (symmetrical) or different (complementary). In symmetrical interactions, the individuals are of equal status, and the behavior exchanged can vary from affection and caresses to insults and blows. An escalation of symmetrical conflict can vary from anything-you-can-do-I-can-do-better through physical violence, but retains the form of equal exchange. In complementary interactions, the individuals are of unequal status, such as boss–worker, parent–child, or sadist–masochist, and the differing kinds of behavior exchanged can also vary over a wide range. An escalation of complementary conflict can lead to a spiraling of status inequality, as every act of submission is followed by a corresponding increase in domination. Interestingly, a complementary escalation can be damped by a symmetrical move (e.g., the person who is one-down fights back), and a symmetrical escalation can be damped by a complementary move (e.g., one of the participants makes a concession).

The symmetrical/complementary distinction is based on a consideration of interactional patterns rather than the behavior of individuals, and takes hierarchy into account. While both symmetrical and complementary interactions are mutually reinforcing, systemic thinking highlights differences at the interactional level that would otherwise go unrecognized. As a result, new possibilities are opened up for understanding and changing behavior.

Systems thinking also makes use of other interactional concepts such as negative and positive feedback. Negative feedback, which reduces the discrepancy between an actual and ideal state, is already familiar to behavior therapists. In the case of the mother who is unwittingly reinforcing her child's tantrums, if she ceases to attend to them they will at first increase in frequency and intensity (an extinction phenomenon), thereby—at least initially—punishing her for ignoring and making it more likely that she will attend again.

On the other hand, positive feedback (alluded to briefly above), which increases the discrepancy between an actual and ideal state, is not familiar to most behavior therapists. Here is an example. My wife and I had a dual control electric blanket that we once hooked up backwards by mistake, so that each of us controlled the heat on the other's side of the bed. When one of us felt cold, that person raised the temperature, making the other side of the bed too hot, so that the other person lowered the temperature, leading the first to raise it more, and so on.

As one can see, negative feedback tends to perpetuate ongoing patterns of interaction, while positive feedback is disruptive of them. Thus, strategies based on positive feedback offer a great potential for changing problem behavior, by disrupting the interactional sequences of which it is a part. Such strategies are often called paradoxical because, by encouraging an increase in problem behavior to the point where it self-destructs, they appear to the uninitiated to be contrary to the goals of therapy. While behavior therapists have long used paradoxical interventions with "resistant" or uncooperative individuals, they have not attempted to push an interactional pattern among three or more people beyond its limits. Once again, I see no theoretical reason why they should not—they just don't seem to think this way.

To read the systems literature, one would imagine that such interventions inevitably lead to remarkable change. My own experience is that, just as using behavioral strategies got my clients to change more rapidly than did working psychodynamically, using systemic strategies has accelerated the change process even more. However, in what seems to me to be about a third of the cases, I have seen change that appears not only more rapid, but also qualitatively different. An example would be "individual" therapy with a depressed woman (but with interactional interventions, such as paradoxical assignments regarding her behavior with others). She ceases to be depressed, breaks up with her lover, and enters a new career, while her lover unexpectedly quits his job and enters graduate school, and her chronically miserable parents unexpectedly seek out a marital therapist.

In other words, my experience is that sometimes just the problem behavior changes, and sometimes all sorts of things unexpectedly change with all sorts of people. I would like to know why. Behavior therapists, with their empirical bent, could help to shed light on this; but for the most part they are unaware of systemic strategies. Systemic therapists seem uninterested in such empirical questions.

Meanwhile, some systemic therapists eschew individual concepts like personality only to reify the system. For example, instead of saying that Johnny has a school phobia because of his defensive structure (his personality is afraid), they assert that his family needs him at home (his family system is afraid). This is quite different from describing a repetitive sequence of events of which refusing to go to school is a part.

Behavior therapists also reject the concept of personality because it exaggerates the degree to which human behavior has structure, permanence, and independence from environmental influences (especially those of other people). Their behavioral skepticism could be put to good use in cleaning up systemic concepts, if only they could be persuaded to move from the individual to the interactional level of description.

So this is how one therapist's thinking evolved. The story is replete with unexpected influences. I chose my graduate school and postdoctoral program, but they also chose me. If they hadn't, I would have had other experiences, and my thinking—in fact my whole life—would have gone off in other directions. Once I was enrolled in training programs, where others arranged much of my learning, I had experiences and developed in ways that none of us would have predicted. The location of my training led me to meet my wife and she in turn led me in other directions. In a similar way, written works, people, and life events led me to other written works, people, and life events, all of which influenced my clinical thinking and behavior in ways I could never have anticipated. They continue to do so.

Interviewers often ask graduate school applicants, "What would you like to be doing professionally ten years from now?" I have asked this question myself—it is an attempt to understand the direction people are aiming in. But if someone had asked me after my first year of graduate school, I would have said, "I'd like to be a psychoanalyst in private practice." Instead, I wound up in an Indian village in the interior of Brazil, trying unsuccessfully to obtain a Krikati man's life history in Portuguese.

My guess is that this unpredictability is not atypical—over time, all people's lives take unexpected turns. I believe that such unanticipated directions are not only inevitable but a source of strength. Each therapist has a unique life trajectory that provides a unique set of experiences and offers the opportunity to see things from a unique perspective. Therapists can create a dialog between these experiences and their theoretical outlook, rather than bending them to fit that outlook. If they do, both they and others can reap the rewards of that dialog.

5

Elements of a Therapeutic Orientation

This chapter is an attempt to bring some conceptual order to the process described in the four preceding ones. Perhaps it should be titled "lessons learned thus far," since the process is an ongoing one. These elements of a therapeutic orientation have to do with therapy itself, with the therapeutic relationship, with the context of therapy, and with learning to learn.

THERAPEUTIC PRINCIPLES

1. *Try something different, and see what happens.* This is the principle of formulating a therapeutic strategy based on a theoretically intelligible hypothesis, intervening to change the problem behavior, comparing the results to predicted outcomes,

and revising the hypothesis and strategy accordingly. It involves abandoning the conceptual and sequential separation between diagnosis and therapy for an interactive process of participant-observation. That is, attempts at assessment affect behavior and thus have the effects of interventions; and therapeutic interventions reveal information about behavior, and thus have the effects of assessment. This feedback process also emphasizes observable behavior and doing over inferred behavior and understanding.

It should be mentioned that making explicit predictions is a humbling experience. Predictions—especially initial ones based on limited information—tend to be wrong, or at least partially wrong. What is important is the corrective mechanism provided by feedback, which ultimately leads to interventions that do change the problem behavior.

2. *Change expectancies of problem behavior.* This is what Jerome Frank (1961, 1973, Frank and Frank 1991) wrote about in *Persuasion and Healing*, what I wrote about in *Placebo Therapy* (Fish 1973), and what Irving Kirsch (1990) wrote about in *Changing Expectations.* Individuals and groups make the continuation of problem behavior more likely by expecting it to occur, and modifying those expectancies even slightly can set off a positive cycle of change.

3. *Change the interactional context of problem behavior.* Rather than viewing problems as located within individuals, it is useful to think of problem behavior as occurring as part of interactional sequences among individuals. Haley (1963b, 1973, 1980, 1984, 1987) and Madanes (1981, 1984) have written extensively about this. Therapeutic strategies include changing the order of who does what to whom, and rearranging relationships among third parties—especially hierarchical relationships—that affect problem behavior.

4. *Focus on behavior change.* While thoughts and feelings are important, they are often most fruitfully understood as the

appropriate results (or effects, or side effects, or outputs, or outcomes) of the actual life circumstances individuals find themselves in. A change in the larger social reality of which problem behavior is a part will generally lead to a change in that behavior, and changed thoughts and feelings will accompany the behavior change. This is not to say that cognitive change cannot produce behavior change, just that a changed environment is generally more powerful in changing behavior than are words. As with principle 1 above, this focus once again emphasizes observable behavior and doing over inferred behavior and understanding.

A focus on behavior change is also associated with an explicit discussion of the goals of therapy. When the goals are clear, all the participants know why they are involved and can tell whether anything is happening. Attempts to formulate goals, and to elucidate different people's attitudes toward them, tend to shed light on the interactional complexities of which problem behavior is a part. Once the change process is under way, it may go well beyond the goals of therapy and may affect people beyond the problem bearer and even beyond other participants in therapy (e.g., colleagues at work, or relatives in another country).

5. *Take the sociocultural context of behavior into account.* Much of behavior in general, including problem behavior, is a specific instance of social and cultural patterns in the larger society. Considering problem behavior in relation to these larger patterns offers additional ways of understanding and dealing with it. Part II of this book is devoted to discussing these issues.

I am hesitant to attach a label to a therapeutic orientation, since labels have consequences. I have been arguing for therapists innovating and exposing themselves to the natural consequences of their work, so that their orientation can continually evolve. If a therapist says, "I am an X," that implies that he or she thinks in certain ways and does certain things and not others, and thus the theoretical label X might limit further development. Nevertheless, we need words to talk about things, so I reluctantly offer these five principles as a reasonably open-ended definition of a sociocultural orientation. In its long form, I referred to it in the Preface as sociocultural (5) interactional (1 and 3) cognitive (2) environmental determinism (1, 3, 4, and 5).

THE THERAPEUTIC RELATIONSHIP

A cooperative, problem-focused therapeutic relationship avoids many of the complications produced by relationship-oriented therapy. Brief therapies—especially problem-oriented ones referred to by the labels behavioral, cognitive, strategic, and systemic—share this task orientation.

Within a problem-focused relationship, a therapist can assume a one-up (Haley 1987, Minuchin 1974, Minuchin and Fishman 1981), one-down (Fisch et al. 1982), or symmetrical position vis-à-vis the client, and can be self-disclosing, or neutral (Selvini Palazzoli et al. 1980). It seems to me that any of these can be effective, depending on the case, and that the therapist should do what is most comfortable but be willing to change it in the face of evidence that it is ineffective or counterproductive (principle 1, above). For example, I generally assume a one-up position, which has advantages for gathering information and assigning tasks, and am self-disclosing, in order to foster trust and reciprocal self-disclosure from clients. However, I might shift to a symmetrical stance with a client who shows concern about issues of our relative status (e.g., a therapist or other professional), and might take a one-down position with someone who is oppositional or uncooperative. Similarly, I might divulge less information about myself if I thought that satisfying the client's curiosity about me was distracting us from the task at hand.

Within the therapeutic relationship, influence among therapists and clients is mutual (each influences the other), hierarchical (therapists influence clients more than vice versa), circular (affected by positive and negative feedback), and affected by unpredicted or random events inside and outside of therapy. For these reasons, therapy is interactive and evolutionary (the result of all the interacting influences is unforeseeable at the outset, though it is the product of deterministic forces and is affected by therapists' actions along the way). In addition, the therapeutic relationship is part of larger networks of social interactions that therapists and clients participate in, affect, and are affected by.

In general, the therapeutic relationship is important because it can foster or interfere with the attainment of therapeutic goals, so progress toward these goals can be used in evaluating its effectiveness and modifying it where necessary.

THE CONTEXT OF THERAPY

There are three contexts that are most relevant to this presentation. These are the social context of therapy, the cultural context of therapy, and the interpersonal climate within which therapy takes place. (The first two will be discussed in more detail in Part II of this book, but I will allude to them briefly for present purposes.)

The social context of therapy refers to institutional pressures and other forms of patterned social interaction in the larger society that affect the therapeutic process. This includes licensing laws, referral networks, pressures to avoid potential liability suits or bad publicity (leading to the practice of "defensive therapy"), professional codes of ethics, and institutional politics, as well as mental health insurance and managed care bureaucracies, other social factors affecting economic cost-benefit ratios of different courses of action, and similar elements. For example, in consulting with therapists who practice in mental hospitals, it is generally helpful to have some kind of official organizational chart, and information on the informal organization, informal channels of communication, organizational politics, and economic issues (e.g., the funding source of salaries, and economic priorities of the unit or team or other entity where the therapist works). Therapy, like politics, is the art of the possible. When a course of action that might change the client's problem behavior might also jeopardize the client's health insurance reimbursement or disability status, or the therapist's job or license, or the hospital's discharge rate or insurance compensation, not much is possible. Knowing what can't work (even though it might under other circumstances) makes it easier to see what, if anything, actually has a chance of succeeding.

The cultural context of therapy refers to the fact that therapy itself is culturally defined and calls attention to the culture within which it takes place. There is considerable variation within contemporary American culture, which calls for corresponding variation in therapist behavior. The amount of variation that is called for continues to increase as one considers the practice of therapy within cultures that diverge increasingly from American norms. Similarly, the more the cultural backgrounds (including social class backgrounds) of therapists, clients, and involved others differ from one another, the more cultural issues have to be taken into account in therapy. For example, what constitutes a satisfactory marriage, or appropriate behavior by a child, is by no means constant. Since both the goals of therapy and the evaluation of progress toward them need to be mutually understood by all participants, adequate communication across cultural gaps is important.

In discussing the interpersonal climate within which therapy takes place, authors have traditionally emphasized the therapist acting in ways to encourage clients to feel trusting and accepted so as to foster their self-exploration. While trust and acceptance are certainly desirable, this book is not about therapy as self-exploration in the context of an intense realtionship. It is about therapy as behavior change in the context of a cooperative, problem-focused relationship. So the question is what sort of interpersonal climate fosters behavior change.

If the essence of behavior change is doing something different, then experimentation, innovation, and creativity are to be valued by the therapist. We tell our shy clients to take risks. Not wild risks—don't seek out a motorcycle gang to prove you can't be intimidated; prudent risks—compliment someone you like, or protest an unfair put-down. Similarly, therapists who want to change behavior would do well to overcome their timidity and take some risks. Not wild risks—just a little bit of experimentation, innovation, and creativity in their interventions. (For example, I once gave an anxious client a birthday present of a T-shirt that read "The calmer I look, the scareder I feel.") From time to time, when a case is really stuck, they could try something they've never done before, or perhaps no one has ever done, but that seems intriguing—and see what happens.

A therapist who approaches a client's problems with curiosity and an openness to experimentation, innovation, and creativity may even encourage similar problem-solving behavior on the part of the client.

Since we want clients to do something different, acting in unexpected or unconventional ways can be quite useful in interrupting their unproductive behavior. For this reason, the use of humor, surprise, confusion, or paradox can create an atmosphere that fosters the occurrence of different and even novel responses. Once again, therapists needn't be wildly unpredictable or bizarre. Social behavior in general, and that of

licensed professionals like therapists in particular, is quite regular, so it doesn't take much to create an atmosphere of "Something odd is going on here; the usual rules don't seem to apply."
If the rules don't apply, or if clients are laughing, surprised, or
confused, or have all their usual responses blocked, then they
might blurt out concealed information, consider their problem
from a new perspective, or do something different.

LEARNING TO LEARN

In order for therapists to promote the evolution and growth
of their orientations, they have to learn from their experiences.
To do so in traditional ways, they can read books and articles
about therapy, attend workshops, receive supervision from
people with differing expertise, discuss cases and theory with
colleagues, and try out new ideas from these sources. They can
also learn directly from their clients, by trying to take lessons
from their ongoing cases, apply these lessons, and see what
happens. These are familiar ways of learning, and the more
therapists follow them, the more they will learn.

Of course, true believers in an official orientation can limit
their contact to approved literature and equally convinced
colleagues, and their interventions to those supported by the
official version of reality, so that they become increasingly
narrow over time. However, if one reads with some breadth, has
reasonably diverse colleagues, approaches clients with an open
mind, pursues ideas that seem useful or intriguing, and attends
to the effects of thinking and acting in clinically different ways,
it would be difficult not to improve.

These are ways of learning that therapists already have
mastered. With antecedents at least in the beginning of graduate
school and throughout their professional careers, therapists
have long since learned how to learn in these ways and from

these sources. Thus, if they want to expand their horizons, to learn in new ways with unanticipatable results, they will have to expose themselves to new kinds of experiences. There is no guarantee that they will learn something qualitatively different if they expose themselves to qualitatively different experiences; but it is quite likely that they won't if they don't.

Once again, I am talking about taking risks—prudent risks, not wild risks—in order to learn how to learn in new ways. By exposing themselves to different kinds of intellectual and emotional experiences, which operate by different rules, therapists create the possibility of seeing the world from new perspectives. When they do so they also gain experience in, and improve at, the process of learning to see the world from new perspectives.

How can therapists do this? To begin with, they can try learning in familiar ways, but from unfamiliar sources. For example, they can read books and articles that they are curious about, or might become curious about, and that are not about therapy but come from a closely related field, or a distantly related field, or even an apparently unrelated field. They might think about the implications for therapy of such readings, and about what they might do differently as a result. Then again, if that makes the task too onerous ("work" instead of "play"), they might not think about therapeutic implications, but simply continue to pursue those aspects of the reading they find interesting. *They cannot fail to be influenced by their experiences.* The fact that they are unable to say, "My reading X article led to my doing Y differently with Z" doesn't mean that exposing themselves to new information and ideas had no effect. It simply recognizes that many environmental effects take place without awareness.

Recognizing that cognitive change (including theoretical change) often follows behavior change, therapists can try changing their own behavior and see what they learn from it. This includes not only attempts at self-therapy for personal problems (perhaps making notes or recording data so they can try with hindsight to see what led to what) but also exposing themselves to different situations, with different sets of rules, in which they will have to act differently.

In their private lives, therapists can occasionally shed their professional identities and expose themselves to new kinds of people and situations. Individuals from other social classes, subcultures, and cultures act differently and see the world from different perspectives. Therapists might learn something by attempting nonjudgmentally to enter into their worlds.

I know that becoming a therapist is an arduous and costly experience. Often it is an individual's hard-won ticket to the upper middle class (or even to the middle class). Having achieved respectability at great personal sacrifice, some therapists may not be eager to associate with foreigners or those of lesser prestige. (Of course, they can also learn something from people of greater prestige. It's just that members of the upper class tend not to be enthusiastic teachers [cf. Domhoff 1974].)

Not to worry! Such therapists can go back to being respectable right after the experience, and no one will know the difference. They can even keep it a secret. Friends, relatives, and colleagues will not suspect that they wanted to associate with such people; and even if it becomes known, they don't have to let on that they found the experience interesting, or even enjoyed it.

The point is that by interacting with people whose social forms can be described as following different rules (e.g., members of another culture) they will have to learn how to learn those rules—or at least to function according to them—and can then transfer this skill to therapy. Similarly, by doing things to themselves and seeing what happens (e.g., self-therapy), they can get a different perspective on the change process from that acquired by doing things to others. Since the way one learns to learn is by learning, such experiences provide the added bonus of whatever one happens to have learned along the way. For example, therapists might learn something about another culture or about themselves in the process.

It is true that exposing oneself to new social contexts and different kinds of people can be upsetting. Taking even prudent risks can be uncomfortable, annoying, and sometimes even worrisome, though it can also be stimulating. But it is worth the effort because of what one can get out of it. By having broader experiences one can become a better learner and a broader person, and in this way can become a better therapist.

PART II

SOCIAL AND CULTURAL ISSUES

Introduction

A sociologist I know once said, "People say culture is subtle, but it's not, it's obvious—except your own." Cultural misunderstandings (Carroll 1988), which occur when the same behavior has different meanings in different cultures, are fascinating; and therapists need to become more sensitive to them. At the same time, intercultural experiences are also replete with unexpected, amazing, startling, humorous, shocking, and embarrassing events, whose meaning rapidly becomes clear, and which reveal major differences in perspective, style, and values. We are unaware of the air we breathe until we are deprived of it, and in the same way it is the absence of our cultural moorings that reveals them to us. It can be a daunting task to confront cultural diversity.

My intention in writing Part II was to provide some theoretical and practical guidance for therapists in taking their first steps toward understanding culture, and to offer encouragement for their efforts at learning to learn. Part II can be viewed as a theoretical and clinical outgrowth of the kinds of cross-cultural experiences described in Chapter 3. (An initial draft of most of Part II was written in Brazil during the latter part of my stay there and in the years following my return to the United States. While I delayed putting this draft in publishable form until it could be part of a larger work, my sense of its relevance for American therapy has, if anything, increased in the interim.)

Chapter 6 deals in a preliminary way with sociocultural awareness and introduces the relevance to therapy of perspectives focused on groups larger than the individual. Chapter 7, which deals with theoretical issues, shows how social learning concepts of individual behavior can be integrated with sociological and anthropological conceptions of larger social groups. This integration allows therapists to understand clients' behavior from a unified theoretical perspective, rather than having to shift theories (e.g., from intrapsychic to interactional) when moving from patterned individual behavior to patterned group behavior. Chapter 8 discusses practical therapeutic implications of the conceptualizations in Chapter 7. Chapter 9 presents some basic knowledge about race from physical anthropology and cultural anthropology, and draws implications for therapeutic practice. (I should mention that publishing this chapter fulfills a personal mission for me. It is an amazing testimony to the durability of cultural beliefs that such important information, which has been possessed by anthropologists for a couple of generations, has not diffused to the general public—or to the overwhelming majority of therapists.) Chapter 10, which offers a crosscultural glimpse of Brazilian psychologists, pursues the theme elaborated in Part I of focusing the explanatory lens on oneself (or, in this case, on one's profession) as well as on others.

To the extent to which this book encourages a view of the therapist as a pragmatic iconoclast, Part II can be seen as challenging many therapists' assumption that the only or best or most useful way to understand clients' behavior is from an individual perspective.

6

Sociocultural
Awareness
and Therapy

In a remarkable paper, the eminent anthropologist George Peter Murdock (1972) attacked the theoretical bases of contemporary anthropology, and in so doing repudiated much of his life's work. After dismissing the theoretical assumptions of both social anthropology and cultural anthropology, he concluded that human activity could be understood only as the behavior of individuals. Within this context, he suggested that it is the function of psychology to describe the *mechanisms of behavior*, such as perception, cognition, and learning, and of anthropology to describe the *conditions of behavior*—that is, the conditions under which the mechanisms operate to produce different forms of human behavior.

In other words, the subject matters of psychology and anthropology are inextricably intertwined. This interdependence is recognized in ironic (and fortunately, only half-true) definitions of psychology, such as "the study of the behavior of American college students, taking introductory psychology, in experiments or on paper and pencil tests lasting no more than one hour." Naturally, any "laws of behavior" discovered in this way are of questionable applicability to South American peasants or tribal peoples of New Guinea (and to many other Americans as well).

Since psychology and anthropology cannot be separated, it follows that therapy as an application of psychological principles can be understood only in the context of particular social and cultural conditions, and can be effective only by taking these conditions into account in the treatment process.

While many therapists are intellectually aware that therapeutic interactions have meaning only within a cultural context, it is also true that therapists come from rather homogeneous backgrounds (Henry et al. 1971). I have known few American therapists who are fluent in a language other than English or have lived for any extended period of time in another culture. Certainly, therapists who have lived in a non-Western culture—especially a nonliterate one—are rare indeed.

As a result of their limited cross-cultural experience, therapists as a group can be expected to display the sort of well-meaning but naive ethnocentrism that characterizes other highly educated but culturally narrow groups. Their preference for clients like themselves in terms of American socioeconomic, religious, and racial categories (Lorion 1978, Parloff et al. 1978) confirms this expectation.

An unfortunate consequence of cross-cultural narrowness is that it prevents therapists from seeing their own limitations. Cultural difference may easily appear unimportant to therapists whose clinical experience is limited to clients with backgrounds similar to their own. For such therapists, the most important differences are in subtle person-to-person variations, which are often viewed as the result of intrapsychic forces (perhaps in part because of the absence of obvious environmental antecedents). This shortsightedness is possible only because the wide range of cultural variables is reduced virtually to a set of constants by their restricted range of experience.

This point bears repeating, because it is so important a clinical shortcoming. For decades, therapists were inquiring into the nuances of their female clients' feelings of inferiority. It took the women's movement, however, to point out the obvious: women felt inferior because in our society they were inferior. Only by overcoming discrimination and changing the patterns of relationships between the sexes could these facts be altered. This is not to deny that any given woman developed her unique feelings of inferiority through a unique set of experiences with other people. Rather, it is to put the matter into perspective and say that the social pattern is overwhelmingly important to her feelings, and that having had one set of negative experiences rather than another is responsible only for the particular coloration of those feelings.

The way in which clinicians systematically distort their diagnostic and prognostic evaluations, by exaggerating the importance of subtle individual differences and minimizing the importance of more powerful predictors, has been well documented (e.g., Mischel 1968[1]). To the dismay of personality

---

1. Mischel's book set off the person-situation debate over his contention that people's behavior is much more situationally determined than they or others believe. A sort of middle ground has been reached with the idea that people display some kinds of behavior relatively consistently across different situations while other kinds of behavior occur relatively consistently across individuals in the same type of situation. Still, an individual's behavioral consistency across situations might well diminish if the situations became very different—for example, by moving to another culture. Bicultural people whose

researchers, the more powerful predictors have generally been obvious ones. Psychologists, in their attempts to be subtle or deep, have referred to these accurate predictions as "the Barnum effect," thereby stigmatizing clinicians who make them as charlatans and those who are impressed by them as gullible. (It was P. T. Barnum who said, "There's a sucker born every minute.") A well-known type of experiment—which may owe part of its popularity to the opportunity it affords harried psychology professors to one-up their students—is conducted as follows: After completing personality tests, students receive written personality descriptions supposedly based on the test results. They then complete ratings of the accuracy of the descriptions, and show a high degree of confidence in them. Finally, one student reads the "personalized" report aloud, and they discover to their dismay that they all received the identical report (Bachrach and Pattischal 1960, Forer 1949, Manning 1968, Ulrich et al. 1963). In such studies, the high confidence of students in the reports was the result not of their individual accuracy but of their applicability to American college students in general. Elements that were included in the reports, such as a need for peer approval or problems in sexual adjustment, were characteristic of the group as a whole. As a result, such statements were likely to be true of the students as individuals. The predictions are accurate precisely because they refer to group uniformities—in statistics they are referred to as "high base rate" statements. However, the critics go astray in dismissing such predictions as unimportant, and insisting that only low base rate statements, which differentiate the individual from the group, are of psychological interest.

The reason for this distorted emphasis appears to be the

"personalities" undergo dramatic shifts as they move from one of their cultures to the other illustrate this possibility, as do the behavioral changes associated with culture shock.

critics' limited cross-cultural experience: high base rate predictions seem trivial only because the critics are also Americans. Statements characteristic of American adolescents are not necessarily characteristic of non-American adolescents or of nonadolescent Americans. The fact that virtually all American adolescents experience problems in sexual adjustment doesn't make such problems unimportant to them as individuals. On the contrary, it implies that they are likely to be more important than idiosyncratic problems, such as a fear of moths.

The question is, what therapeutic use can be made of these high base rate psychological inferences? I would suggest that they can be used to help people achieve what might be called sociocultural awareness, as opposed to the personality insights that traditional psychotherapy provides. For the purposes of this book, sociocultural awareness can be defined as an awareness that one's specific behavior and experiences are not unique, but are characteristic of a class of people with similar backgrounds in similar situations; and a sociocultural explanation can be defined as a communication aimed at the client's achieving sociocultural awareness. Thus, in the experiments described above, a desirable result would be not for the students to realize how gullible they are, but rather for them to realize how similar their problems are as a result of being American adolescents.

What I am calling sociocultural awareness is quite like the sociological concept of class consciousness, except that it is an awareness relating to membership in virtually any group with similar backgrounds or in similar situations, and not just to economic classes. Thus, insights based on one's membership in a group of people with a similar age, sex, race, religion, physical handicap, hobby, language, profession, or other characteristic in common, which provides similar environments for them, would come under the definition.

Regardless of our (American) desire that everyone be

treated as an individual, it is a fact that sociocultural variables are powerful determinants of how people actually treat each other. Thus, therapists' blindness in this area cannot be the result of dullness or insensitivity—as a group they are bright and sensitive—but only of intensive misguided training. We therapists had to study long and hard and be involved in absorbing therapeutic and didactic encounters, in order to learn to close our eyes to the obvious.

In describing the effects of training on clinical sensitivity, Mischel (1968) made a point that applies equally well to sociocultural awareness:

> Judges, because of their clinical training, became more sensitive and responsive to what they perceived to be individual differences. As a result, they also became less accurate than if they had based their predictions on relatively undifferentiated stereotypes. Training programs devoted to enhancing accuracy of interpersonal perception therefore may actually decrease accuracy by sharpening the trainee's attention to individual differences. [p. 115]

In the sociocultural area, however, therapists do not need to choose between an exaggerated emphasis on individual differences and undifferentiated stereotypes in working with their clients. There is a relevant body of knowledge in the other social sciences, especially anthropology and sociology, that can supplement psychological knowledge in giving a more complete understanding of their clients' behavior. Even without mastering the detailed knowledge of other fields, therapists can gain an understanding of the frames of reference of these disciplines. It is my belief that, by integrating such an understanding into their therapeutic outlook, they will be able to think and interact with their clients in a more sophisticated and, hence, more effective manner.

Therapists who attribute overwhelming importance to internal states as determinants of behavior naturally believe that a crucial part of training should be devoted to increasing sensitivity to those states. Hence, they have emphasized the desirability of therapists undergoing therapy themselves so as to acquire this sensitivity (e.g., Freud 1963a, Rogers 1951). Apart from the sociological function of such therapy—an emotionally intense persuasive experience leading therapists to maintain their theoretical beliefs despite contradictory clinical and experimental evidence (Fish 1973, Frank 1961, 1973, Frank and Frank 1991)—the idea of therapy for therapists is a logical consequence of psychological theories emphasizing the importance of subjective experience. It follows, from a sociocultural stance, that it would be equally logical to suggest that therapists expose themselves to an intensive cross-cultural experience as part of their training. For example, it might be required as a part of a therapist's training to spend at least a year in a non-American culture, developing an appreciation of its complexities—if not a facility in dealing with them—and learning the language.

I have no illusions that such a suggestion would ever be implemented, or even taken seriously, but I raise it anyway because I believe that it would have a salutary effect on American therapy. The current superabundance of highly trained professionals may lead some therapists to gain cross-cultural experience for economic reasons, even if their inclinations are to the contrary.

At the very least, it would seem desirable to increase the interconnections between therapy training programs (in psychology, psychiatry, social work, pastoral counseling, education, and nursing) and departments of anthropology and sociology at the same universities. In addition, minority and foreign students and faculty within the programs, especially those who have academic as well as experiential sociocultural knowledge, can be a resource for their monocultural colleagues.

Trainees could be provided with field work experiences with immigrants and members of minority groups. Approval could be expedited for internships that provide cross-cultural and multilingual training within the fifty states, or in bureaucratically acceptable nearby places like Puerto Rico or Québec. While it would be difficult to obtain approval for overseas internships, university-based training programs could at least begin the process by initiating contacts with psychiatric hospitals or mental health centers affiliated with universities abroad. They could also include in their program applications questions about experience with cultures other than American, facility in languages other than English, and participation in programs such as the Peace Corps or a junior year abroad. The point of emphasizing cross-cultural experience would be to increase mental health professionals' sensitivity to socio-cultural variables affecting their clinical work.

The meaning of culture-specific communications is essentially arbitrary, just as the meaning of a given word is arbitrarily associated with particular sounds in a given language. When learning a new language, one is often surprised or amused to find that a word one knows well has an entirely different meaning (for example, *flèche*, pronounced "flesh," means arrow in French). In a similar way, particular sentences or gestures may communicate entirely different meanings in different cultures. Thus, the danger of a therapist's misunderstanding a client from a different cultural background is not greatest when the client acts unexpectedly. The very strangeness of the behavior is a clue that something is happening that merits further investigation. Rather, it is when the therapist and client behave in entirely understandable ways—each misinterpreting the other's behavior from a different frame of reference—that real damage can be done, without either party recognizing what has happened (Carroll 1988). A famous example (Hall 1959, 1966) concerns a neutral conversation between an Arab and an Englishman, in which the Arab sees the Englishman as cold and the Englishman sees the Arab as intense and intrusive. The reason for the misunderstanding concerns extreme differences in the expected physical distance between persons having a casual conversation in the two cultures. If a second Arab stood as far away from the first as did the Englishman, he would be cold; and if an Englishman moved as close to one of his compatriots as the Arab did, he would be intrusive. The misunderstanding occurred precisely because the distance between the two speakers had well-defined meanings in both cultures, albeit different ones.

In other words, the process of becoming sensitive to sociocultural variables necessitates developing a therapeutic "third eye" for sensing the presence of minimal cues to sociocultural patterns analogous to the "third ear" (Reik 1949) for detecting partially hidden signs of individual uniqueness.

In order to understand the difference between listening with the third ear and watching with the third eye, let us consider an interaction between a client who complains of not feeling understood and a therapist who recognizes that anger is being expressed. If the therapist views the client's hostility as representing a projection of negative feelings that were once appropriate to someone else—probably one of the client's parents—then he might try to help the client develop insight into its unconscious cause.

Let us assume, for the sake of argument, that the therapist is a 40-year-old man from a northern white urban middle-class background who now lives in a white upper middle class suburb of a northern city with his wife (from a similar background) and two elementary school children, in an eight-room house with two cars in the garage. He is the director of a university counseling center and also has a part-time private practice. Let us further assume that his client is a 19-year-old woman from a southern black rural lower-class background who is working as a waitress and living in a rooming house in a black lower-class neighborhood of the same northern city while attending courses part-time at the local university at night. Finally, let us assume that she is in therapy at the university counseling center because she is lonely, depressed, unsure of her academic objectives, and having difficulty with her coursework.

Given this information, instead of looking for unconscious causes, the therapist might come to the following tentative conclusions:

The painful feelings that led her to therapy are appropriate to her real-life situation. She is probably lonely because she is alone, living in an unfamiliar environment without friends or family for support. She is most likely depressed because there are few rewards in her life: she is constantly working or attending class, has few social contacts, and experiences difficulty in her courses and a lack of direction in her personal, work, and academic life. Her academic problems are probably due in part to the academic and counseling deficiencies of southern rural schools in preparing students for northern urban university life.

Her feelings of not being understood by the therapist are also appropriate, since he has had no experience with her world (nor she with his). It is natural for a client to feel frustrated and angry about not being understood; and there is no need to appeal to more complex concepts such as projection or transference for an explanation. Much more likely explanations for his difficulty in understanding her can be found in differences between them on the socio-cultural variables of sex, age, social class, race, and urban-rural background, as well as on interactions among these variables. I am making a point of enumerating the variables because by now American therapists are hypersensitized to the importance of racial differences. There are frequent sociocultural misunderstandings between therapists and clients of different American racial classifications that have nothing whatsoever to do with race. In the current example, if the client were white it would be easy to imagine the difficulties in communication with the therapist that could result from her being a woman, from being less than half the therapist's age, from coming from a lower class-background, or from growing up in the rural south. It would be just as unfounded to automatically attribute these misunderstandings to race, just because the client is black, as to attribute them to unconscious processes.

Since her psychological suffering is appropriate to her real-life situation, and her feelings about the therapist are appropriate to her interactions with him, it follows that *the problems that brought her to therapy need not be related to her feelings about the therapist.* Either could change without affecting the other. The theoretical assumptions that therapy is a microcosm of the client's psychological world, that all important problems manifest themselves in the therapeutic relationship, and that problems can be resolved only through a resolution of their manifestations in therapy, can be seen as unnecessary.

In consequence of the above, *the therapist's focus on subtle personality processes and internal states could have blinded him to obvious sociocultural aspects of the client's problems.* This point underlines the danger of therapists' theoretical orientations distorting their perceptual and conceptual processes.

Finally, *directing therapy toward possible hidden meanings of her anger could have led the therapist to avoid the more appropriate task of finding realistic solutions to her problems.* Such solutions would probably include vocational counseling and remedial training for her educational deficits. However, it is the realistic treatment of her depression and loneliness that would be at once the most interesting, challenging, and difficult therapeutic task. In brief, a major therapeutic goal would be to help her to enter into northern urban African American social life, so that she could build up a network of friends and support.

Since the therapist has no intimate knowledge of this subculture, his task would be one of encouraging her to make enquiries and get involved in social activities. Then, after listening to her southern rural African American understanding of the northern urban African American subculture from his northern urban European American point of view, he would have to make suggestions as to how she might better be able to succeed in her new environment. Naturally, this approach would involve considerable trial and error for both therapist and client, with both of them learning from their mistakes. Difficulties could arise because the client might observe inaccurately, because the therapist might misunderstand her observations, or because he might propose a solution that would be culturally untenable despite an accurate understanding of the situation.

This type of therapy would involve rather different role relationships between the participants from the traditional ones. In brief, therapy could be seen as taking place between a therapist/anthropologist and a client/informant. From such a frame of reference, it is clear that any colleagues, friends, and personal or educational experiences in therapists' backgrounds that give them special knowledge of the cultures in question, or enhance their ability to understand other cultures, can be a great asset. Furthermore, in therapy involving cross-cultural problems, therapists' lack of understanding of their clients' cultures is balanced by the candid information they can give about their own. In the example under discussion, the therapist would be able to give his client inside information about campus life, faculty attitudes, and ways of getting to know European American students on campus and entering into predominantly European American activities.

It is clear that this sort of therapy requires a reasonably open and trusting relationship between therapist and client. Therapists must surrender much of their authority and prestige because in the cultural area, where so much cannot be anticipated, they are bound to make embarrassing mistakes and inaccurate assumptions. Therapists who can't relax and laugh at their own occasional demonstrations of naiveté are going to wind up looking silly.

It is my impression that clients and therapists alike are considerably more defensive about discussing matters such as their ethnic, religious, social class, and racial beliefs and identifications than they are about discussing their masturbatory fantasies or feelings about their parents. Evasiveness in discussing sociocultural areas is a major barrier to getting the kind of concrete information that is essential to problem solving. Thus, accepting the client's cultural difference (i.e., representativeness of a group of people different from the therapist) and communicating this acceptance is every bit as crucial to therapy as accepting the client's personal uniqueness. The implication is that, to do this kind of therapy, therapists must truly value cultural diversity and accept attitudes, feelings, and behavior different from their own.

In short, for most therapists, enhancing their view of therapy to include a prominent role for social and cultural variables will involve making changes in their theoretical approach, personal values, and therapeutic style. If they rise to the challenge, they can expect to gain the fascination of viewing the world from a more comprehensive perspective and the satisfaction of applying their new understanding in more effective therapy whenever sociocultural variables are salient.

7

Sociocultural Theory

The aim of Part II of this book is to indicate the clinical relevance of some established points of view in the social sciences. To do so requires at least provisional adherence to a model of human behavior. I am including the following condensed theoretical discussion in order to indicate the kind of understanding I believe is useful both for dealing with clinical realities and for taking into account cultural complexities.

All people learn, and continually relearn or modify throughout their lifetimes, patterned ways of thinking and of interacting with others in recurrent types of situations. This learning occurs both by active social participation and by passive experience such as reading or watching others, and includes the development of elaborate systems of thoughts, feelings, and values, in addition to overt behavior. Formal and informal patterned behavior is shared by members of groups ranging in size from nations (pledging allegiance to the flag or drinking Coca-Cola) and religions (going to confession or hunting for Easter eggs), down through ever smaller ethnic groups, professions, businesses, and other work groups, local fraternal organizations, neighborhood bars, extended families, and nuclear families. Ultimately, we can see such behavior transmitted, and maintained, modified, or rejected, within specific triads (e.g., mother–father–child) and dyads (e.g., husband and wife, or employer and employee).

Since the content of such patterned thoughts and behavior is largely arbitrary and unpredictable a priori, a person who enters a new group will be unprepared, at least to the extent to which the group differs from those previously experienced. In general, the individual will have to develop new patterns of thoughts and behavior to adapt to the new environment (while possibly influencing it to some extent as well) or will have to leave—regardless of the size of the group involved. At the national level, people suffer culture shock when moving to a new country. In dyads, people who change jobs or remarry have to learn to adapt to their new boss's or spouse's initially unpredictable behavior, although modifying it to some extent by their own actions.

Several comments about this model of human behavior are in order:

1. The model applies to all humans. The new spouse or the inhabitants of the new country also act in patterned ways, based on the totality of their own previous experiences.

2. Since people affect their environment, the process of influence (and its inverse, adaptation) are interactive. This interaction is characteristic of both the social environment—parents adapt to their children as well as vice versa—and the

physical environment, as ecologists have demonstrated so graphically.

3. Since people influence their environment and their environment influences them, it follows that people have an effect on their own behavior. Furthermore, individuals may respond directly to their own behavior, as in feeling guilty because of something they have done; and thus, in an analytical sense, a person is a part of his or her own stimulus environment. This means that long chains of "individual–environment interaction" may consist of a person's responding to his or her own behavior and providing consequences for it, while the external environmental setting and consequences are salient only at the beginning and end of the chain.

4. People can develop generalized adaptational skills (e.g., learning to learn) that apply to broad classes of situations. Anthropologists who have done field work in several different cultures often claim to get better at the initial process of adjustment. Similarly, polyglot friends have told me that language learning gets easier after mastering several unrelated languages.

5. The importance of the situational context to learning cannot be overemphasized. The time, place, and consequences of behavior are central determinants of the learning process, and subtle situational differences may lead to entirely different patterns of behavior. With regard to behavior while eating in our own culture, different situations—a formal dinner, an "elegant" restaurant, a "family" restaurant, a fast food joint, dinner at someone's house, dinner for company at home, a family reunion, and an everyday dinner at home—lead to quite different ways of acting. These differences shrink into insignificance, however, when cross-cultural variation is taken into account; a belch in some cultures is a desirable compliment to one's host, while in others one may eat with one's hands and

find it revolting to think of using utensils (which may once have been in someone else's mouth).

6. Recurrent behavior may be viewed as static or dynamic. Static behavior can be seen as adapted to an environmental niche, with no pressures for it to change or remain the same (e.g., one learns how to shake hands and then performs the behavior in appropriate situations). Dynamic "homeostatic" processes of mutual influence may be responsible for the consistency of other behavior (e.g., pressures that keep participants in a work group focused on a disliked task or prevent members of a family from discussing an important but taboo subject).

7. Deviation-amplifying "positive feedback" processes of mutual influence may lead either to the internal restructuring of a group or to its breakup. For example, an escalating conflict between two subgroups might lead an organization to reorganize into two distinct subunits, or to restructure itself in some other way, or to expel members of the weaker subgroup one or several at a time, or to split into two or more new entities, or even to self-destruct altogether.

8. None of this is meant to deny the importance of genetic or physiological influences on behavior. While standards of beauty vary widely from culture to culture, the body one has is largely determined by genetics (though environmental influences such as diet and health care are also important). In our culture, physical appearance may still be the most important determinant of many women's social mobility. Similarly, the anxiety and depression of someone with appendicitis is better treated by an appendectomy than by therapy.

This, then, is a sketch of how I understand human behavior. It is clear that it differs from the outlook of many therapists, especially in the much greater importance attributed to the ongoing effects of the environment. For example, internal events such as thoughts and feelings are viewed mainly as the result of previous learning rather than as primary causes of behavior (though, once acquired, they are among the factors that determine how the individual will act in a particular situation).

Since this point of view understands human behavior as inextricably bound up with its social context, it is necessary to discuss that context in somewhat greater detail. It is interesting to note that serious works on personality and psychotherapy rarely give more than passing mention to this important topic.

As outsiders to the vast and important fields of anthropology and sociology, therapists should not lose their critical perspective in accepting the useful insights these fields have to offer. Many of the theoretical shortcomings of our field are amply present in these other areas, and we must be aware of them as we go along.

Perhaps the greatest fallacy in personality theory comes from reifying descriptive concepts and then using them as causal explanations. For example, instead of using the term *extroverted* to describe people who make friends easily and talk a lot, we erroneously say that they are friendly and garrulous *because* they are extroverted. It is as if extroversion suddenly became a thing the people had a lot of, which caused their behavior—rather than a concept used by the observer. (Even individual differences in activity level or conditionability lead to different behavior in different individuals as a result of different life histories.) Another common psychological example is the contrast between the descriptive use of the adjective *unconscious*—to refer to acts that one is not fully aware of doing, or to the implications of such acts—and the causal use of the noun *the unconscious* to explain behavior. The latter can be seen in explanations such as "the devil made him do it" or "his unconscious made him do it."

In a similar way, social and cultural concepts may easily be turned into things and made to function as explanations. Consider the following: middle-class people believe therapy can help them with emotional problems (descriptive) versus John believes therapy can help him with his emotional problems because he is middle class (causal). The middle class is an abstraction and not a cause. Only specific interactions with people, books that John has read, and similar experiences can be seen as causal in his belief. Consequently, the correct statement is: people referred to as middle class have similar environments that lead them to a similar belief that therapy can help them with their emotional problems; and John is one of these people.

Like the term *personality* in our field, *society* and *culture* are the leading candidates as the most reified concepts in sociology and anthropology. (I have been using the terms *society* and *culture* informally for smoothness of exposition, and will continue to do so; but the following distinctions can be understood to be implicit throughout the book.)

Some social theorists have been fond of comparing society to a living organism. Usually a human is the organism of choice, doubtless because of its audience appeal. Less differentiated organisms such as the jellyfish, extinct species like the dinosaur, or figments of the imagination such as the unicorn seem not to be used. In the analogy, different groups within society have different functions, just as do different organs of a living creature, but all parts must perform their functions harmoniously for the organism to exist.

This striking comparison highlights certain aspects of the way groups of people live together; but, as with any analogy, this virtue comes at the expense of ignoring other important parts of the phenomenon under consideration. While pointing up differences between groups and harmony among them, it ignores similarities among groups and conflicts between them. When taken as an explanation, instead of a description of mixed virtues, it can easily become a justification for inequality and the status quo. Thus, it has been argued that leaders, as the head of the organism, are justified in being better off than the workers, or hands, because such inequalities are necessary for the organism as a whole to function successfully. Naturally, such explanations have always been more appealing to leaders than to workers. Finally, as with any analogy, the organismic view of society can be pushed too far. It would be hard to see what group would be identified as the gall bladder.

Keeping these cautions in mind while expanding on the earlier theoretical sketch, we can return to the issue of understanding the behavior of individuals. Such behavior can be seen as resulting from the interaction of three kinds of antecedents: biological factors, individual psychological factors, and social psychological factors. Under biological factors, I am lumping together both those aspects common to all human beings, and the genetic and other physical idiosyncracies of the individual. Homo sapiens is a species, which means that all humans biologically resemble one another more than any individual resembles another creature from the animal or plant kingdoms. Still, when we look only within the human species, it is the relatively minor differences in genetic makeup, nutrition, and medical history that appear to emerge as important determinants of behavior. Even these biological variations interact with the social environment to produce differences in behavior, as we can see by a cross-cultural comparison of the sick role, standards of beauty, or attitudes toward people with physical handicaps.

Representative and idiosyncratic biological factors can for most purposes be lumped together, since all humans share the former. Only when groups of humans differ in some biological way, as in sex, must distinctions be made in order to better understand the relation between biology and the behavior of individuals.

This is not the case with psychological factors. While some psychological processes such as learning or perception may function in virtually identical ways for nearly all humans, the human content of what is perceived or learned is never univer-sal. Thus, it is important to distinguish between an individual's idiosyncratic learning experiences—the effect of growing up in a particular family, or of working for a given employer—and an individual's experience of specific instances of kinship or labor patterns that characterize large groups of people.

While considerable attention has been paid to the role of idiosyncratic learning in developing personal uniqueness, the issue of how social patterns transform themselves into the behavior of individuals is generally not discussed. Sociologists and anthropologists, whose interest is in the society as a whole rather than in individuals, generally refer to the "socialization" process. That is to say, people learn to be like others in their society by growing up among them—a truism that is not very informative about the mechanism by which this process occurs. On the other hand, since psychologists work from within American society, social and cultural patterns form an irrelevant background to their studies, and are in general not dealt with. These patterns become apparent only when the America of today is seen as but one of many ways in which large numbers of people live together.

Any discussion of social and cultural factors in therapy must concern itself with the individual–social interface, because the therapist needs a conceptual framework to bridge the gap from general patterns in society to the specifics of the client's prob-lems.

The two main kinds of patterns of behavior dealt with by sociologists and anthropologists may be referred to as social patterns and cultural patterns. This distinction is an analytical one, as between form and content, rather than one of subject matter. Thus, in a given instance, it is possible to discuss the social and cultural aspects of the behavior in question without being forced to make a choice between these two aspects.

In general, a social pattern refers to a repetitive form of

interaction that occurs among specifiable groups of people, as between drill sergeants and privates or priests and penitents. The giving and obeying of orders or the offering and receiving of absolution are repetitive forms, linked to social institutions, that are repeated regardless of the individuals involved, as if the social patterns had a life of their own. Such patterns take place within delimited bounds of acceptable deviation: the private does not give orders to the drill sergeant nor does the penitent offer absolution to the priest.

Cultural patterns, on the other hand, refer to the specific content of beliefs, behavior, and objects that characterize specifiable groups of individuals. There is a sense of arbitrary choice among innumerable possible variations, and a conceptual independence of the cultural content from its social context. That a soldier wears a green uniform rather than a blue one, that he salutes with one hand motion rather than another or with his foot, that a church is decorated with baroque or folk art, are all cultural variations that can be independent of the social patterns.

While social and cultural patterns are analytically separable, they are in practice intertwined. Social conditions may determine cultural content, as when, during World War II, the need for women's labor resulted in their performing many traditionally male tasks and led to a modification of the American belief that a woman's place is in the home. Cultural content may also determine social patterns, as can be seen in the separate existence of the kosher meat industry with its unique combination of religious and butchering personnel. This social network exists because of a set of beliefs held by American Orthodox Jews.

These examples of the interaction between social and cultural patterns also illustrate another important point. Their apparent independence of each other or of the individuals involved is an illusion. They are independent conceptually in the eye of the observer; but concepts are not things, and it is important to avoid reifying concepts. Cultural and social patterns continue across time because particular individuals learn them in consistent environmental contexts. A dramatic change in the physical environment (e.g., an earthquake) or social environment (e.g., being conquered by another group) can lead to sudden transformations in social and cultural patterns that previously appeared immutable because their environmental context was unaltered for an extended period of time. In this way, working in a factory or saying a prayer over an animal carcass can be seen as human behavior that takes place in a social context. It is only natural that variations in the social environment should lead to variations in human behavior—no matter what conceptual terms are used to describe either the environment or the behavior.

An integration of this discussion with the view of human behavior presented at the beginning of this chapter is illustrated in Figure 7–1. Since the figure was designed to highlight the role of social and cultural influences on an individual's behavior, I have omitted for purposes of clarity the feedback effect of the

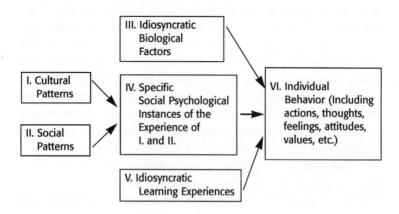

Figure 7–1.   Influences on Individual Behavior

individual's behavior (and of the awareness of the various influences) on these and other influences, interactive effects among the influences, and non-human factors (e.g., the physical environment), which have effects on all elements included. It is the inclusion of elements I, II, and IV in this diagram that distinguishes it from most therapists' view of human behavior.

Cultural patterns can be seen as learned by the growing child (and later, adult) in a series of social contexts as outlined at the beginning of this chapter. Some behavior patterns are learned from parents who learned them from their parents, some from teachers who learned them from their teachers, and some from playmates who learned them from their playmates. (A few present-day American children's games have been traced as far back as ancient Rome.[1])

Since social patterns are defined as repetitive forms of interaction, the individual learns by observing and engaging in examples of these patterns. Through contacts with men and women, adults and children, rich people and poor people, whites and blacks, natives and foreigners, and bosses and workers, as well as through information gained indirectly about such contacts, the individual learns how it is appropriate to act with such people in modern America. This learning includes the effects of the ways others label one and expect one to act, and one's own development of a repertoire of expectancies and labels for others. Another way of putting this is that the system of statuses and roles (which are viewed sociologically as positions and corresponding behavior patterns within a social structure) can be seen psychologically as an abstraction of patterns of interactions among individuals.

The relationship between these points of view, focused on

---

1. This is discussed by Stone and Church (1957, pp. 209–211), especially in footnotes 3 and 4, p. 237, which refer to Mills and Bishop (1937), Leopold (1952), and Bolton (1888).

the social pattern and focused on the individual, can be summarized as follows. From the social point of view, each person occupies various age, sex, professional, and other statuses, each of which is characterized by a distinctive pattern of behavior or role. Role behavior is interactive and is displayed in complementary pairs—such as employer/employee or doctor/patient—in which each actor communicates an expectancy of reciprocal behavior by the other, and reinforces it when it occurs. (It is also displayed in and shaped and maintained by triads and more complex interactive groups, but the principle is the same, so I will deal only with dyads for expository purposes.) Thus, a person who is naive about a given role performance is trained for it by the complementary role behavior of those with whom he or she interacts (as well as by observing others in the role, reading about it, and through other indirect forms of learning). The more varied boyfriends and professors a college student has, the more skillful she becomes in the girlfriend and student roles. Thus, the preexisting pattern of social interactions guarantees that particular individuals will have similar learning experiences in given situations, and thereby makes certain their socialization into appropriate roles.

Individuals are born into societies, each of which comes ready made with a pattern of statuses and roles, and grow up with the impression that it is permanent. That is, the pattern appears to constitute an enduring social "structure"—and in very stable and isolated societies individuals may encounter little evidence to challenge this perception. Over time, however, increasingly complex forms of social organization have evolved on the planet, based on increasingly complex and productive subsistence technologies developed to feed increasingly large populations (Harris 1980, Lenski and Lenski 1974). Thus, while individuals' behavior may seem to be shaped by enduring social patterns with an independent existence, we can see that these patterns are themselves the product over extended periods of time of interactions among individuals. The social influence processes of these interactions can in turn ultimately be understood in terms of laws of psychology.

Given that the learning of both cultural and social patterns of behavior takes place in patterned social contexts, it remains for this chapter only to discuss the antecedents of what is learned. Just as cultural and social patterns are conceptually different though substantively intertwined, so are their determinants. Nevertheless, for the purposes of this discussion, it suffices to say that cultural patterns are determined primarily by tradition, while social patterns are determined primarily by power.

To say that cultural patterns are determined by tradition is practically a tautology. What is contributed by making the statement is to emphasize the socially arbitrary nature of such patterns and the lack of any necessary relationship among them. Naturally, some traditions may once have been selected from among alternatives because of their harmony with a preexisting social pattern. For example, the handshake once had the social function of demonstrating a lack of weapons. The arbitrary nature of the American handshake can be seen by comparing it to the pattern that evolved in many other countries, of men embracing as well as shaking hands. That the embrace-plus-handshake is a culturally distinct pattern is evidenced by most American men's awkwardness when they encounter it.

To say that social patterns are determined by the distribution of power requires a pause to look at the concept of power. Unlike personality, society, and culture, which appear to be theoretically misleading reifications, it does seem possible to anchor the concept of power in verifiable terms that reflect important phenomena. The problem with the concept of power is that it lumps together under one rubric various phenomena that need not always be highly interrelated. The concept is rather like Krasner and Ullmann's (1973) concept of behavior

influence—though perhaps the term *social influence* is preferable, to emphasize the human nature of power and omit biological variables and those in the physical environment that also
have an effect on behavior.

If power is defined as control of the resources necessary to
influence the behavior of others, then we can distinguish at the
very least among the control of rewards, the control of punishments, and the control of information.[2] These can be approximately translated into familiar types of power. The control of
money, goods, and services, the most common rewards, may be
called economic power. The control of violence, especially the
punitive resources of police and military organizations, may be
referred to as political power. The control over the various
sources of information concerning facts (e.g., the mass media)
and values (e.g., religious authorities) may be referred to as
persuasive power.

If power is understood as social influence, then it follows
that its use must obey the principles laid down earlier in this
chapter. In particular, the use of power is interactive and
situation-specific. The interactive nature of power means that
the future use of the control of economic, political, or informa-

---

2. In this discussion I am attempting to make subject matter
distinctions rather than traditional theoretical distinctions to highlight
the social aspects of my argument. Thus, I am using the terms *reward,
punishment,* and *information,* rather than *positive reinforcement,
negative reinforcement, punishment,* and *extinction* (nor do I discuss
the informational aspects of these processes) and do not allude to other
social psychological and cognitive processes. My aim in doing so is to
focus attention on the social phenomena rather than on the intricacies
of their theoretical explanation. Persuasive power is extremely
complex, since the ability to convince others that one possesses
economic or political power can be as important in influencing their
behavior as the actual possession of that power.

tional resources depends on the consequences of its past use by the same people. The situation-specific nature of power means that the same resources cannot be used with equal effect to influence all behavior by all people. A dictator may be able to mobilize armies at his personal whim, but his wife may have the power to tell him what tie to wear.

It is important to remember that the single term *power* encompasses a variety of distinct phenomena, and if we accept the use of the term for theoretical convenience, we must be careful not to confuse subject matter distinctions. For example, it might seem paradoxical that American generals are much more powerful than corporation presidents, yet are much less wealthy. The paradox disappears when we realize that the generals' control of violence is substantively different from the corporation presidents' control of economic resources. Given the American system, it is much easier for a corporation president to bribe a general than it is for a general to force a corporation president to act in a given way; in other societies (e.g., military dictatorships) the reverse is true.

The argument that the specific patterns of social structure are determined primarily by power runs more or less as follows. For any large and complex society to function, its activities must be organized, and for the various organizations within society to function, there must be people at the top with the power to set and enforce policy. Naturally, such elite groups want to protect their privileged positions, and they do so by manipulating the rewards, punishments, and information they control. Their positions enable them to pay well those who act in their service, to punish those who act against them, and to justify their special status by self-serving ideologies. The divine right of kings before the American Revolution, and the more recent notion that the best people rise to the top through successful competition, are essentially ideological justifications by the powerful and rich, whose function is to get others to accept their superior position as merited. (The inheritance of wealth or the use of criminal tactics to gain it are not stressed in the American mythology of success.)

Any discussion of the distribution of power must distinguish between past learning and controls and those of the present. For example, control over information in the socialization process of education leads to an "internalization" of values. Adults may do things "voluntarily"—with minimal ongoing reward and punishment—whereas much greater environmental control would be necessary to achieve similar behavior without the early learning history. The extent to which Americans have learned to believe that success and failure are merited is reflected in the psychological depression and feelings of worthlessness of people who lose their jobs during a recession. Even though they know that economic conditions and not their performance were responsible for their dismissal, they react as if the reverse were true.

Those in positions of power must of necessity delegate some of that power to skilled people who can devote themselves full time to keeping them at the top, maximizing their power, and implementing their policies. The powerful are willing to pay well for these services, and the American ideology of success has been exceptionally effective in generating an intense competition among underlings to rise to high managerial positions. In this way, in certain situations, the ideology of success can become a self-fulfilling prophesy. Naturally, once managers receive some of this delegated power, they can use it in their own interest, much as those at the very top have done. Thus, it is possible for a corporation president to receive two million dollars a year (rather than, say, two hundred thousand) because his services are worth that much in a free market. On the other hand, if he were to demand too much (e.g., a hundred million dollars), the powerful stockholders for whom he really works would not hesitate to fire him and risk suffering the consequences. Naturally, when the people who hold the ultimate power are also the top managers—as in huge corporations owned and run by a single family—such conflicts are much less likely.

As the managers structure and restructure their organizations to achieve given ends, a network of statuses and role relationships is continually created and modified throughout the organization. This hierarchical pattern can be found in the various sectors of society, for example, industry, the military, and organized religion. The results of such structure are the repetitive types of interaction that take place among people in different positions, both within and between different organizations, as was discussed above.

Each individual is a member of many different groups or classes of people, each of which is exposed to a particular pattern of environmental experiences. Because of the "zero-sum" nature of many resources (each person or group can gain something only at the expense of other persons or groups), groups within society must inevitably conflict with one another. For example, American adolescents find themselves at an economic, political, and informational disadvantage in relation to their parents. Therefore, it is understandable that they should band together into peer gangs or clubs, develop separate ideologies and means for their communication (including specialized mass media and slang), and often engage in activities antagonistic to parents-in-general, and to their own parents in particular.

Because everyone is a representative of many such groups—some in conflict with each other—all individuals find themselves enmeshed in a fabric of inconsistent and shifting alliances and conflicts. For example, American college students from rich and poor families may have sex together, drink together, read the same magazines, listen to the same music, and generally see themselves as allies against their parents. Twenty years later, economic factors may well be more important in their lives, and former allies may find themselves aligned with former opponents against each other.

Since conflicts generate alliances, conflicts among overlapping groups generate overlapping alliances. In this way, conflicts among groups can serve an integrative function for "society" as a whole (i.e., all the groups taken together) by crisscrossing it with a network of alliances. For example, within a single family confronting various disputes in the wider society, parents and adolescent children may find themselves on opposite sides of a generational conflict, they may simultaneously all take the same side in an ethnic conflict, and father/son versus mother/daughter coalitions may develop around gender issues.

The network of overlapping alliances also produces individuals who are simultaneously members of two or more conflicting groups—for example, children of a racial, religious, ethnic, social class, or other intermarriage. Pressures to maintain group boundaries on both sides of a conflict discourage intermarriage.[3] These include myths, such as the "tragic mulatto," which imply that multiple group membership places intolerable demands on the individual. In fact, while one might

---

3. This taboo can be seen as the counterpart to the incest taboo—the larger social group can best be maintained by discouraging alliances both with those who are too close, since this could lead to the breaking away of subgroups, and with those who are too distant, since this could lead to the fragmentation of the larger group. This social explanation—that prohibitions against both incest and intermarriage serve to maintain the integrity of the larger social group—has two advantages over Freud's explanation that the incest taboo is based on the universality of the Oedipus complex. First, it explains more by bringing together two apparently unrelated phenomena. And second, it avoids the Lamarckian assertion of the inheritance of the experiences of previous generations. Instead, one need merely argue that both prohibitions exist because of their social consequences in the past.

choose—or be pressured—into identifying with one or another group, this is not the only alternative to being torn apart by conflicting loyalties. One can also retain membership in both groups and enjoy the "binocular" advantages of biculturalism. Furthermore, people from mixed backgrounds can play an important integrative role for society, by serving as cultural bridges among the different groups they belong to.

The same kind of overlapping network of alliances can be seen in the larger society and can have a similar "familial" integrative function. Naturally, this is only the case as long as the conflicts are not too intense and are of relatively equal magnitude. When one conflict becomes of overwhelming importance in relation to others (e.g., economic conflict during a depression, or religious or ethnic conflict as in Northern Ireland, Cyprus, the former Yugoslavia, or the Middle East), then its social effect can only be disintegrative, since it forces people to choose sides in an all-out struggle.

Even while attempting to avoid the reification of concepts like society and culture, this presentation has, perhaps unavoidably, implicitly painted a picture of social organization as relatively enduring. Such a presentation may give undue weight to social mechanisms fostering continuity (deviation-reducing feedback) rather than those fostering change (deviation-enhancing feedback). The United States has a remarkably stable regime, with the Civil War as the only threat to its continuity in more than two centuries. In contrast, much of the world lives under regimes whose longevity can be measured in months or years rather than centuries. Not surprisingly, social organization may appear more capricious and less enduring to such people. The breakup of the Soviet Union is a recent reminder that all forms of social organization change over time.

In an attempt not to expand this presentation unnecessarily, I will not deal with interactions among societies. Even though issues like migration, trade, foreign policy, and warfare are not discussed, they may still be quite relevant to understanding and changing the behavior of clients from other cultures.

In conclusion, it should be reemphasized that social and cultural patterns are substantively intertwined, even if they are distinguishable analytically. Class or group differences *are* cultural differences. The upper class is privileged in relation to the lower class because of the unequal distribution of power in society. However, rich people have different values, eat different foods, dress differently, have different manners, and engage in different activities from poor people for reasons of cultural tradition as well as economic advantage (Domhoff 1974, 1983, Ostrander 1984). This is part of the explanation for why the nouveaux riches have such difficulty in being accepted—they have acquired the requisite economic power for their new status, but have not been exposed to the cultural traditions necessary for the smooth execution of their new role. Similarly, resistance to social change is usually due to a combination of social conditions (countervailing sources of power) and the inertia of cultural tradition. Finally, cultural and social features may conflict with as well as complement each other, as when differing cultural traditions among the members hamper the functioning of a social alliance based on economic interests.

Any discussion of causes runs the risk of turning into an infinite regress. It would be possible to discuss the influence of the level of technological development on the distribution of power, then to attempt to explain factors affecting technological development, and to continue in the same vein unendingly. However, any further exploration of the causal chain would lead to areas of little relevance to the therapist's understanding and treatment of clients and their problems. Thus, despite the academic interest of such matters, I have decided to resist the temptation to deal with them. Those who are interested might begin by consulting the works of Marvin Harris (1980, 1981, 1989) and Gerhard Lenski (1966, Lenski and Lenski 1974).

8

Applications to Therapy

The previous chapter was deliberately aimed at highlighting social and cultural determinants of behavior that are usually ignored in discussions of therapy. Therapists need only view such factors from the perspective of clinical interaction to take them into account in their work. New ways of thinking about clients and dealing with their problems follow easily from such a consideration; and the present chapter provides illustrations of this approach.

Perhaps the simplest place to begin is with clients who encounter difficulties because of conflicts over differing cultural traditions. Such traditions are omnipresent in every person's speech, dress, food preferences, manners, and other kinds of behavior, and mark individuals as similar to or distinct from others with whom they come in contact.

In general, an approach to such problems when they arise in therapy involves three parts. The first consists of the therapist's recognizing the cultural patterns involved, pointing them out to the client, and having the client become aware of them too. This is the process of sociocultural explanation and awareness referred to in Chapter 6. It involves having the client recognize that both his or her own behavior, and that of others involved in the problem situation, are representative of culturally homogeneous groups of people who, because of similar backgrounds, act in similar ways.

Cultural misunderstandings are common when the same behavior has different meanings in two cultures. For example, in French culture (among others), interrupting someone is a way of showing interest in what he or she is saying, while in American culture it is inconsiderate. Conversational behavior that an American would view as attentiveness would appear to a French speaker to show a lack of interest (Carroll 1988). While correcting such misunderstandings requires specific knowledge of both cultures, it is easily accomplished once A understands that B's intended meaning was different from the one A inferred and vice versa. In this case, both the interrupting French person and the silent American intended nonverbally to communicate interest in what the other was saying.

The second part of the therapist's approach involves communicating the value of cultural relativism. That is, the therapist expresses a belief to the client, and attempts to influence the client to adopt this belief, that no one cultural pattern is better than another. Rather, the therapist communicates that different patterns are merely alternative variations to which different groups of people have become accustomed.

This is an important point. The therapist in this instance is using a special status and role to influence the client—directly or indirectly—so that the latter will adopt a change in values in the direction of this particular value of the therapist. It has long been known that therapists influence their clients' values in the direction of their own (Parloff et al. 1960, Pentony 1966, Rosenthal 1955, Welkowitz et al. 1967). It is evident that therapists *cannot have no effect* on their clients' values. Thus, therapists must take responsibility for the influence they inevitably have, use it judiciously (and effectively—crass propagandizing is counterproductive), and not hope that by ignoring the issue all will come out for the best.

There are good reasons for not imposing most values on clients. It would seem against professional ethics, as a waste of the client's time and money, to attempt to change values unrelated to the problems for which the client is seeking help. Furthermore, since values are often strongly held, attempts to influence them may backfire and may undermine progress in therapy, or even lead to the client quitting abruptly. It is for these reasons among others that I have advocated a strategy of supporting the client's values in ways that can make the attainment of therapeutic goals more likely (Fish 1973). In addition, tolerance for differing points of view is consistent with American values, as enshrined in the First Amendment to the Constitution, and so should not appear morally unfamiliar to clients.

Still, where a client's values and therapeutic goals are contradictory, we must change one or the other. Since all individuals in the modern nation state must live with others who are culturally different from them, it is inevitable that everyone will face problems related to cultural difference. Ethnocentrism as a value is bound to create difficulties for the client; there is, therefore, a pragmatic argument for the therapist's imposition of the value of cultural relativism in the context of therapeutic work.

Finally, there is the sociological argument that people who seek therapy for help with their problems are more likely at least to pay lip service to the value of cultural relativism than are those who seek other sources of help. As a result, the therapist's attempts to inculcate such a value usually meet with acceptance, and even enthusiasm, when the client sees the day-to-day relevance of a value that was previously held only intellectually. Even so, the fact that the therapist's efforts are aimed at strengthening rather than weakening one of a client's values is not an exemption from the professional self-image of an influencer of values.

Once the client has become aware of the cultural patterns involved and the therapist has communicated the value of cultural relativism, the intensity of the problem diminishes. If clients accept that their behavior and that of others are merely alternative ways of acting, each understandable and appropriate within a given cultural context, then issues of who is right or wrong, good or bad, disappear as irrelevant. In their place is the third part of this approach: rational efforts at problem solving.

Conflicts between people from different cultural traditions are especially common in marriages where the spouses come from different backgrounds—including social class backgrounds since, as I already pointed out, class differences include cultural differences. The threefold approach I have been describing can be illustrated by the way I dealt with a minor incident in a marital therapy case.

The husband, who was from an upper middle class background, was used to eating on a tablecloth; the table seemed bare without it, and his wife's refusal to use one seemed inconsiderate. The wife, who was from a lower middle class background, felt that a tablecloth for everyday meals was pretentious, and that by asking for one he was pointing up her "inferior" background to make her feel miserable.

It is true that the ways in which they argued about the tablecloth were characteristic of the ways in which they argued about other matters, and these were dealt with elsewhere in therapy. On the other hand, the subject matter of the tablecloth was typical of the cultural conflicts between them, and such conflicts were one important source of problems in their marriage. To focus only on the way they fought, and not on what they fought about, would have been an incomplete form of treatment, focusing on psychological issues to the exclusion of cultural ones. Hence, I dealt with the tablecloth issue in the following manner.

I acknowledged that they had grown up in families with different patterns of tablecloth use, and in environments where each family's behavior typified that of other families known to them. I added that, in fact, these were just two patterns from a much wider range of culturally relative behavior; that many cultures didn't have tables, let alone tablecloths, and that their languages didn't even have a word for such a concept (e.g., a Navajo friend told me that, in her language, *table* is approximately translated as "the log the white man uses to eat from"). Thus, I concluded, their differences had no great psychological significance, and the question could be decided by straightforward negotiations. Among possible solutions would be tablecloths for some meals rather than others or on some days rather than others, division of labor (if he wants a tablecloth, he has to put it on the table and wash it) or any other mutually acceptable compromise. Following this, I worked with them to decide on a solution that would function best for them and pointed out how this type of problem solving could be applied to other cultural differences between them.

The pragmatic utility of the value of cultural relativism is especially evident in marital therapy such as this, where opting for one cultural pattern as being preferable to another would contradict the impartiality of the therapist role and make it difficult to function. Therapists who do not assert the value of cultural relativism may imply by omission that they might take sides in a future cultural disagreement. Even in individual therapy, the stance of cultural relativism puts the therapist in a neutral position vis-à-vis the client's relationship with people from other cultural backgrounds. Such an attitude is consistent with the professional role of being paid to give expert advice, rather than being paid to agree with the client. Because of this, it is uncommon for clients to challenge the therapist's advocacy of cultural relativism.

Problems stemming from the client's positions in political, economic, and ideological groups are treated in much the same way. Despite difficulties arising from the complex nature of power relationships, the principle remains unchanged that such problems are realistic and that, to the extent to which they can be solved, they are solvable by realistic means.

Unlike some therapists' optimism regarding "neurotic" problems—that they are all solvable by therapy—I must express pessimism regarding the therapeutic prognosis for many problems of socio-cultural origin. Many of a client's miseries resulting from poverty, for example, are unlikely to yield to even a decade of intensive therapy, while a rapid influx of money might work a miracle that would be the envy of any therapist. It is my view that a large proportion of the problems for which people come for help are essentially realistic consequences of social conditions and are unsolvable by therapy. It is only because therapists are untrained in sociology and anthropology, and because they see their clients one at a time, that they often do not realize that they are attempting to treat individual instances of sociocultural patterns.

Perhaps a medical analogy can aid in making this point. Considerable progress has been made in combating disease during this century, and many people are not aware that the law of diminishing returns has set in. It is costing ever more huge sums of money to develop ever more subtle and complex procedures and equipment to treat ailments that affect ever smaller numbers of people. Smoking, drinking, overeating, and accidents—especially traffic accidents—are increasingly responsible for loss of life nowadays, and these are patterns of social behavior resulting from consistent types of environments experienced by increasing numbers of Americans. Americans by the thousands are dropping dead of obesity while much of the world is starving. It is incredible that many therapists attribute the phenomenon to insatiable oral cravings and not to factors such as the ready availability of food, lessened exercise in a highly industrialized society with diminished demand for physical labor, and similar social causes.[1]

In the same way, I believe that the day is not too far away when the law of diminishing returns will set in for therapy. Ever more time and effort will be expended to develop ever more subtle techniques to treat ever rarer personal problems. As this occurs, I believe that it will become increasingly clear that the major unresolved causes of psychological misery, like the major untreated sources of physical suffering and death, have their origins in sociocultural patterns.

If my pessimism were complete, I would not be writing this book. While many problems that have their origins in social conditions cannot be helped by therapy, some can. For example, therapy clients may not be making the best of objectively bad situations. They may not perceive their situations accurately; they may lack the skills to deal with them effectively; they may not know how to make the best use of their resources. There are a wide variety of ways in which a therapist can be of help—even though the goals of therapy may have to be quite limited.

One positive aspect of work with problems of social origin is this: once the problem has been identified, therapy can

---

1. Despite Schachter's work on obesity (e.g., 1971), the fact remains that even stimulus-bound people will gain less weight if they exercise more or have less food to eat. Presumably, the same percentage of people in Bangladesh and America are more responsive to external than internal cues. Certainly a larger percentage of the former are hungry a greater percentage of the time.

become quite straightforward, and often brief. When the client understands the objective limitations of a situation, it can be much easier to make the best of a bad position. For example, hardships can be examined for hidden advantages or can be viewed as challenges.

Participation in a variety of patterns of social interaction inevitably involves an individual in conflicts; and such conflicts are the most important societal source of personal problems. In social terms, the conflicts are between groups of people. However, in terms of personal experience, the individual suffers as a member of one or more groups who encounters difficulties with others when they display the patterned behavior of their own groups. In schematic form, when two groups conflict, the client may be a member of one or both. Membership in one of two conflicting groups can be illustrated by labor problems, where the client might be a worker aligned with other workers against management. In such a situation, he or she might experience anxiety (e.g., fear of losing a job), anger (e.g., at the boss), or a variety of other unpleasant feelings attributable to the social situation rather than to unconscious conflicts. In one study of a teachers' strike, for example, the degree of anxiety experienced by teachers was found to be related to their position within the educational hierarchy (Cole 1969, Chapter 8).

An individual's membership in two or more conflicting groups makes the experience of role conflict inevitable. That is, behavior that would be satisfactory with regard to one group might prove disastrous with regard to another. In general, the solution to role conflict is for the client to keep the situations that require different types of behavior as separate as possible. For example, I knew a man who served as a Protestant minister for a conservative congregation while he was enrolled as a graduate student in a social science program with a radical reputation and employed as a psychologist in a mental hospital that was bogged down with a tangled bureaucracy. He was able to function well in all three settings because he was in contact with different people in each one. He did not read his term papers to his congregation on Sunday mornings; he did not sermonize about the moral level of ward meetings; and he did not discuss his diagnostic evaluations of inpatients with fellow students of the sociology of deviance. He functioned well in all three situations and was aware that he could continue to do so only by keeping them separate. If it had been impossible to do so, he would have suffered embarrassment, and might have had to give up one or more of these activities.

Role conflict is a fact of life; there is no one way of acting that is tenable in all situations. Personality theorists who claim the possibility—let alone the desirability—of an individual's achieving a single harmonious and internally consistent self are overreaching. People who actually try to live this way inevitably come to grief as their "honesty" is attacked as disloyalty by members of one or more groups, or as they feel torn apart by "internal conflicts." Such conflicts are externally rather than internally caused by an environment that makes it impossible to be all things to all people, but are self-inflicted to the extent to which the individual blindly insists on trying to achieve the impossible. Such people can sometimes make a contribution to intergroup understanding by interpreting each group's behavior to the other. But they will have better self-esteem if they accept their ability to act in two (or more) ways as an asset—evidence of a broader behavioral repertoire.

The most a person can hope for is to be reasonably consistent in thoughts, feelings, and actions in similar types of situations. To unrealistically demand more of oneself creates a kind of misery analogous to that experienced by those who set unattainably high standards for themselves and then fail to reach them. Just as such people must learn to lower their sights, those who insist on being totally authentic, centered, and possessed of an internally consistent personality that forms a harmoniously structured Gestalt would do well to adjust their self-expectations to a more humble, realistic, and human scale. To do the best possible under the circumstances as a spouse, parent, and worker is a reasonable goal. To hope to act in the identical "authentic" way with one's marital partner, children, and fellow workers is self-defeating.

In dealing with problems of economic or political origin, the therapist must consider questions such as the following: How is a client's economic or political position related to personal problems? What are a client's realistic opportunities for action in the current situation? What are the immediate and long-range consequences of various actions likely to be? What individuals or groups of people are in similar economic or political positions and what are their possibilities for action? Are alliances with them or other individuals or groups possible?

In general, the therapist's task is to evaluate the client's economic or political power and related problems in specific situational terms—avoiding global generalizations—so as to be of use in the problem-solving process. This is by no means an easy task, since power relationships are often unclear or deliberately concealed, as are many decisions and objectives of those in positions of authority. A company, for example, may have an impressive organizational chart and a list of official policies such as the efficient production and distribution of a worthy product in order to maximize profits. To the extent that its managers make decisions aimed at their personal advancement or enrichment by evading the established decision-making process or working against the company's policies, they must camouflage their acts or motives or both.

This means that naive efforts by the client to get relevant information by simply requesting it, or to understand superiors' strange behavior by asking them for explanations, can be dangerous. In such a way, he or she might be informing those with power of the attempt to get at hidden information—thus compounding difficulties with them—without being any wiser as a result. Often, the therapist must aid the client in developing subtle trial-and-error tests of hypotheses so as to gradually build up a picture of realistic courses of action and alternatives that are clearly untenable.

At times, therefore, it may be necessary for the therapist to help the client to be "hypocritical"—to say one thing and do another—as part of the process of helping him or her to overcome psychological suffering resulting from a difficult economic or political position. Affirming obligatory beliefs, while doing what works even when it contradicts them, is often the only way the client may investigate and deal with pragmatic realities. In short, for the client's political position to improve, the therapist may have to help him or her to become a more effective politician.

For this reason, an ironic sense of humor can be a valuable asset for a therapist working with such problems. It can help in preventing clients both from getting embittered about the situation they find themselves in and from labeling themselves as hypocrites when forced to act in necessary but disagreeable ways.

The question of the therapist's values, which is inescapable in all therapy, assumes a central position where problems such as these are involved. The therapist must refuse to work toward a morally objectionable end (e.g., "How can I become a better crook than my boss?"). In addition, a therapist's general moral evaluation of a client must enter into the treatment plan. When teaching social skills, a common strategy is first to show the client how to act in particular situations, and then to work toward self-control. That is, the client is helped to develop more general skills so as to facilitate improvisation in unanticipated social dilemmas. In the present case, however, the therapist may deliberately have to avoid helping certain clients to go beyond a solution to their immediate problem. If a ruthless administrator came for therapy because he was miserable at the way he was being unjustly treated by an equally ruthless but more powerful colleague, I might consider helping him to develop psychological tactics to improve his present situation. If I felt that he was perspicacious enough to figure out how to use such tactics unjustly against others in the future, however, I would refuse to help him.

Problems related to the client's economic and political position most frequently arise in the work situation. An example of a realistic solution to one such realistic problem can be seen in the case of the head of one of the therapeutic departments of a government-run mental hospital. While she arrived at the solution without the aid of therapy, the fact that she was a therapist and that the problem involved the care of mental patients makes the illustration an interesting one.

While a number of efforts to improve patient care had received the overt blessings of the director of the hospital, they had run into inexplicable bureaucratic complications. When the administrator received several confidential tips from employees about the director's unsavory personal connections and financial and political involvements, it began to appear that her therapeutic efforts might be running into difficulty because they were inconsistent with conflicts of interest and other unethical endeavors of the director. Further inquiries revealed that a large proportion of the workers at the hospital lacked the formal qualifications for the positions they were in. As such, they were earning higher salaries than they might otherwise receive but were also ineligible to become permanent civil servants. In other words, lacking the protection of the civil service apparatus, they served at the director's whim and could be fired at any time.

As the dimensions of the problem became evident to her, the administrator became increasingly anxious and depressed. Her feelings began affecting her family life, and interfered with other activities she had previously enjoyed, as the question about what to do with the hospital situation became the central preoccupation of her life.

Gradually, the following reasoning about her position evolved:

1. Continued insistence on her part about improving certain aspects of patient care would inevitably lead her into a direct conflict with the director.

2. In such a situation she would have to either fight the battle out to its conclusion or resign.

3. Since she had no legal proof of the director's misconduct, since he was in a more powerful position than she, and since he could control the behavior of a large part of the hospital staff, she would almost certainly lose in any direct confrontation.

4. Even so, she might fight a losing battle, just for the principle of the matter. However, even assuming she won, she had no strong personal commitment to that particular hospital and would probably leave within a few years anyway. Furthermore, considering the emotional toll the situation was already taking, the thought of the suffering that an open battle would cause was too much to bear.

5. As a result, she decided to begin looking for another position and to inform the director of her choice as soon as she had found an acceptable alternative.

Once she made the decision to leave, the downward spiral that her feelings had taken was immediately halted. Within a few months, she found another position, immediately gave appropriate notice, and continued to cheer up as she counted off the days until she left the hospital. A brief vacation before assuming her new position completed the process of restoring her spirits.

Some months after she had left, she received rather disagreeable news that confirmed her analysis of the situation. While at the hospital, she had worked closely with the heads of a few other departments in her efforts to improve patient care. Apparently, a large number of employees had signed a petition directed to the head of the government body that administered mental hospitals, protesting the behavior of those department heads on the grounds that they were undermining the morale of the hospital. She felt relieved that she had gotten out before matters took a turn for the worse.

In considering this example, it must be admitted that some people would have been less upset than she by the conditions she found, and others would have chosen to fight rather than move on. Still, it is clear that the resolution of her psychological distress was brought about by analysis of the external situation and actions she took, rather than by excavating hidden aspects of her feelings. It is conceivable that her feelings about the director were related to her adolescent—or even oedipal—disillusionment about her father. However, one might question whether such insights would have had the dramatic effect on her misery that was evident in her change of jobs.

Psychological problems arising from membership in ideological groups most frequently occur in situations where one's beliefs are different from those of a dominant surrounding group. Academic psychologists are aware of the embattled predicament of a behaviorist teaching in a department of psychoanalysts or vice versa. Psychology departments sometimes even hire a professor of a different theoretical persuasion in a laudable attempt to offer their students a broad background—and then gang up on him or her as the revulsion at having to live with a heretic grows insupportable.

Since this chapter deals with implications for therapy, it is necessary to restrict our discussion to beliefs not too deviant from those of the dominant culture. The reason for this is simple—where the difference is too great, the person suffering from the consequences of having a particular set of beliefs simply would not seek out a therapist's help. A miserable Anglo college professor would be much likelier to try therapy than an even more miserable Cherokee colleague.

In general, the therapeutic strategy for individuals suffering because of their group's beliefs involves three main goals.

First, the client can be helped to avoid allowing ideological conflicts with members of the dominant group to grow into personal conflicts. The American ideology regarding freedom of thought, when cheerfully hinted at ("Variety is the spice of life," rather than "You're immoral for denying me my right to believe what I wish") can be useful in this regard, as can acting generally friendly and helpful in ideologically neutral situations. When all else fails, the client can minimize contact with all or at least the most disagreeable of his or her antagonists.

Second, the client can be encouraged to build a social life away from the conflict setting—that is, with people for whom the ideological conflict is irrelevant. In the example from academia, the professor could be encouraged to enlarge social contacts away from the university, or if having professors for friends seems desirable, to find them in academically unrelated disciplines.

Third, and most people with such problems are already doing this anyway, the client should be encouraged to maintain contact with others of similar beliefs. This can be accomplished both with individuals, through visits, telephone calls, letters, and E-mail, and with the group as a whole, as by attending mass meetings or subscribing to its periodicals.

By progressing toward these three goals, the client can develop a sense of not being alone, and of having sufficient rewards available to make suffering for one's beliefs bearable. Where the client lacks the requisite social skills to achieve the

goals, the therapist can teach such skills through real-life assignments of graded difficulty, role-playing and role reversal, and
similar commonly used techniques.

Naturally, all of this assumes that for some reason the client
wishes to stay or has some overriding interest in staying in a
situation where his or her beliefs are deprecated. As in the case
of the psychologist at the mental hospital, the possibility of
simply leaving a bad situation is always available. Similarly, the
option of changing one's beliefs to those of the dominant
group—while not a highly prized solution in our culture—has
been found advantageous by many Westerners ever since the
Inquisition.

I have argued that psychological distress arising from the
client's position in political, economic, or ideological groups is
essentially a reaction to realistic difficulties and that, to the
extent to which it can be bettered, the improvement can be
achieved only by realistic means. This does not mean that the
process is always an easy one. Having clients recognize that they
are upset because of an objectively bad situation can be very
painful to them. Similarly, challenging some of a client's social
assumptions—which turn out to be the self-serving ideology of
groups with power over the client—can be a disillusioning
experience for him or her.

It would seem a good idea to limit such disagreeable
sociocultural explanations to those necessary for achieving the
goals of therapy. This suggestion is made for ethical, pragmatic,
and humanitarian reasons.

In ethical terms, since the client is coming for help with
specifiable problems, it would seem a waste of time and money
to challenge beliefs unrelated to those problems. Pragmatically,
the more the client's strongly held beliefs are challenged, the
more likely the client is to mistrust the therapist ("Any therapist who believes *that* must be one of them instead of one of
us.") or even to leave therapy. Finally, while the therapist needs

to see the client's situation clearly (to help determine a productive course of action), it would seem inhumane to force clients to realizations that will only make them unhappy, and about which they can do nothing. One would hope that therapists would not live up to Tom Lehrer's definition of a philosopher: someone who gives advice to people who are happier than he is.

With regard to not bringing up certain topics, I would like to suggest a possible explanation for why politics, money, religion, and sex are considered taboo in many social gatherings. Therapists who understand behavior in terms of inner motivation might suggest that talk about sex and religion threaten defenses against oedipal conflicts, money does the same with anal conflicts, and politics is threatening to defenses against either or both. From this book's frame of reference, it would appear more likely that such topics are avoided because their discussion would so frequently reveal fundamental differences of group alignment (political, economic, and ideological) and thereby provoke conflict among participants during what was supposed to be a harmonious occasion.

A number of suggestions can be made to facilitate the application of a sociocultural approach to clients' problems.

In trying to understand the relationships between clients' problems and the social groups which affect them, therapists can consider the issue from two perspectives:

1. In what ways do the social groups produce clients' problems and how might they affect proposed solutions? (This is the group-to-individual approach.)

2. How do clients conceptualize themselves, their problems, and possible solutions in relation to various social groups? In what ways do they see themselves as affecting those groups' members' perceptions of and actions toward them? (This is the individual-to-group approach.)

From a theoretical point of view, these are the complementary perspectives of an objective, social science understanding of the client's problems and the client's subjective understanding of these problems (the client's sociocultural awareness). In practical terms, with regard to the first perspective, the therapist can attempt to look for social functions—as opposed to purely personal functions—in the client's "neurotic" behavior. Furthermore, it is often possible to view "symptomatic" behavior as resulting from sociocultural sources of stress and to direct therapy toward aiding the client to develop new ways of coping with them. With regard to the second perspective, therapy can be directed toward considering the social effects of possible solutions to these problems, as well as to considering the possibility of removing the sociocultural sources of stress or distancing the client from them.

Another suggestion is that, since therapists work with people whose behavior is deviant, it follows that many clients either come from deviant subgroups or can make a better adaptation to life as a member of a deviant subgroup than as part of the mainstream of society. The surge in urban anthropology has provided a wealth of clinical detail about lifestyles within groups that may be alien to the therapist's experience—for example Esther Newton's study (1979) of drag queens. Such studies might suggest a subgroup where the client could be happier as is, rather than having to make major lifestyle changes to adapt to his or her present situation. Alternatively, a greater knowledge of a subgroup to which the client already belongs can be helpful in facilitating adaptation to its nonmainstream demands. The treatment of an impotent homosexual has a different social component from that of an impotent heterosexual, as is the case for a timid woman who does a disproportionate amount of the housework in a commune as opposed to within a nuclear family.

When the client does come from a deviant subgroup,

therapy can be seen as a case of culture contact, in which the therapist is a representative of the mainstream way of life. From this point of view, one would expect—as in all culture contact—not only excitement, creativity, and innovation, but also lack of understanding, frustration, bewilderment, and despair. To the extent to which therapy is no more than the contact between two ways of life (and "relationship-oriented" therapists might claim this is all it can be), one would expect the great successes and failures characteristic of culture contact to be reflected in its results. Allen Bergin's finding (1966, 1971) that psychotherapy leads to greater variability of results than no treatment—both greater improvement than controls, but also a deterioration effect—is consistent with this picture.

It should be mentioned that this increased variability of outcome does not apply to more focused kinds of therapy, such as behavior therapy, where particular treatments are applied to specific types of problems. In addition, Bergin argues persuasively for the existence of psychonoxious therapists who make their clients worse. Also, the culture contact argument wouldn't apply when, as is usually the case, the therapist and client are from the same background. Where they are from different backgrounds, however, one would expect more deterioration than improvement, as is the case for contact between groups. This last point is an important warning for therapists interested in cross-cultural therapy aimed at change by means of the therapeutic relationship rather than through problem solving. Whatever the attractiveness of such an approach to psychodynamically oriented practitioners, in cultural terms the cards are stacked against its success.

In conclusion, given the salience of conflict as a fact of life, it follows that a major element in any client's interpersonal problems is likely to consist of realistic interpersonal conflicts growing out of partially or wholly irreconcilable conflicts of interest. The view that people would all love one another if the world could become a giant encounter group (where everyone could deeply understand one another) is a delusion, however well intended. It is at least equally likely that the amount of hate and grim combative resolve would increase, as people became aware of irreconcilably conflicting goals and realized that in many cases the only way to get what they want is to take it by force. The fact that many therapists believe and attempt to convince their clients that realistic social problems are neurotic psychological problems clearly functions in defense of the status quo.

The therapeutic approach described in this chapter can be briefly summarized as follows:

1. Assess the ways in which and extent to which a problem reflects social and cultural patterns, as opposed to the client's idiosyncratic personal background.

2. View these patterns from the standpoints of cultural relativism and power distribution among relevant groups.

3. Work on rational solutions to sociocultural aspects of the problem, bearing in mind that such solutions may be quite limited or even nonexistent.

9

A Therapist's Guide to Race

Despite all the interest in cross-racial therapy, therapists are by training remarkably uninformed about the subject of race. In part, this is a natural instance of the difficulty in obtaining information that clashes with a society's dominant ideology. However, there is a subcultural conflict as well, which impedes communication in this area. It is the mutual incoherence of the scholasticisms of psychology and anthropology. This chapter is my attempt to communicate an understanding of the topic of race in the hope that therapists will, when they think in terms of their own race and that of their clients, do so more lucidly and respond in a more sophisticated and sensitive manner.

Perhaps I can best begin the discussion by describing a hypothetical example I have used in my teaching. Whatever race may be, I have said, let us consider a hypothetical mating between one person who has only genes for "whiteness" and another of the opposite sex who has only genes for "blackness." What proportion of "blackness" genes will the offspring have? My students invariably give the correct answer of one-half. Then, suppose one of these offspring mated with someone who has only "whiteness" genes—what percentage of "blackness" genes will the children of this union have? Nearly all students give the incorrect answer of one-fourth.

It is easy to see why they would make such an error. Despite their knowledge of elementary genetics, they are culturally American. As such, when thinking about race, they do so in terms of American folk concepts: someone with one black parent has one-half black blood; someone with one black grandparent has one-quarter black blood. But American culture is not biology and genes are not blood. When I point out to the students that the correct answer is a range, from zero to one-half, depending on which of the "mixed" person's genes happen by chance to be involved, it helps in understanding that biological variation and the social concept of race are quite different.

I will first discuss biological variation so as to provide a basis for contrasting it with the social classification of race, a concept of greater interest to therapists. First, let us review some definitions.

A species consists of those organisms that can mate together and produce fertile offspring. Thus, gorillas, chimpanzees, and humans are three distinct species. Two kinds of borderline cases exist. First, horses and donkeys are separate species because, although they can mate, the offspring they produce—mules— are sterile. Second, there are examples of species spread out over great distances, such that those at point A can breed with those at point B; those at point B can breed with those at point C; but those at point C cannot breed with those at point A.

The complex chemicals that control heredity are called genes, and they occur together in groups called chromosomes. Humans have forty-six chromosomes (twenty-three pairs), which are made up of about 100,000 genes. The members of each pair of chromosomes are similar, but not identical. In reproduction, a sperm or ovum contains one member from each of the twenty-three pairs; and which member is included in a particular germ cell is determined independently for each pair. Since, in a given mating, any conceivable sperm might mate with any conceivable ovum, there are $2^{23} \times 2^{23} = 2^{46}$ possible arrangements of chromosomes that might occur in the offspring of given parents. This astronomical figure, however, assumes that the chromosomes in each pair retain their integrity before separating into two groups of 23. On the contrary, through a process known as crossing over, they exchange unpredictable amounts of genetic material with each other before separating into germ cells. Hence, the figure of 2^{46} is but an infinitesimal estimate of the number of possible offspring that could be produced from the mating of two humans. It is for this reason that it is safe to say that—with the exception of identical twins— while we are all members of the same species, each of us is genetically unique.

The relationship between an individual's genes, or genotype, and their physical expression, or phenotype, is a complex one. The phenotype produced depends, to differing degrees in different instances, on genetic factors, environmental factors, and complex interactions among them. Thus, a man with brown hair (his phenotype) may or may not carry genes for blond hair. The important point is that the hair color of his offspring will be determined by the genes that he and his mating partner carry, and not by the color of his hair. Two phenotypically brown-haired people may, and often do, produce blond offspring. (An explanation of this phenomenon would lead us into a discussion of dominance, penetrance, and polygenetic determination—topics whose treatment is not necessary for the present discussion.)

With this brief background it is possible to explain the closest biological concept to race, that of a breeding population. A breeding population consists of members of a species which breed among themselves more frequently than they do with other members of the species. As a result, the breeding population comes to differ from other populations of the species in the frequencies of certain genes. In general, this distinctiveness arises through the mechanisms of mutation, natural selection, and genetic drift.

Mutations, or changes in genetic material, occur infrequently. Since their phenotypic expressions are most often disadvantageous, they tend not to show up in populations where they occur (e.g., death occurs before the organism expressing the mutation has a chance to reproduce). When they are neutral—conferring neither a reproductive advantage nor disadvantage—they may continue on through the generations. If two groups do not interbreed, perhaps as a result of physical distance between them, then the appearance and survival over many generations of different mutations in each group may occur.

Those rare mutations that are adaptive—which increase the chances of survival to reproductive age, or increase the likelihood of producing more offspring who will breed successfully—will, over the course of generations, spread to ever larger percentages of the population where they occur. The increase in the frequency of adaptive genes is called natural selection.

It is important to remember that populations contain variations in both genotypes and phenotypes for any given trait, and that what is adaptive in one environment may be maladaptive in another.

Archaeological evidence indicates that our earliest ancestors evolved in Africa and then spread out through the rest of the world. As they migrated into Europe, Asia, and into the New World,[1] they encountered widely varying physical environments. It appears—though it is not certain, since skeletal remains give only limited clues about the skin that once covered them—that many of the features that are regarded by our culture as racial signs had adaptive value. Thus, dark skins may have been selected for where they served a protective function against the tropical sun, while light skins may have been selected for in cold regions, where people wore clothes, because they were helpful in maximally utilizing sunlight for the production of vitamin D. This would explain the parallel evolution (independent selection for similar forms in similar environments) of skin color around the world. Indigenous peoples of tropical Africa and South America have dark skins, while groups in northern North America and northern Europe have much lighter skins. Even within Africa, the Bushmen of southern Africa have lighter skins than their neighbors to the north.

By contrast, the additional (epicanthic) fold of skin which many Asians have on their eyelids appears to have been adaptive as extra protection for the eye against the extreme cold of northern Asia. Unlike skin color, this trait seems in no way maladaptive in other climates; and so it can be seen among the indigenous peoples of North and South America who are descendants of these Asians.

While some of the physical traits that were probably selected for in particular climates are regarded by our culture as racial signs, other equally obvious physical traits (which were most likely also the result of natural selection) are not so

---

1. They were able to follow game from northeast Asia across the Bering Strait because, during the last ice age, so much water was in the form of ice that the lower sea level created a land bridge.

regarded. A case in point would be body shape. The smaller the surface area of an object of given mass (i.e., the more like a ball) the more slowly it loses heat; and the larger the surface area (i.e., like the pipes of an old-fashioned radiator) the more rapidly it loses heat. Thus, it is likely that the rounded bodies of peoples like the Eskimo in northern North America were selected for as heat conservers, while the elongated bodies of African groups like the Masai were selected for as heat dispersers. The relevant point to understand is that our culturally specific categories for the racial classification of people arbitrarily include certain dimensions (e.g., light vs. dark skin) and exclude others (e.g., round versus elongated bodies).

A key factor that makes natural selection possible, and that thereby protects the survival of a species, is genetic diversity within the species. As environments change, certain low-frequency traits may become highly adaptive, and thus more widespread in successive generations. A famous example concerns a species of English moth whose light coloring served as camouflage against light tree bark and protected it against predatory birds. With the coming of the Industrial Revolution, soot from the factories darkened the bark and provided a contrasting background that made the moths easy prey. As a result, the previously rare dark-colored moths of the same species rapidly spread while their lighter-colored brethren were decimated. Within a few years, the color of the species appeared to have changed miraculously.

This is the essence of natural selection: genetic diversity plus the selective pressure of the environment. It is not a process of "survival of the fittest" in which members of a species slug it out against each other, like teams of sportsmen at elite private schools or like cutthroat businessmen in an unregulated market-place—though Darwin's contemporaries may have viewed it in this way. Nor is evolution a process whereby mankind struggles heroically ever onward toward perfection (this is known as the

Teleological Fallacy). Species appear to reflect their Creator's grand design in their harmonious adaptation to the environment because the inharmoniously maladapted brethren of their ancestors died off before reproducing, leaving the survivors to define themselves as the model of perfection. Members of a species who are well adapted in one environment would have a poor chance of survival in another. When the entire range of genetic variability is insufficient to adapt, the species itself becomes "inharmonious" and dies out.

While mutations and natural selection are dramatic explanations of ways in which different human breeding populations come to differ from one another in the frequencies of certain genes, genetic drift provides both a humbler explanation and one that may account for a larger proportion of such differences. Genetic drift refers to accidental changes in gene frequencies. When some members of a tribe break away and migrate or when disaster strikes a population (e.g., an earthquake or a volcano) it is virtually impossible for such events not to affect gene frequencies. Just by chance, the people who move away or who survive the calamity are bound to differ in the frequencies of various genes from those who do not. Even physical separation over many generations will eventually lead two equivalent populations to differ in the frequency of genes—as people with some genotypes in each group reproduce more than their counterparts in the other. Assuming that the genes that accidentally increase in frequency have no effect on survival to reproductive age, their higher frequencies will be maintained as the population increases in size.

With this background, we can compare the biological concept of breeding population with the concept of race. First of all, breeding populations are merely statistical subgroups of species, which may be defined in whatever way is useful for research purposes. For example, one might wish to examine populations characterized by 99 percent inbreeding over twenty generations (there are no such human populations) or one might investigate populations characterized by 51 percent inbreeding over two generations (there are millions of such human groups). Second, it is important to remember that all breeding populations belong to a given species. Humans from anywhere in the world, regardless of physical appearance, are capable of producing fertile offspring with other humans from anywhere else. Finally, even when a group qualifies as a breeding population according to some statistical criterion, it can merge with other groups and cease being a breeding population in a single generation. Modern transportation has increased gene flow around the world, so that the number of breeding populations according to any given statistical criterion is rapidly declining.

It is easy to see that the biological concept of breeding population is different from the social concept of race to which we are accustomed. In particular, social judgments of race are largely based on physical traits, such as skin color. Clearly, one cannot tell a person's breeding population from phenotypic information. Neither, however, can a person's breeding population be determined by a knowledge of genotype. Suppose, for example, that 20 percent of the members of a particular race have the gene R, while 40 percent of other humans have the gene. The fact that a given individual does or does not carry the gene is of no help in deciding whether or not the person belongs to the breeding population in question.

Given the distinction between a breeding population and the social classification of race, it is worthwhile pointing out that neither whites nor blacks constitute a breeding population. Whites are not a worldwide breeding population because whites in America breed with blacks in America more frequently than they do with whites in Australia or Russia (i.e., whites do not breed among themselves more frequently than with others). And blacks are not a worldwide breeding population because blacks in America breed with whites in America more frequently than they do with blacks in Ghana or Tanzania. In contrast to blacks and whites, residents of an isolated small town are a good example of a breeding population because they do breed among themselves more frequently than with others.

Given that blacks and whites aren't breeding populations, what can we say about their physical appearance? First, we can say that they aren't at the opposite ends of a single racial continuum. If this were so, then characteristics considered by our culture to be racial would vary together: a "totally white" person would have a white skin, straight blond hair, blue eyes, narrow nose, and thin lips; a "totally black" person would have dark brown skin and eyes, tight curly black hair, broad nose, and thick lips; and people in between would have, to a correlated degree, skin, hair, and eyes of intermediate color, loosely curly hair, noses of medium width, and lips of medium thickness. Anyone who takes a look around can see that this is not the case. These features vary independently. It is not only perfectly possible to have a person with dark brown skin, straight dark hair, narrow nose and thin lips, but in another culture (northeastern Brazil) that has a different social conception of race, there is actually a specific term to designate people who look like this.

Just as cartographers color a map of the world according to the height of the terrain, it is possible to color a map of the world according to the mean value of some biological feature of the inhabitants. Thus, it is possible to create a world map of average skin color, or of average hair form or nose breadth (actually, the ratio of breadth to length), or of an average index of lip thickness (evertedness), or of the average proportion of people with a given chemical in their blood, or of any other characteristic that is supposed to be an index of race.

If blacks and whites really were different biological entities, then these maps should coincide. In fact, they do not. What happens is much more interesting. Not only do the different features vary independently, but they do so gradually and in different directions along lines known as clines. The reason for this finding is easy to understand. Suppose that several breeding populations are situated along a line, where the members of A have some contact (including sexual contact) with those of B, B with C, and so forth. If the population of A has a high frequency of some gene that is absent in the other populations, then it is likely that some of the offspring of their contacts with B will carry the gene. Since A and B are separate breeding populations, the frequency of the gene among the members of B will never reach its level among A. Some of the carriers in B will transmit it to the offspring of their matings with people of C, though the frequency of the gene among the members of C will never reach its level among B, and so forth. In this way, over many generations, the trait will spread out in declining frequencies the further one is from A.

The hodgepodge of clines, running every which way all over the globe does not suggest that humans consist of a small number of distinct entities that developed separately. Rather, the data are more what one would expect from a species in which different groups migrated to all corners of the earth in differing numbers and at different times, splitting apart, becoming isolated, merging with new groups, and generally combining and recombining in myriad ways across time and space. The model of evolution that best explains human variation is not that of a branching tree, but rather a lattice.

The social classification of race, which plays such an important part in our everyday lives, is a conceptual domain strikingly different from biological variation. It is what anthropologists refer to as a folk taxonomy; that is, a culturally (as opposed to scientifically) based system of categories. For example, in the American folk classification of edible plants, the avocado is a vegetable: people eat it with oil and vinegar in a salad. In Brazil, the avocado is a fruit: people eat it with lemon juice and sugar for dessert. While the botanical classification of the avocado is invariant across cultures, its folk classification does vary.

Just as edible plants are biological organisms categorized in different places according to differing pseudobiological plant classifications, so human beings are biological organisms categorized in different places according to differing pseudobiological racial classifications.

The American system of the social classification of race is based on the concept of "blood," or the racial classification of one's parents. It is a system according to which various groups in society are ranked according to their racial status; when parents come from different groups their children are classified as belonging to the lower status group. For this reason, the system has been called one of hypo-descent (Harris 1964). Thus, all children of couples with one parent classified as white and one parent classified as black—regardless of the physical appearance of the children or their parents—would traditionally be classified as black. If some of the children had straight blond hair, blue eyes, white skin, narrow nose and thin lips, they would still "really" be black. If, on growing up, they associated primarily with whites, and never let on about the racial classification of their parents, they would be said to be "passing" for white—that is, dishonestly pretending to belong to a higher-status racial category. (I am spelling out these details—although they are obvious to my American audience—because they appear so alien to people whose systems of racial classification are different from our own.)

It is true that the words *mulatto, quadroon,* and *octoroon* exist in our vocabulary, but given the short genealogies and high mobility of our nation of immigrants, they are rarely used in classifying people. The only term I have heard used in conversation—and that very infrequently—was *mulatto,* used by whites in referring to a child of a black-white marriage. Those who used the term had no knowledge of the racial classification of the child's grandparents (e.g., the black parent might have been a mulatto, thereby making the child a quadroon) and were employing it as a shorthand way of saying something about the parents—that one was black and the other white—while ostensibly speaking about the child. It was not used to imply, and could not have been so used in our racial system, that the child was neither black nor white, but belonged to some third category. The closest that one can come to this status in America is to be considered black by whites and white by blacks.

It is possible that the rankings of groups of intermediate racial status may vary regionally, so that people of Latin American descent have higher status in areas where they are scarce, and people of Native American ancestry have higher status where there are few of them. Hence, it is possible that a child who had one parent from each of these groups might be classified as an Indian in South Dakota and as Hispanic in New York City. Such regional variations would emphasize that race is a social label rather than a biological attribute.

New immigrant groups sometimes challenge American racial categories, and go through a period of adjustment while negotiating with the larger society over what to call themselves. Thus, Cape Verdeans found they had to choose between being white and black, and immigrants from India seem to be in the process of confronting a choice among white, black, and Asian.

In addition, as the American population becomes increasingly diverse, with ever more marriages producing offspring that are hard to classify, it is possible that a new "multiracial" or "multicultural" category will emerge. A child whose four grandparents are black, white, Asian, and Latin American stretches the American system of racial classification beyond its limits. The fact that categories have to be invented or changed to accommodate to social realities highlights once again the fact that race is a social rather than biological concept.

In contrast to our racial system based on ancestry, Brazil's system of racial *tipos* (which varies regionally, and is most elaborate in northeast Brazil) is based on physical appearance, as modified to some extent by social status. Detailed discussions of this system can be found in Harris (1964, 1970) and Degler (1971).

Since the American racial system is based on ancestry, all children of a given marriage receive the same racial classification. In a marriage between an African American and a European American, this means that all children are regarded as black, despite the usual genetic outcome of a range of phenotypes. In Brazil, however, each child is classified according to its physical appearance. Since large families abound, it would not be unusual for a couple in the city of Salvador, Bahia, to have children of a half-dozen different racial *tipos*.

Brazilians and Americans, because of a lack of familiarity with each other's cultures, are often not aware that their racial systems are different. Since Portuguese and English often use cognate terms, communication on the already sensitive topic of race often becomes bewildering. For example, in Brazil a *mulato* is someone with tight curly black hair and light tan to brown skin, who probably—but not necessarily—has dark eyes, thick lips, and a broad nose. A *moreno* is someone who looks similar, except without tight curly hair and with a slightly lighter range of possible skin and hair colors. *Mulato* is a darker and less prestigious racial classification than *moreno*. A marriage between a *moreno* and a *morena* might well produce a *branco* (white) or *mulato* child, or even both.

This result, of parents producing children with a higher or lower racial classification than either of them, is impossible in the American system of hypo-descent.[2]

---

2. It should be mentioned that Brazil does have social stratification based on "race," though it is weaker than that in the United States. On the other hand, Brazilian discrimination based on class is

One informant[3] from northern Brazil explained to me that a certain person was a *mulata* and not a *preta* (black) because she "doesn't have that really kinky hair and black skin that Africans have." The fascinating aspect of this report is that both my informant and I knew that the woman in question was the daughter of African immigrants to Brazil. Hence she was one of the few Brazilian citizens of whom it could be said with conviction that she was of 100 percent African ancestry. Not only was the racial *tipo* assigned without regard to ancestry, but the folk explanation of its origin was offered (by a college educated informant) in disregard of evidence to the contrary. In this respect, neither Brazilian nor American stereotypes take into account the breadth of physical variation that is to be found among Africans (Alland 1971).

A New Yorker who would be called a *moreno* in Brazil is perplexing to his fellows in the United States because he is not easily classified. In meeting people, he must endure interrogations of the what-was-your-name-again-and-where-do-you-come-from variety, as his audience tries to decide whether he is black, white, or Hispanic. By contrast, he is an immediately recognizable *tipo* in Brazil and creates no confusion for others there.

Two categories used in northeastern Brazil, unknown in the more Europeanized south, are *sarará* and *cabo verde* (after the

---

stronger than American racial discrimination. Perhaps as a result, Brazilians say that "money whitens." That is, the more money dark-skinned Brazilians have, the lighter the *tipos* they would use in self-classification, and the lighter the terms others would use in referring to them.

3. This term, which is neutral to anthropologists, conjures up images of stool pigeons to psychologists and other outsiders, much as our use of *subjects* sounds demeaning to nonpsychologists. This is one more example of the difficulty in communication among the social science subcultures.

Cape Verde Islands, where it is common to find people who look this way). What is interesting about these *tipos* is that, since they are opposite to each other, they form a dimension in the Euro-African domain, and that this dimension is independent of the black-white dimension (Harris 1970). That is, a ranking can be made along the black-white dimension (with approximate equivalents offered parenthetically in American English) as follows: *louro* (blond), *branco* (white), *moreno* (in the Northeast, a kind of white), *mulato* (a kind of black), *preto* (black). However, *sarará-cabo verde* forms an independent dimension; people categorized as either *tipo* are considered to be neither black nor white. A *sarará* is someone with light (red or blond) tight curly hair, light (blue or green) eyes, light skin, broad nose and thick lips; a *cabo verde* has black straight hair, dark eyes, dark brown skin, narrow nose, and thin lips.

These few *tipos* should be sufficient to give the reader the flavor of the Brazilian racial system. There are dozens, and in some regions even hundreds, of such racial terms. I have not even referred to the Indian-white (e.g., *mameluco*) or Indian-black (e.g., *cafuzo*) *tipos*, to avoid going into unnecessary detail.

I hope it is clear from all this that a person's race is not a biological characteristic of his or her own, but a cultural label applied by others to certain aspects of the person's physical appearance, ancestry, or social attributes. To the extent to which it is treated as a biological entity, race becomes a reified concept. The everyday process of racial classification is learned behavior; people exposed to different environments learn to categorize differently. A person may change race by moving from one place to another (e.g., from the U.S. to Brazil). What changes is not the individual's physical appearance or ancestry, but the behavior of the people labeling it.

In personal terms, I must say that after having lived in Brazil, I can no longer look at people and say what race they belong to. I have to know where they are from and to whom I am speaking. Even then I find that I can be more precise by qualifying my answer culturally. For example, I met a family in New York that I would describe in this way: the father was black here and a *mulato* in Brazil; the mother was Hispanic here and a *morena* in Brazil; and their daughter was black here, a *mulata clara* (light *mulata*) in southern Brazil and a *sarará* in northeastern Brazil.

The function of social classification is to serve as a guide to action. Whether or not a given piece of beef is kosher will determine its edibility for Orthodox Jews. Whether an avocado is a fruit or a vegetable makes a difference for Brazilians and Americans regarding how it is to be prepared and during what part of a meal it is to be eaten. In a similar way, knowing whether people are black or white fills the important social need (no matter how inaccurately) of predicting how they will behave. That is, among groups who use systems of racial classification, there are stereotypes associated with the different racial categories, that create specific expectancies regarding the behavior of each race. These stereotypes grew up for historical reasons (e.g., conditions during slavery and thereafter). Like similar phenomena elsewhere—as a therapist, diagnostic labeling comes to my mind first—racial stereotypes are notoriously resistant to change. Factors perpetuating racial stereotypes include social patterns (e g., the distribution of power going against those groups unfavorably stereotyped), cultural patterns (e.g., children learning and relearning them from parents and peers), and psychological patterns (e.g., the resistance to extinction of intermittently reinforced responses—some people can always be found who act as the stereotypes predict—and the self-fulfilling prophesy of people conforming to negative expectations).

Since racial stereotypes function to predict behavior within a cultural setting, it follows that such stereotypes are culturally relative. This contrast can be seen between stereotypes of women's beauty and sexuality in northeastern Brazil and the

United States. In the United States, blondes are considered the most attractive and sexy ("Blondes have more fun."), while in northeastern Brazil, blondes are seen as cold. The most beautiful women there are the *morenas*—a category we do not have, but that is in any event much closer to our concept of a brunette. In the United States, black women are considered sensual, while in Brazil this stereotype is applied not to the *preta* but to the *mulata* (another category we do not have).

Given this brief introduction to biological variation, social race, and the stereotypes associated with the latter, it is possible to consider the therapeutic relationship from a new perspective. For purposes of simplicity, I will discuss the one-to-one relationship and leave it to the reader to elaborate these points for therapy of interracial marriages, of families with cross-racially adopted children, or of interracial therapy groups.

Whenever a therapist and client get together we can be confident that each categorizes the other in racial terms and draws behavioral inferences from the categories applied. More specifically, the therapist knows that he or she belongs to a given race A, that the client belongs to another race B, that As are one kind of person, that Bs are another kind of person, and that As and Bs commonly interact in a pattern P. Meanwhile, the client knows that he or she belongs to a race B', that the therapist belongs to another race A', that B's are one kind of person, that A's are another kind of person, and that B's and A's commonly interact in a pattern P'. Difficulties in communication arise from the fact that A and A' may not be the same, nor may B and B', nor P and P'.

In terms of increasing complexity (and perplexity, for the participants), the therapist and client may come from the same culture and be of the same race,[4] they may come from the same

---

4. I am using both *culture* and *race* as admittedly inadequate shorthands because of the lack of vocabulary to avoid the reification of

culture and be of different races, or they may come from different cultures and be of different races.

The simplest case, and the one that has characterized most therapy ever since Freud, is where the therapist and client are from the same culture and of the same race (i.e., white). In this case, issues related to race need never affect the therapeutic relationship—not because they do not exist, but because there is no occasion for them to arise or to affect the clarity of communication between therapist and client. This is a typical instance of a cultural variable appearing to be a constant in a limited cultural context. If therapist and client come from the same economic or educational background these issues too might never cause confusion. One might even suggest that a therapist who has a sociocultural background identical to that of his or her client would have the least difficulty in understanding or communicating in the therapy situation and the least likelihood of opening the client up to new vistas. By contrast, a therapist from a different background would most likely have greater difficulties in understanding and communication. As these were dealt with, differing assumptions of therapist and client would emerge and might well lead to the consideration of alternative courses of action. Naturally, the greater the difference in backgrounds, the greater would be the likelihood of misunderstandings occurring; and bad ones might even lead to the abrupt termination of therapy. Despite this risk, the potential for change in what might otherwise have been an unrecognizable direction remains an important counterbalancing benefit. This

---

culture referred to in Chapter 7 or tne conceptual confusion associated with race discussed in this chapter. To say that nearly all Americans hold a similar pseudobiological view of what it means to be white is not to imply that there is one clearly structured and all-encompassing American culture, nearly all of which is shared by nearly all Americans.

kind of thinking suggests the hypothesis of a curvilinear relationship between the amount of sociocultural difference between therapist and client and the likelihood of the client developing useful sociocultural awareness from the resulting therapy.

It is when therapist and client are from the same culture but of different races that the complications begin. The nature of these complications depends on the culture in question; but I will limit my discussion to the American case. I will consider the example of the white therapist with a black client for illustrative purposes, because it is the most common, but most of the same observations would apply, *mutatis mutandis*, with a black therapist and white client, or with members of any two American racial classifications.

In this case, the therapist believes that he or she is white, that the client is black, and that each is a member of a different race. The client holds the same beliefs. Because they share the American system of racial classification, it is unlikely that difficulties in communication will arise concerning the "biological" categories they are supposed to belong to. On the other hand, each holds stereotypes of what it means to be white, what it means to be black, and how whites and blacks interact. It is unlikely that these stereotypes and expectancies are the same for both participants, since they were learned in different subcultural settings. Hence, difficulties in communication are most likely in this area.

For example, if the client is a woman whose dress and hairstyle are distinctively African American, a white male therapist might well assume that she holds militant political views and might even blame him personally for the oppression of blacks. Such conclusions might lead him to nonverbally communicate a stance either of defensive coldness ("It's unjust of you to prejudge me like that.") or of ingratiating egalitarianism ("Actually, I'm one of the good guys opposed to racism, so you don't have to be angry at me.''). In fact, the woman might have chosen her hairstyle because she considers it attractive, and might be wearing a dashiki because it is loose-fitting and she is pregnant. In such a situation, the therapist's nonverbal stance (based on unfounded but culturally determined assumptions) would likely be disruptive of communication between him and his client.

In a similar way, many younger white therapists dress casually for sessions, at least in part because they believe that this will put their clients at ease. However, an African American client might view such dress as an expression of disrespect and be put off rather than relaxed by it. If the therapist is not aware of subcultural differences in the importance and meaning of clothes, such undetected assumptions might also undermine the quality of the therapeutic relationship.

I will not treat separately the case of the therapist and client who are from different cultures but of the same race, because it is really dealt with in other parts of this discussion. That is, to the extent to which the two cultures have the same system of racial classification, with regard at least to race, the therapist and client are really from the same culture; and to the extent to which the two cultures have different systems, the therapist and client are by definition of different races. Hence, the only remaining case to be discussed is that of the therapist and client who are from different cultures and of different races.

Here we have extraordinary possibilities for misunderstanding. Whether or not the therapist and client recognize that they are of different races, neither claims to be a member of the race to which the other would assign him or her. Most likely, neither really understands that the other categorizes race differently, or even that racial categorization involves social as opposed to biological judgments. Needless to say, the stereotypes that each associates with various racial categories differ from those of the other. If the categories are associated with identical or cognate words, so much the worse. Should the subject of race be dealt with explicitly, friction is likely to result when they each apply their own stereotypes to a word that actually represents the other's category.

The difficulties arising in such therapy can be illustrated by the hypothetical treatment of a rich Brazilian businessman who is setting up an office of his company in the United States. Let us assume that he looks like a *mulato,* as defined earlier in this chapter, and that he is being treated by a white male therapist. Because of what Brazilians describe as the remarkable "whitening" power of money, he might think of himself as white (*branco*) and be accustomed to being treated as a member of this prestigious racial category. Since prejudice increases as one ascends the social hierarchy in Brazil (the opposite of the United States), he might well make an occasional anti-black remark. While such comments (e.g., regarding the incompetence of black servants) might be made unthinkingly, if there were a motive behind them it would most likely be one of demonstrating solidarity between himself and the therapist, as white men of importance and power. He would probably be shocked to find that the therapist regards such remarks as racist— especially because the client believes himself to be free from prejudice and is proud of coming from Brazil, the world's only racial democracy. For a Brazilian, his belief stands in stark contrast to America's obvious racism, which labels as black many people who are not, and unjustly discriminates against them.

From the therapist's point of view, he is treating a black Brazilian. Perhaps it would occur to him that the black Brazilian experience might be different from the black American experience. If so, the client's anti-black comments might remain a question mark for him, rather than a basis for hastily concluding that his client's conflict over being black was manifesting itself in denial, reaction formation, identification with the aggressor,

or some other defensive reaction. It is unlikely that he would
guess that the client made the remarks because he thought of
himself as white, and even less likely that he would imagine that
Brazil's system of racial classification is different from our own.
While this example may seem extreme to white American
therapists with little or no cross-cultural experience, the fact of
the matter is that people classified as black in the United States
are culturally heterogeneous and not at all the single group that
our system makes them out to be. For example, there is a large
population of Americans born in the Caribbean area, from
English-, Spanish-, French-, or Dutch-speaking backgrounds.
Each island or colony developed a separate set of social and
cultural patterns—including linguistic ones—in relative isola-
tion from the others; and each created a unique breeding
population from disparate elements. The mixture of isolated
indigenous groups with conquerors from one area of Europe and
slaves from other areas of Africa ultimately resulted in each
island or country having a unique range of physical variation
associated with its unique range of social and cultural variation.

It is only natural that such diversity includes differences in
systems of racial classification. (Haiti and Puerto Rico, for
example, have systems that are quite different from each other's, and quite different from those of Brazil and the United
States.) The classification of New Yorkers living in Harlem into
the categories of white, black, and Hispanic cannot begin to do
justice to the myriad ways they classify themselves and each
other, not to mention the broad range of stereotypes associated
with the various categories of the differing systems.

One consequence of this is that some people from the
Caribbean, who are regarded by Americans as black, think of
themselves as white. This can lead to bizarre situations such as
the equal opportunity hiring by American whites of immigrant
"blacks"—who think of themselves as white, and whose hiring
only antagonizes American-born blacks who view them as ille-

gitimate competitors from an alien culture. In a similar way, Hispanics in New York include both culturally American descendants of Spanish speakers and people who actually grew up in a Hispanic culture. In each of these groups there are large numbers of people whose cultural identification is Dominican, Cuban, or Puerto Rican (not to mention groups from other areas). Hence, there are at least six major groups of Hispanics who classify one another in varying ways.

It is unclear exactly what the outer limits of the Hispanic category are (as used by most New Yorkers to make judgments on the basis of casual social contact). Certainly it includes Brazilians, who speak Portuguese. At times, I think it must extend to anyone with dark hair and/or skin who has a Spanish or unrecognizable accent (e.g., a Pakistani might not be classified as Hispanic, since his accent would probably identify him as Indian).

The point is, once again, that race is a cultural as opposed to a biological phenomenon. If we, as therapists, can recognize that the racial categories and stereotypes we apply to ourselves and to our clients are a subtle and pervasive result of our cultural training, we will have lifted from our eyes an important veil that distorts our interpersonal vision. To the extent to which we succeed in doing so, we can be available to deal rationally with this aspect of the therapeutic relationship and with our clients' problems in this area.

The Human Side of Brazilian Psychology

One of the main objectives of this book is for therapists to understand themselves (as well as their clients) from a sociocultural perspective. A good way to illustrate this process is to look at ourselves and our discipline—psychologists and psychology—in another culture.

While the existence of the term *psychology* might suggest that it is everywhere the same, just as a physical object would be the same in two different places, there are notable cross-cultural differences in its content. This chapter, which attempts to illuminate such differences, is based on my experience while I was a visiting professor in Brazil (at a university in a city in the interior of the state of São Paulo) from June 1974 to August 1976—though I have returned six times, for periods of three weeks to three months, since then.

Brazil has changed in the intervening years, and even at that time the behavior of psychologists in the more cosmopolitan state capital of São Paulo would have been somewhat different from that at my university. Also, because of my specialty, this chapter may give disproportionate emphasis to clinical psychology, even though it is the largest area within Brazilian psychology. Finally, I should at least mention three issues that I will not be dealing with (though they merit consideration in a different kind of discussion). They reflect the growing pains both in psychology and in Brazilian higher education in general. They are:

1. The youth of psychology (the profession was recognized by law only in 1962).

2. Nationwide licensing procedures, including the characteristically Brazilian bureaucracies associated with the field's legal status. Licensure in Brazil is at the undergraduate (five-year) level.

3. The organization of academic psychology within institutes, including the scarcity of library and laboratory facilities, and the widespread use of *apostilhas*[1] in undergraduate education (and, at times, even in graduate education).

---

1. *Apostilhas* are mimeographed productions, prepared either by a group of professors or by a single professor teaching a given course at a university. Their contents vary from direct translations of entire textbooks (which are rare) to summaries of or translations of excerpts from textbooks (these are the most common) to compendia of summaries or translations of excerpts from various texts. In general, these *apostilhas* are prepared by busy professors who rarely have more than a bachelor's level education. As a result, the quality of the *apostilhas* is quite variable, and frequently on the low side. Students attending undergraduate courses are commonly required to read an *apostilha* (usually around 100 pages) as an American might have to read a textbook.

Rather than deal with the institutional structure of Brazilian psychology, however, I would like to examine the field from an interpersonal perspective, focusing on the psychologists themselves. From this perspective, my time in Brazil can be viewed as ethnographic field work among the subculture of Brazilian psychologists. They are very different people from their American counterparts and view themselves and psychology through culturally different lenses. (This, I believe, is what makes my observations from the mid-1970s still of interest.) Because of their difference from their American counterparts, Brazilian psychologists are in the process of creating a psychology that differs in significant ways from that found in the United States.

The story of Brazilian psychologists is in large measure the story of middle- and upper-class educated Brazilian women. Unlike the situation in the United States in the mid-1970s, when roughly three-fourths of psychologists were men, psychologists in Brazil were and are overwhelmingly female; approximately 95 percent of graduate students in clinical psychology are women. (While American psychology is moving in the Brazilian direction, it still has a long way to go before becoming a women's discipline.) One effect of this situation, despite Brazilian *machismo* with its demand for men to fill important posts, is that there simply are not enough competent male psychologists to go around. Thus, even though men occupy disproportionately many important posts within psychology, the field is one where qualified women have a much greater possibility of achieving high status than elsewhere within the society. At the same time, the feminine image of the field, coupled with its subdoctoral entry level training (compared to that of psychiatry) combine to give it a less prestigious professional status than it has in the United States. Psychology's subordination to psychiatry is increased by the fact that psychiatrists are nearly all men, creating something of a parallel to the relationship between psychiatry and social work in the United States.

In the same vein, it should be observed that men who choose psychology as a profession find their masculinity more open to question than it would be in other fields. One compensation for this is that the lack of male competition makes it relatively easier for men to succeed—albeit in an area that is identified as a women's specialty.

While the development of a Brazilian middle class has led to the recruitment of unprecedented numbers of university students from the families of minimally educated or illiterate parents, psychology in general, and clinical psychology in particular, has remained a field predominately for the elite. The typical graduate student whom I taught was a woman in her mid-twenties who was married and had one or two children. Most likely, either she or her husband came from families of professionals, or of traditional wealth. Her husband was very likely a professional, perhaps an engineer or a physician, and she was a part-time undergraduate university professor and probably also worked part-time in a group private practice or at a mental hospital. She and her husband lived in a house bought with the assistance of one or both of their families and had at least one full-time maid and cook. In addition to teaching her classes and performing her clinical duties, she was entirely responsible for running the house, which, while it involved almost no physical labor, did involve raising her children and supervising servants. These diverse responsibilities led to a lifestyle in which the psychologist was desperately short of time. Nevertheless, as a modern woman with a career, she felt very fulfilled and lucky not to be merely a *dona de casa* (a woman who—like her mother—runs the house but has little status beyond her decorative value).

In her relationship with her husband she was likely to focus more on how fortunate she was that he allowed her to have a career than on the fact that her career had to be subordinated to his needs and her household responsibilities. (This observation may have been less accurate in some Brazilian urban centers than in the relatively traditional city where I was located.) After all, she knew many women whose husbands did not allow them to practice psychology despite their training. One woman, the envy of the institute, had a husband who actually allowed her to go by herself to attend an international psychology convention in Argentina, where she saw *Last Tango in Paris*—which was banned in Brazil at the time—and was able to report back that she didn't think it was a very good film. Unlike her mother, the typical psychologist didn't see sex as a distasteful duty she had to perform, but rather she viewed herself as a modern woman with positive attitudes toward sex who was proud of her ability to satisfy her husband. While she may have felt somewhat cheated at the way in which his ardor had cooled since their marriage, she most likely did not feel that her needs were sufficiently pressing to demand satisfaction either within or outside of marriage.[2]

Naturally, this picture is a composite one, and like any generalization is at best only partially accurate for any individual. Its shortcomings are particularly apparent for single women (who, nevertheless, seemed for the most part to think of themselves as premarried, at least through their thirties) and legally separated (*desquitada*) women,[3] not to mention the few male

---

2. While I was teaching at the university, the local district attorney responded to his wife's having a lover by stabbing her to death. He was found not guilty on the grounds that her behavior was an intolerable affront to his honor. The verdict had a demoralizing effect on my students. When I mentioned that some American therapists viewed the question of whether or not to have affairs as one to be made by the couple, one of my students said sardonically, "Oh sure. You tell your husband you want to have an affair and he'll kill you first!"

3. Divorce was still illegal while I was teaching in Brazil; and the number of legal separations appeared to be growing. Now it is legal, but hard to obtain. Brazil has gone through a sexual revolution in recent years, timed sadly to coincide with the spread of AIDS.

psychologists who actually did exist. Even so, I believe that it presents a striking contrast to the typical American psychologist who was a man at least ten years older, held a doctoral degree, and thought and viewed the world from a rather different perspective.

The relevance of the Brazilian racial situation to psychology also deserves mention, though what I have to say is equally applicable to other disciplines. In my contacts with hundreds of Brazilian psychologists (both students and professionals), I met only one who would be viewed as black in the United States. Considering Brazil's self-proclaimed status as a racial democracy, and its much greater proportion of African genetic makeup than the United States, this is an extremely disturbing state of affairs—protests to the effect that discrimination is economic, rather than racial, notwithstanding.

In interpersonal terms, Brazilians, as opposed to Americans, are warmer, better conversationalists, more interpersonally skilled, and more skilled at interpersonal manipulation. (Naturally this is a broad generalization with many exceptions). As a result, they are natural therapists. The mistake I have so often found among novice American therapists, of naively trying to apply textbook principles in a literal way to a client for whom such an application would be grossly inappropriate, seemed not to occur. On the contrary, I am tempted to hypothesize that the Brazilian dual consciousness (the official bureaucratic way of doing things versus the informal, manipulative *jeitinho*[4] way of

---

4. Unfortunately, no dictionary adequately conveys the sense of the culturally central expression *dar um jeito* or *dar um jeitinho*. The concept includes elements of adaptability, creativity, problem solving, flexibility, innovation, interpersonal manipulation, and bribery. Perhaps the closest English equivalent would be "to finagle." Even this is an inadequate synonym, and it has a negative connotation in contrast to the term's generally positive one (if often only ironically so) in Portuguese.

getting things done) creates, at times, the opposite danger of psychologists not synthesizing the textbook theory with the here-and-now clinical reality. That is, I sensed a danger in some of my students of talking one way, albeit with full conviction, about theory, and acting quite another way with clients— without ever feeling the necessity to reconcile the two. This is a parallel to the way Brazilians recognize the official bureaucratic requirements and the unofficial way of getting things done, without feeling a need to reconcile the two.

The cultural style of thinking of Brazilian psychologists appears in many ways to be more European and philosophical, with a love for a coherent system of thought that explains everything (whether by psychoanalysis or operant conditioning). This contrasts with the pragmatic American orientation toward data and problem solving, using concepts only insofar as they are helpful in achieving results. For example, I arrived to set up a graduate area of concentration in behavior modification. Unbeknownst to me, Fred Keller had been in Brazil during the 1960s and had left behind him a dedicated Skinnerian following. When I tried to introduce various cognitive concepts (cf. Chapter 11), I encountered great resistance because my students had already developed a system of thought in which all problems had arisen for operant reasons (such as schedules of reinforcement) and could be solved by appropriate forms of contingency management. Rather than asking what the evidence was for the concepts I was introducing, and what their explanatory value was in understanding and changing behavior, my students were resistant because these concepts challenged the integrated theoretical system they had adopted as a whole.

Brazilian psychology in its youth had to start with the psychology that already existed. That is, it began with approaches principally from the United States but also, to a lesser and diminishing degree, with those from France (e.g., Lacanian psychoanalysis). Characteristically, the psychology that has been developing has superficially resembled its foreign models, while on close inspection it has operated in practice in quite a different way. For example, there was great interest in applying the techniques of sex therapy in Brazil, but the taboo nature of the subject led to major informal revisions in clinical technique. In the "dual consciousness" style alluded to above, Brazilian therapists tended to refer to what they were doing as an application (or perhaps adaptation) of the techniques of Masters and Johnson (1970), rather than as a new Brazilian form of sex therapy.

If I were to predict the future for Brazilian psychology, I would guess that it would continue to develop in this dual (or, from an ethnocentric American viewpoint, contradictory) manner. That is, as Brazil continues to industrialize, and as its system of higher education becomes more (superficially) like our own, Brazilian psychology and psychologists' roles will also (deceptively) seem more like their American counterparts. Meanwhile, in a more fundamental sense, the growth of Brazilian psychology should inevitably become more distinctively Brazilian, since it will in large measure involve studying and treating Brazilian issues in a Brazilian way. That is, as the words become more American, the music should become more Brazilian.[5]

---

5. When I wrote these conclusions, Brazil was at the end of its "economic miracle." Now that the country has been lurching from one economic catastrophe to the next for a number of years, it is not so much my predictions about Brazilian psychology that seem wrong to me (I still think they're reasonable) as my implicit assumption of economic progress. Brazilian psychologists, like all Brazilians, have been trying to avoid personal economic disaster. Until Brazilian universities and psychologists can operate under minimally predictable and economically viable conditions, Brazilian psychology will be in a survival mode—focused more on avoiding personal and institutional calamity than on growth and achievement.

BEHAVIORAL AND COGNITIVE THERAPIES

Introduction

Parts III and IV are briefer than and different from Parts I and II in that they consist of chapters that were written at different times in the evolution of a sociocultural orientation. They are included as much to illustrate that evolution as they are for their substantive content. (While they were articles written concisely in part because of the scarcity of journal space, their brevity also argued for choosing them instead of longer ones because they allow for illustrative variety without occupying an undue portion of the book.)

Part III consists of four brief chapters written for behavior therapists and from a behavioral perspective. All of them were selected because they involve some sort of shift in perspective or challenge to implicit assumptions, and in this sense are congruent with the advocacy of therapists adopting an outlook of pragmatic iconoclasm.

I got the idea for the assessment schema presented in Chapter 11 as a way of introducing cognitive concepts to my Brazilian students, so as to expand the Skinnerian outlook Brazilian therapists had developed as a result of Fred Keller's influence. Taking the operant unit (discriminative stimulus + operant + reinforcing stimulus[1]) as a given—or even a metaphor—I stretched it to include a variety of social and cognitive skills and strategies so that my students, and therapists who shared their orientation, would look beyond the most obvious consequences of a client's behavior in understanding it.

Playing with the operant unit is once again the theme of Chapter 12, which discusses behavioral irony. Since behavior therapists as a group aren't all that playful, an implicit message that I wanted to convey was "lighten up." Unfortunately, when I attempted to publish the article in a prominent behavioral journal, it was rejected because some of the consulting editors were upset by it. So I published it in a more general journal. The original title was *1983,* and *A More or Less Functional Analysis of Behavioral Irony* was the subtitle. Since the pun involved in 1983—not quite 1984—lost its impact by 1985, I have dropped the title and kept only the subtitle.

Chapter 13 was written to challenge the implicit assumption of some behavior therapists that they are the influencers and their clients are the influencees. Recognizing that the process of influence is mutual, this chapter suggests how the influence of clients on therapists can sometimes be harnessed to the therapists' advantage. In addition, since this book is concerned with the evolution of a therapist's orientation, it seemed relevant to include something about supervision. Finally, I

---

1. For the present, nontechnical purposes (and omitting discussion of extinction and punishment), an operant is almost any behavior, a discriminative stimulus is one in the presence of which the behavior has some chance of being rewarded, and a reinforcing stimulus is the reward.

included this discussion of supervision (as well as the one in Chapter 17) in a book about therapy to emphasize that the same principles of behavior change apply to supervision—or any other relationship—as to therapy.

Chapter 14 is a case study from my postdoctoral year that involves an early example of a paradoxical intervention in behavior therapy. The case is also significant because it looks at an interacting system rather than individual behavior and attempts to understand paradox in terms of concepts from general psychology. The chapter's social-cognitive theoretical analysis can be seen as in some ways antedating the more comprehensive discussion of Rohrbaugh and colleagues (1977).

Schema for the Assessment of Problem Behavior

An accurate assessment is more essential to behavior therapy than to other therapeutic approaches. This is true not only because specific treatments are applied to the specific problems identified, but also because the application of such treatments is both highly structured and of relatively brief duration. Thus, if a problem area for behavioral intervention is not identified during the assessment phase, it is possible that the treatment phase will provide neither the time nor the context for the problem to emerge. For this reason, heuristic devices aimed at making assessment as thorough as possible are of great help to the practicing clinician. For example, Lazarus (1973, 1974) has used the acronym "BASIC ID" to remind therapists to explore Behavior, Affect, Sensations, Imagery, Cognitions and Interpersonal relations as possible targets for modification, as well as to consider the relevance of Drugs to their treatment of the case. While his acronym is aimed at identifying problems that need therapeutic attention, the elevenfold schema below is a heuristic aid to the detailed assessment of a problem once it has been identified.

Behavior therapists recognize that behavior can be understood only in its situational context. The unit of behavior is typically understood as being made up of three parts: discriminative stimuli, the behavior itself, and reinforcing stimuli. However, an attempt to translate this behavioral micro-unit directly into the macroterms of the client's problems encounters both theoretical and clinical difficulties. In a two-person interaction, for example, it is possible to translate "what the other person does" as "discriminative stimuli," "what the client does" as "the behavior itself," and "how the other person reacts" as "reinforcing stimuli." While these three overt elements are essential to understanding what happened, and are perhaps the most important elements, they omit consideration of the sorts of social psychological and cognitive variables that have been emphasized in the writings of clinicians such as Lazarus (1971) and myself (Fish 1973). Ultimately, it is assumed that such covert processes are learned, and can be broken down into specifiable contingencies. B. F. Skinner's book *About Behaviorism* (1974) is in large measure an attempt to show how this might be accomplished. Thus, the hasty definition of a client's problem as nothing more than its overt elements may blind a therapist to relevant targets for modification—targets for which appropriate treatments already exist.

In theoretical terms, then, the other eight parts of the elevenfold schema below are in principle reducible to simpler learning components. Similarly, there is nothing sacred about the number eleven, and the number of parts might be extended ad infinitum. Rather, the schema has the heuristic function of systematically directing the clinician's attention to covert aspects of the client's problem that might otherwise be ignored.

THE ELEVENFOLD SCHEMA

When inquiring about a client's problem behavior, I suggest that the therapist obtain information about the following areas.

1. *The situation* (e.g., what the other person did). This is the same as the "discriminative stimuli" of the three-part unit, and includes verbal and nonverbal behavior as well as contextual cues.

2. *The client's ability to observe the situation* (e.g., to recognize what the other person did). Naturally, a client who observes relevant aspects of a situation inaccurately or partially, or is even oblivious to his or her surroundings will respond inadequately.

3. *The client's understanding of the situation* (e.g., the client's view of why the other person acted as he or she did). This is a complex element and involves the sophistication of the client's understanding of interpersonal relations in general as well as in the specific situation. An assessment of the cultural or subcultural context of the situation is relevant: foreigners or people living in cultural settings other than those in which they were raised may misunderstand the behavior of others, as well as contextual environmental cues. A background in anthropology and experience living in another culture can be invaluable aids to a therapist in identifying such problems. Furthermore, as Toffler (1970) pointed out in *Future Shock*, our own culture is changing at such a rate that we are all deficient to some extent in understanding the cultural rules of the moment.

The client's understanding of the situation also includes

both the accuracy of his "naive psychology" (Heider 1958) and of the way in which causation is attributed to the environmental situation. For example, it is relevant to know whether the client believes that the other person wished to act pleasantly (or unpleasantly), or was compelled to act in that way, why the client believes it, and to the extent possible, the accuracy of the belief.

The way in which the client labels other actors in the problem situation also has important effects (Krasner and Ullmann 1973; Ullmann and Krasner 1969). Those of us who have mistaken patients and therapists for each other in mental hospitals are aware that inappropriate behavior can easily be generated by inaccurate labels.

In brief, a client who is able to observe problem situations accurately may still respond inadequately if his or her understanding of the situation is deficient.

4. *The client's behavioral repertoire.* Even if the client has observed the problem situation accurately and understands it clearly, he or she may still be unable to respond adequately without the appropriate skills. Assessment of possible behavioral deficits should be undertaken with a broad definition of what constitutes the client's behavioral repertoire. Thus, not only abilities directly relevant to the situation at hand but also more general strategies of self-control (Goldfried and Merbaum 1973) and problem solving (D'Zurilla and Goldfried 1971) are important areas to be considered. A therapist whose molecular treatment of a few situations fails to "generalize" may be overlooking a molar deficit in cognitive strategies.

5. *The client's ability to predict how others will understand and respond to his or her behavior.* Clients who have observed the problem situation adequately, understand it, and have an adequate behavioral repertoire may still respond inadequately if they are unable or unwilling to predict the consequences of their behavior—or simply don't bother to do so. An

unfortunate by-product of some encounter groups and "therapy of joy" has been incredibly naive behavior in which clients "shared their feelings" with others and then were hurt by unforeseen but easily anticipatable responses.

6. *The client's behavior.* This is the same as "the behavior itself" of the three-part unit. After the above five steps, the client actually does something, and the familiar goal of assessment is to know as clearly as possible what that something is. Once again, behavior should be defined as broadly as possible to include verbal and nonverbal behavior, physiological responses, sensations, images, thoughts and feelings—in short, to use existential instead of psychoanalytic imagery, the BASIC I.[1]

7. *The client's ability to observe his or her behavior.* (e.g., to recognize how one responded with one's BASIC I). A faulty ability in self-observation, especially in recognizing one's social stimulus value, is a common reason for inappropriate behavior. In particular, a client who is unaware of how he or she behaves is unlikely to be able to predict how others will respond (cf. item 5 above). The relative contributions of avoidance, learning deficits, and inaccurate learning to this problem are relevant areas for assessment, since they call for different treatment approaches (extinction, training, and/or retraining).

8. *The client's understanding of his or her behavior* (e.g., one's post hoc view of why one responded as one did with the BASIC I). This includes clients' understanding of their sociocultural, familial, peer, work, romantic, and other social environments and learning histories, as well as the effects on their behavior of social-cognitive variables such as self-labeling

---

1. As Lazarus's acronym has been reified into a school of therapy, the irony of a behavior therapist treating the id has been transformed into the sober identification (I.D.) of problems to be treated. I continue to prefer the original image. A danger for the behavior therapy movement is that a loss of self-referential humor could lead to a dulling of self-criticism.

(Krasner and Ullmann 1973, Ullmann and Krasner 1969), the attribution of self-causation to behavior (Davison and Valins 1969), and the belief that they acted freely (Brehm 1966).

9. *The environmental consequences* (e.g., how the other person reacts). This element—which includes positive and negative reinforcement, punishment, and extinction—is the same as the "reinforcing stimuli" of the three-part unit.

10. *The client's ability to observe the environmental consequences* (e.g., to recognize how the other person reacted). This is similar to item 2 above.

11. *The client's understanding of the environmental consequences* (e.g., the client's view of why the other person reacted as he or she did). This is similar to item 3 above.

DISCUSSION

The elevenfold schema presented above emphasizes three main areas sometimes overlooked in the assessment of problem behavior:

A. The client's ability to observe his or her own behavior (7) and the behavior of others (2 and 10).

B. The client's ability to understand his or her own behavior and the kinds of labels the client applies to him- or herself (8), the client's ability to understand the behavior of others and the ways in which the client labels them (3 and 11), and the client's ability to predict how others will understand and react to his or her behavior and label him or her (5).

C. The client's behavioral repertoire, including strategies of self-control and problem solving (4).

Information obtained in the course of an elevenfold analysis of several problem situations may point to targets for change in any or all of these areas (in addition to implying changes in the client's overt behavior or environment). Once such targets have been identified, they can be broken down into their components and treated with the same specificity as any other behavior.

12

A More or Less Functional Analysis of Behavioral Irony

It is natural for behaviorists to be ironic, since a moment-to-moment analysis of environmental contingencies leaves little room for epic forces to intervene between behavior and reinforcers. From an environmental point of view, profound undertakings such as Science, Religion, and Psychotherapy often appear pretentious—or even quaint—when viewed as the scientific, religious, or therapeutic behavior of their adherents. Ironic insights like these have occasionally found their way into print; and this chapter is aimed at carrying the process to its logical conclusion, by looking at behavioral irony from an ironic behavioral perspective.

In essence, behavioral irony involves a transformation of covert verbal behavior into overt printed responses (PR). The highest probability of occurrence of PR is in technical journals and textbooks—the two most important discriminative stimulus media (*DSM-II*[1]). B. F. Skinner would have agreed with Marshall McLuhan that journals and books are limited in their potential for influencing behavior. Hence, it is not surprising that many behaviorists have reservations about *DSM-II*, and participate at times with ironic PR.

The response class of behavioral irony can be divided into two subclasses, based on the type of imagery employed. The first, which especially upsets existentialists and individualists, may be referred to as futuristic-computerized irony; the second, which tends to vex theologians and psychoanalysts, employs the imagery of magical or religious pseudoscience. Since the classes of irony are not mutually exclusive, and since people distressed by one type of irony may also be distressed by the other, it is sometimes possible for a single article to antagonize many groups at one time.

Behavior modifiers have stressed the important consequences of labeling on behavior (Krasner and Ullmann 1973, Ullmann and Krasner 1969). They know that people usually judge a book by its cover. Hence, while irony sometimes appears in the body of a behavioral work, it can most fruitfully be sought after in the title.

Classic examples of futuristic-computerized irony can be seen in Krasner's (1962) article "The Therapist as a Social Reinforcement Machine" and Skinner's (1971) book *Beyond Freedom and Dignity*. The former was published at a time when research and other client-centered PR were gaining support for the Rogerian view of the therapist as a loving, open, honest,

---

1. This pun on the second edition of the *Diagnostic and Statistical Manual of Mental Disorders* of the American Psychiatric Association—which might more accurately be known as the *Diagnostic Stereotypes Manual*—loses some of its effect now that we have reached *DSM-IV*. Even a fourth edition is not a reductio ad absurdum, since *DSM-V, -VI*, and others will doubtless follow.

understanding person. It comes as no surprise that therapists, like anyone else, enjoyed viewing themselves in so positive a light. In this context, the metaphor of the therapist as a machine had a particularly jarring effect. A subsequent behavioral metaphor is of the therapist as an actor playing a role aimed at influencing clients. While this metaphor involves behavior more characteristic of the human species, it too denies the therapist so beneficent a self-image. Christie and Geis's finding (1968, 1970) that psychiatrists scored high on their scale of Machiavellianism seems consistent with this denial.

Beyond Freedom and Dignity, like the social reinforcement machine metaphor, is a title that evokes imagery of *Brave New World* or *1984*. And like the Krasner article, the controversy it provoked seemed directed more at this imagery than at the content of the book.

It is possible to view B. F. Skinner as the E. E. Cummings of psychology—an *enfant terrible* whose provocative way of saying things was for some people a source of penetrating insights and for others of exasperation. (He even eschewed names for initials.) For example, Skinner's original use of a word like *control* was bound to provoke more controversy than the scientifically neutral *cause* or the socially milder *influence*. In a similar manner, the message of *Beyond Freedom and Dignity* was not—as the title seems to imply—"Let's work for a world where we can all be undignified slaves."

Irony expressed in the imagery of magical or religious pseudoscience is especially prevalent in the psychotherapy literature. As with any other profession, what practitioners do must go beyond the limits of the scientific knowledge they are attempting to apply. In this context, the proliferation of new schools of therapy, each of which claims in its PR to have The Answer, is a natural object of behavioral irony. Thus, when Lazarus (1973, 1974) wrote about multimodal behavior therapy, he used the acronym BASIC ID to call attention to possible therapeutic targets for a sophisticated behavioral approach (Behavior, Affect, Sensations, Imagery, Cognitions, Interpersonal relations, plus the use of Drugs when appropriate). Similarly, I entitled my book (Fish 1973) about social influence in psychotherapy *Placebo Therapy*. (One clinical psychologist said of the title, "Is nothing sacred—or secret—anymore?")

As with new schools of therapy, the case study is often a vehicle for extravagant claims and as such is a logical area for behavioral irony. Thus, the case study that I am including as Chapter 14, of the treatment of three women who claimed to be the same person—a kind of multiple personality in reverse—is entitled "Dissolution of a Fused Identity in One Therapeutic Session." While it describes the way in which I persuaded my clients that they were in fact three people, psychologists who read the case study when it was first published, but who apparently missed the irony, occasionally asked me challengingly, "How do you know their identities really merged?"

Surely the finest case study of this genre is Upper's (1974) "The Unsuccessful Self-treatment of a Case of 'Writer's Block'." The article is a blank page! As with its other controversial articles, the *Journal of Applied Behavior Analysis* prudently included the Comments by Reviewer A: "I have studied this manuscript very carefully with lemon juice and X-rays and have not detected a single flaw in either design or writing style. I suggest it be published without revision . . ." (p. 497).

One final example, which at one time illustrates the various themes thus far discussed, should be sufficient to close this section on the nature of behavioral irony PR. It is entitled "Operant Reinforcement of Prayer." The author was listed as Benjamin Franklin (1969), but a footnote indicated that reprints could be requested from B. F. Skinner. The article describes the way in which Franklin helped a military chaplain get his men to pray by having him dole out their allotment of rum only after they completed their prayers. This tour de force includes both futuristic-computerized and religious pseudoscientific imagery, in the format of a case study, and makes ironic use of both the title and author.

From a social learning perspective, the acquisition of behavioral irony can best be understood in terms of modeling and operant reinforcement. With regard to the former, both observational learning (Skinner did it) and vicarious reinforcement (Skinner got rich and famous doing it) appear to have occurred.

As I hinted earlier, two important sources of social reinforcement are peer approval from the behavioral in-group and perplexed aggression from colleagues of depth psychology or transcendental persuasions. In addition, there are the usual academic reinforcers: career advancement as a reinforcer for promotional PR, and international requests for reprints as a reward for stamp-collecting behaviorists.

From the point of view of social psychology, the academic pressure to publish can be seen as a denial of freedom. According to Brehm's (1966) theory of psychological reactance, behavioral irony could then be viewed as an attempt by behaviorists to regain some of their lost freedom by publishing in a way that defies academic tradition. (In behavioral terms, Brehm's theory would be understood as asserting that people are not free not to react against restrictions on their freedom.)

Behavioral irony also poses a paradox (Watzlawick et al. 1967) for nonbehaviorists. If nonbehaviorists disagree with an ironic article by taking it literally, they have no sense of humor; if they dismiss it as not serious, they lack the insight to understand its point. No wonder unsympathetic audiences are angered or bewildered. How is a psychoanalyst to respond, when a behavior therapist asserts that the essence of his approach is to treat the BASIC ID?

It is not surprising that behavioral irony functions as a paradox, since the essence of irony is the discrepancy between what is said and what is meant. A response to either message is inadequate because it leaves the other unanswered. Hence the only effective response to behavioral irony is nonbehavioral irony—which answers the overt message overtly and the covert message covertly. The only problem with this response is the implication it entails. It is hard to maintain the theoretical stance of free will by the use of deterministic tactics like paradox.

Unfortunately, behavioral irony may have untoward consequences. Just as nonbehaviorists may take it literally, naive behaviorists may make the same mistake. While this lack may result merely in an oversimplified theoretical outlook (the world as a gigantic M & M dispensary), it may in the case of futuristic-computerized irony have more ghoulish results. One behaviorist described a psychologist reminiscent of Dr. Strangelove who told him, "I like ziss behavior therapy because it iss very efficient." Similarly, when an article or book is less upsetting than its ironic title, non-behaviorists who might otherwise be persuaded by it will read it with a negative set. All this just goes to show that labeling—even of behavioral PR—really can lead to negative consequences.

In conclusion, behavioral irony—its nature, situational context, acquisition, and effects—can be understood in behavioral terms. But is it as much fun that way?

13

Case Assignment to Ameliorate Therapists' Problems in Behavior Therapy Supervision

The supervision of behavior therapy, unlike that for psychodynamic therapy, has tended to focus on the teaching of specific technical skills such as systematic desensitization or contingency management. Training methods are consistent with a social learning approach to therapy and include modeling, role-playing, and similar techniques. Supervisors of behavior therapy (like supervisors from other orientations) are aware that therapists' personal problems may affect their clinical functioning, and use their own theories and techniques to deal with such problems (Levine and Tilker 1974). These include an emphasis, wherever possible, on attempting to change behavior in the environmental context where it occurs.

In supervising therapists whose personal problems affect their clinical functioning, the above emphasis suggests considering supervisory strategies aimed at making use of the therapist-client interaction to benefit the therapist as well as the client. The point of such strategies is that exposure to upsetting stimuli can lead to the extinction of anxiety for the therapist, while the coping responses that he or she makes, under the supervisor's guidance, offer an opportunity for the therapist to develop a sense of self-efficacy (Bandura 1977a,b) in areas of behavioral deficit.

A useful supervision technique along the above lines is the assignment by the supervisor of cases that present difficulties in the therapist's problem areas. Naturally, the exercise of clinical judgment on the part of the supervisor is critical in such instances and is discussed further below.

The following two examples of supervision are taken from my work while in Brazil. All therapy and supervision took place in Portuguese, since both therapists and clients were culturally Brazilian (cf. Chapter 10; Biaggio 1980).

Case No. 1. The therapist was a competent but rather shy woman, lacking in self-confidence, who worked almost exclusively with children. She did feel confident in relation to children, as a result of differences between her and them in age, physical size, education, and occupational status. The case I assigned to her was that of an impotent man. The discussion of intimate sexual material with a male client posed special problems for a woman therapist in Brazil at that time, and it was an especially strong challenge to shyness. The conduct of the case required the therapist to give the client homework assignments involving masturbation and increasingly intimate forms of sexual contact with women, as well as, by demonstrating her confidence in discussing highly charged material, helping him to overcome his feelings of anxiety. As the case progressed, various colleagues commented on the therapist's increased self-confidence. This improvement was reflected both in her nonverbal behavior and in her willingness to take on increased professional responsibilities, including more therapy cases with adults. Shortly after the conclusion of her successful treatment of the case, she was offered and accepted a position with administrative responsibilities, suggesting that her improved self-confidence was maintained.

Case No. 2. The therapist was a woman whose first baby had been stillborn the previous year. She was pregnant once again, and during supervision she was glum and anxious regarding the pregnancy. I assigned her the case of a pregnant woman with intense fears related to giving birth. The therapist's responsibilities included modeling a comfortable acceptance of her own pregnancy and indicating in her assignment of homework tasks that, as a woman going through the same process, she knew that the client could achieve what was asked of her. The therapist grew more cheerful and self-confident as therapy with her client progressed. She "accepted emotionally" what she had accepted only intellectually before—that the previous stillbirth was a freak occurrence and was unlikely to happen again. Her second baby was born normally, and the therapist described herself as having gone through delivery with no greater anxiety than had preceded her first delivery.

Technical and ethical issues related to this approach involve consideration for the client's welfare, consideration for the therapist's welfare, and acknowledgment of the supervisory contract as one aimed at improving the therapist's clinical performance rather than his or her private life. These issues were dealt with in the following manner:

1. The cases were offered to the therapists as an opportunity for training. This is consistent with the nature of the supervisory contract.

2. I indicated to the therapists that I had suggested that they take on these cases only because I thought that they could handle them. This judgment is a critical one. The judgment itself and its explicit statement are consistent with a concern for the welfare of both therapist and client.

3. I advised the therapists to decline the cases if they felt that it would be too upsetting to treat them. The advice was also given with the welfare of both therapist and client in mind. At the same time, it should be recognized that advising therapists to decline cases has a paradoxical quality (Haley 1963, Rohrbaugh et al. 1977). That is, advising them to turn down the cases may well increase the likelihood of their rising to the challenge and accepting them, while the ethically questionable stance of encouraging therapists to accept the cases might be more likely to provoke feelings of self-doubt and inadequacy.

4. In the course of supervision I focused on issues concerning what the therapist could do to help the client overcome his or her problems and did not call attention to or initiate discussion regarding the therapist's related problem areas. On the occasions when the therapist brought up for discussion her own personal reactions, I dealt with them only insofar as they were relevant to the treatment of the case (e.g., role-playing how to discuss anxiety-provoking material). This was consistent with the treatment focus of the rest of supervision, and with the

nature of the supervisory contract. That is, when case assignment is used to ameliorate the therapist's problems, the therapist's improvement is not seen as the result of the supervisor's treating the therapist. Rather, it is viewed as a by-product of the interactions involved in the therapist's treatment of the client.

14

Dissolution of a Fused Identity in One Therapeutic Session

This case report is aimed at achieving several ends. First, it attempts to provide a glimpse of rather rare abnormal behavior: three people who claim that their identities have merged into one. Next, it exemplifies a social-cognitive approach to therapy, as opposed to the more common emphases on intrapsychic forces or conditioning as determinants of behavior. Finally, it illustrates the use of therapy to alter a preexisting nonfamilial social system, rather than to change separately the behavior of individuals.

Two main techniques characterized the treatment of the present case. The first of these was the use of dissonant communications by the therapist to modify the clients' self-referring attitudes. As Bergin (1962) has shown in a study that was designed to have implications for psychotherapy, communications from a highly credible source—closely resembling a therapist—have marked effects on subjects' self-referring attitudes. The fact that Bergin experimentally manipulated communications concerning his subjects' masculinity-femininity gives his study particular relevance to the present case.

The second technique was a paradoxical intervention (Haley 1963, Watzlawick et al. 1967). Such paradoxes involve telling clients to do what they are doing in order to get them to stop doing it. The technique, which originated with the communications therapists (Watzlawick et al. 1967), is explained by them as follows:

> If someone is asked to engage in a specific type of behavior which is seen as spontaneous, then he cannot be spontaneous anymore, because the demand makes spontaneity impossible. By the same token, if a therapist instructs a patient to perform his symptom, he is demanding spontaneous behavior and by this paradoxical injunction imposes on his patient behavioral change. [p. 237]

Of course, other theoretical explanations of the technique are possible. In behavior therapy terms, paradoxical interventions may in various instances be likened to negative practice (diminishing the frequency of a maladaptive response, such as a tic, by massed practice), stimulus satiation (diminishing the reinforcing properties of a stimulus by providing a superabundance of it), or extinction. However, since negative practice, stimulus satiation, and extinction all require repeated trials, while a paradoxical intervention may lead to an immediate change of behavior, such explanations would appear to be inadequate.

Another possible way of understanding paradoxical interventions is in terms of reactance theory (Brehm 1966). This theory asserts that subjects will experience "reactance" as a result of restrictions on their freedom to act and will therefore react in an attempt to regain their freedom. Two of Brehm's conclusions based on his experimental studies are: "When a free behavior is threatened with elimination, the individual will tend to attempt re-establishment of freedom by engaging in the behavior which is threatened" (p. 121), and "The greater is the absolute and/or relative importance of the freedom threatened or eliminated, the greater will be the magnitude of reactance and its effects" (p. 122). Paradoxical interventions can thus be seen to involve the therapist putting pressure on clients to give up an important area of freedom—their "normal" or "asymptomatic" behavior. As a result, clients are likely to experience considerable reactance and give up their "symptoms" in an attempt to reestablish their freedom.

Finally, paradoxical interventions may be understood in terms of attribution theory. In particular, when subjects attribute to themselves the ability to control behavior that they previously believed to be beyond control, attribution theory predicts that their actual control should increase. Along these lines, Davison and Valins (1969) succeeded in lowering subjects' pain thresholds and increasing their tolerance for electric shocks by a deceptive procedure. Their subjects were first tested for pain thresholds and shock tolerance, following which they swallowed a placebo that they were told was a "fast-acting drug," and they were then "retested" for thresholds and tolerance—although the shock intensities had been halved without their knowledge. At this point, half of the subjects were told that they had received a placebo, while the other half were told that the drug had worn off. At a second retesting, with the original shock intensities restored, "It was found that subjects who attributed their behavior change to themselves (i.e., who believed they had ingested a placebo) subsequently perceived the shocks as less painful and tolerated significantly more than subjects who attributed their behavior change to the drug"

(Davison and Valins 1969, p. 25). In line with this study, attribution theory would suggest that paradoxical interventions work by persuading clients that their "spontaneous symptoms" are really under their own control. By deliberately performing their problem behavior, clients convince themselves that such behavior is under voluntary control; and this new attribution of self-control enables them to discontinue the behavior.

CASE STUDY

On a Monday morning, shortly after the beginning of the fall term, three first-year women students entered the reception room of their university's psychological center. They told the receptionist that they were quite upset, and that they would like to consult a therapist as a threesome as soon as possible. Since I was available for "emergencies" at that time, I agreed to meet with them in the group therapy room. In the presentation that follows, I shall refer to them as Ms. Controlling (who spoke the most, and in an authoritative manner), Ms. Dependent (who spoke softly, and looked to others for reassurance), and Ms. Depressed (whose expression was generally sad and downcast).

The three young women began the session by stating, with wide-eyed looks of anxiety and credulousness, "We've lost our identity. We're the same person."

"I can tell the difference between you," I said with a friendly smile.

They calmed down somewhat at this point but persisted in trying to convince me that their experience was a genuine and upsetting one. They pointed out that they were "always" together, agreed about "everything," and had similar likes and dislikes. They even had a boyfriend whom they all liked, and who liked all of them; and none of them felt jealous. As we discussed the subject further, they continued to explain their experience of a fused identity by means of examples that would generally be called friendship. Each time that I made this observation, however, they restated their presenting problem and insisted that it was more than mere friendship.

Since they appeared unable to communicate the unique aspects of their experience, I decided to try another tack. I inquired why they had come to the psychological center that particular morning, and whether anything special had happened over the weekend.

They explained that they had spent the previous night with their shared boyfriend. All four of them had been lying on the same bed, and my three clients had taken turns holding him and kissing him. While they insisted that they felt no jealousy toward one another concerning that event, their pressured speech as they described it suggested that something about it was still upsetting them.

I reasoned from the postulate "Lips that kiss the same lips indirectly kiss each other," that my clients might be experiencing doubts about their sexual orientation. I therefore asked in an incredulous voice, as if trying to rule out an unlikely possibility, "You aren't afraid that you might be lesbians, are you?"

"No!" they blurted out in unison, with sufficient anxiety to imply that they meant "Yes."

"I'm glad to hear that," I said, "because that's a lot of nonsense." This assessment brought smiles of relief to their faces. However, despite their reassurance over the immediate reason for seeking help, the belief that their identities had merged still remained. In the absence of useful diagnostic information, I considered the hypothesis that, as first-year students, they were lonely in their new college environment. If this were so, then their experience could be

the result of spending an excessive amount of time together
and relying exclusively on one another for closeness, understanding, and support. To investigate this possibility, I
asked them if they had been feeling lonely since arriving on
campus. Their replies, which follow, indicated for the first
time the kind of interaction that they appeared to be
labeling a fusion of identity:

> *Ms. Dependent:* Yes, I think so.
> *Ms. Controlling:* No, I wouldn't say so.
> *Ms. Depressed:* Not lonely, no.
> *Ms. Dependent:* No, I guess I wouldn't really call it
lonely.

When this interchange took place, I pointed out the
way in which their initial disagreement had been smoothed
over, making it appear as if they had all felt the same from
the start. Ms. Depressed and Ms. Dependent expressed
interest in this possibility and seemed to wonder how
general such a pattern of interaction might be. However,
Ms. Controlling disagreed with my description and insisted
that even if it were accurate it did not refer to a general
pattern of interaction. Furthermore, she said that it had
nothing to do with their having become the same person.

I admitted that she might be right, and suggested that
since there was some uncertainty as to what was going on in
the course of their interactions, it would be a good idea to
study how they felt under controlled conditions. Using this
rationale, I asked them to describe in detail when they
would be together during the next day, and what they
would do at those times. It took about twenty minutes to
assemble a complete list of such activities (i.e., two of them
would meet for breakfast before a class they had together
and make fun of their professor over coffee. They would
then go to class, and after class all three would meet in the

library. There, they would talk about how much studying they had to do, but they wouldn't get any done, etc.). Once we had finished, I handed them the list and told them that it was extremely important that they follow it to the letter (i.e., meet for breakfast, make fun of the professor, go to class, meet in the library, talk about studying but not study, etc.). I explained that as they followed the list, they were to remember how they reacted—even making notes, if necessary. We then set up an appointment for the following week, at which time, I explained, we would go over their reactions to see what could be learned from them.

Only Ms. Dependent and Ms. Depressed showed up for their next appointment, which lasted about fifteen minutes. They said that they had started out by following the list, but that they had given up in the middle. Since then, they had been spending less time together and no longer felt as if they were the same person. Ms. Controlling had become upset as they drifted apart and had demanded that Ms. Dependent and Ms. Depressed spend more time with her. When they refused, she threatened to start taking unspecified drugs. They maintained their refusal, regarding her threat as a ploy, and told me that they felt that she would "calm down in a while." Ms. Dependent and Ms. Depressed said that while they were still friendly with each other, they had other friends and a lot of schoolwork, and no longer got together so frequently. I indicated that if either of them wished to continue to see a therapist, I was available (I had Ms. Depressed in mind in making this offer), but they both declined.

Unfortunately, I have no follow-up data on my three clients, other than the memory that several months later Ms. Controlling did consult another therapist at the psychological center for problems unrelated to identity fusion (neither I nor my clients are any longer at the university, and the psychological center has a policy of destroying inactive files). However, the rarity of their condition would suggest that it is statistically unlikely that their identities would once again merge, or that any one of them would experience identity fusion with other protean personalities.

DISCUSSION

"I Can Tell the Difference Between You"

The clients in this case study, as so often happens, arrived for therapy with more than a set of problems. They also brought with them various beliefs and attitudes toward those problems. When clients can be persuaded at the outset to check this extra baggage (including ideation such as "I'm a hopeless case" or "What a remarkable person I am to have such colorful psychopathology"), the therapeutic load can be lightened considerably.

My opening gambit, "I can tell the difference between you," challenged my clients' nonverbal communication that their problem was an awesome one. By humorously emphasizing their physical dissimilarity, I expressed my professional opinion that their problem was not so impressive after all. In addition, I communicated this message in a friendly way to emphasize that it was their experience of identity fusion—and not they as individuals—that appeared mundane to me. Had I responded instead with a concerned and sympathetic attempt to get more information, I would not have been making this important distinction. Although still communicating that I cared about them, I would also have implied that their problem was sufficiently alarming to merit such concern and attention. This sort of counterproductive sympathy is but one of many therapeutic maneuvers that deserve the epithet of "poisoned chicken soup."

"That's a Lot of Nonsense"

My clients' anxiety about their sexual orientation was treated in a similar manner. Since no actual homosexual behavior had taken place, the problem appeared to be one of self-labeling. As Ullmann and Krasner (1969) have pointed out, self-labeling can have considerable effects on subsequent behavior. In the present case, my clients appeared to be considering the appropriateness of applying the psychological label of "latent homosexuality"—or even "homosexuality"—to themselves. Had they done so, the likelihood of their anxiously engaging in unwanted homosexual experimentation as a consequence of their self-labeling would have increased. Since they seemed to fear such a label but had not yet accepted it, and since they were consulting a specialist in part to help them decide on its appropriateness, they were particularly receptive to the communication that it was inapplicable.

Once again, the decisive way in which the dissonant communication was delivered merits special emphasis. Had my clients not feared that they were unconsciously homosexual, I would not have wanted to suggest this worry to them. Given that it did bother them, I wished to dissuade them from such a belief. By asking the question in the form "You aren't afraid that you might be lesbians, are you?" I made it possible to achieve my goal either way. Since my primary emphasis was on changing upsetting self-referent beliefs, I did not ask the exploratory question "You say that you weren't jealous toward one another while kissing him. Were there other feelings that you did have toward one another at that time?" Such a question would by its hesitancy have run the risk of communicating that I thought they had been sexually attracted to one another. In other words, at a time when they were uncertain as to how to label their experience, such a question might well have pushed them in an anxiety-provoking direction.

For similar reasons, when they answered my question with a startled "No!" I agreed with them emphatically. Asking why they had been so upset by the question would only have implied that I thought that they were concealing their basically homosexual natures.[1]

The Paradoxical Intervention

Paradoxical interventions take effect only if clients attempt to comply with their therapists' prescriptions. In terms of Parsons's perspective (1951), clients may be viewed as enacting the sick role vis-à-vis their therapists; and the sick role entails an obligation to cooperate with the ministrations of socially sanctioned healers. Thus, in order to get clients to attempt to comply with a paradoxical intervention, a therapist requires a persuasive rationale to convince them that the instructions constitute a legitimate therapeutic endeavor. In the present case, the rationale was a diagnostic one: to see how the clients felt as they interacted in specified ways. Fortunately, the rationale was successful, and the clients subsequently attempted to follow the script. As they did so, however, they found that their preplanned behavior lacked the chaotic excitement of being swept along by a fused identity.

The Therapeutic Goal

In an extensive review of therapeutic outcome research, Bergin (1971) concluded that global outcome measures should be abandoned and replaced by specific measures tailored to each

---

1. Had this case occurred now (instead of in the late 1960s) when homosexuality is no longer labeled a mental illness and is less stigmatized on college campuses, the entire issue might have been less important.

client. He argues cogently that "if a person seeks help for severe depression, we would tend to measure change in depression rather than his global psychological status" (p. 258).

This case study suggests, by extension, that the goals of therapy and outcome measures for them may even be specific to a social system, without necessarily involving changes in the psychopathology of its individual members. Ms. Controlling, Ms. Dependent, and Ms. Depressed left therapy while remaining controlling, dependent, and depressed, respectively; and yet, therapy was successful. Similarly, marital therapy or family therapy may be judged successful by the client group when its pattern of interaction has been changed to a more agreeable one—even if all the individuals involved retain their initial psychiatric diagnoses. If the therapist is truly a consultant to his clients, he must be flexible in considering the goals of therapy and not inevitably aim toward individual personality reorganization.

PART IV

STRATEGIC AND SYSTEMIC THERAPIES

Introduction

Part IV consists of five brief chapters that attempt to foster communication between systems therapists and behavior therapists, while implicitly advocating pragmatic iconoclasm (doing something different or considering issues from a new perspective) as a useful outlook on theory and practice.

Chapter 15 is an attempt to show that a question on which behavior therapists and systems therapists differ—whether it makes sense to understand psychological problems as resulting from skills deficits—involves a false dichotomy. In arguing that "it depends," the chapter attempts to promote communication between the two groups.

Chapter 16, which is somewhat longer than the others, is a discussion of the concept of discontinuous change. This presentation goes well beyond the implications of discontinuous change for therapy, much as Chapters 7 and 8 dealt with broad social and cultural issues. As with Chapter 15, it was written in part to foster communication between behavior therapists and systems therapists.

Chapter 17 considers paradoxical interventions in supervision. In some ways the outlook is similar to that in Chapter 13, regarding behavior therapy supervision—not only because it deals with supervision, but more importantly because it involves doing something different or unexpected. While the situations in which a supervisor might intervene paradoxically are rather rare, the idea of applying the same principles of behavior change to both therapy and supervision makes the discussion of interest.

In a similar way, Chapter 18, which describes a family game, offers an opportunity for unpredictable change by putting participants in a situation with new social rules.

Chapter 19, which consists of a paradoxical prescription for the family therapy movement, was originally written with ironic intent. Instead, it has turned out to be mildly prophetic. When I included it in the first draft of this book, I planned for it to serve as a coda. But that was before the need arose for an epilogue. . . .

Skills Deficits versus System Reorganization

A major theoretical issue dividing behavior therapists from strategic and systemic therapists has been the relevance of skills deficits to explaining and treating problem behavior. Briefly, behavior therapists have viewed many problems as resulting from clients' inadequate social, work, or other skills. In contrast, strategic and systemic therapists have viewed deficient performance as the result of hierarchical or other organizational patterns that make otherwise appropriate behavior impossible.

These differing views imply contrasting therapeutic strategies. If the problem is one of skills deficits, then the appropriate treatment is training in needed skills; and any time spent on rearranging hierarchies, or contexts, or patterns of communication, is wasted by ignoring the real difficulty. If, on the other hand, the problem is an organizational one, then training in skills that are already possessed is an exercise in futility. Not only does the client learn nothing new, but the therapist is implicitly accepting the status quo as regards the overall pattern of organizational relationships. Strategic and systemic therapists would expect that the client might show some "progress" during skills training, since the skills are already "in the repertoire." They would, however, predict "difficulty in generalization" to real-life situations, or relapses following progress, as the distribution of hierarchical power, homeostatic mechanisms in the organization, or similar systemic features undermine "appropriate" performance.

In the case of a boy with temper tantrums, a behavior therapist might view the mother as lacking parenting skills, particularly the ability to ignore the tantrums consistently and to reinforce age-appropriate behavior. Perhaps the therapist would teach the mother to apply time-out from reinforcement during tantrums by confining her son in his room until he is quiet. The therapist would probably encourage her to "catch him being good" and reinforce many different kinds of acceptable nontantrum behavior when he engages in them.

If this works, well and good. Naturally, strategic and systemic therapists would have a different explanation for the positive result—perhaps in terms of clarifying the hierarchical relationship between the mother and her son. In a similar manner, behavior therapists or psychoanalysts would have alternative explanations for the success of a strategically treated client.

Let us suppose, however, that after some initial progress the boy starts to have tantrums again. The behavior therapist might find that his mother had ceased to follow through on the threefold program of ignoring, using time-out, and rewarding appropriate behavior. A likely inference regarding this difficulty would be that the mother's new behavior didn't persist because it wasn't reinforced. The therapist might then try to get the father to reinforce the mother for implementing the treatment program. If this worked for a while and then failed, the next step might be to seek a source of reinforcement for the father for reinforcing the mother, and so on. In this way, a Rube Goldberg machine of interlocking interventions might gradually be constructed, with the ultimate object of maintaining the mother's newly acquired "skills."

Is it any wonder that strategic and systemic therapists would respond with exasperation: "Why not just change the entire familial pattern of interaction?" Behavior therapists, and social learning theory, have made an important conceptual leap by looking beyond what goes on within a single person to considering the ways individuals affect each other one at a time. However, by shifting conceptual levels beyond this to the functioning of an entire organization, such as a family, strategic therapists and systems theory have made an important contribution. Straightforward interventions become possible in situations that previously seemed extremely complex.

Still, there is much that strategic and systemic therapists have in common with behavior therapists. They share a commitment to brief treatment, a willingness to take presenting problems seriously and to examine them in their interpersonal context (though strategic and systemic therapists tend to look at more context and behavior therapists tend to look at the immediate context more microscopically), and skepticism about the medical model of the origins and treatment of abnormal behavior. In addition, behavior therapists' commitment to clearly defined empirically based concepts, and to experimental examination of their work, serves as a model for therapists of all theoretical persuasions.

With the exception of a few true believers, most strategic and systemic therapists would be willing to concede that real change is possible at the individual and dyadic level—that the entire system need not always be involved in lower-order change. After all, the concept of the holon (Koestler 1972) indicates that one can never deal with the "entire system." Just as the individual and the marital dyad are subsystems of the nuclear family, that family is a subsystem of higher-order forms of organization.

Over the past two or three decades, behavior therapists have developed numerous treatment programs, of varying efficacy and experimental documentation, for a wide range of problems. These include gradual approach methods for over-coming fears, and techniques of sex therapy that antedate Masters and Johnson (e.g., Wolpe 1958). Consider, for example, the work of Azrin and Nunn (1974), who in one session each were able to reduce by 94 percent the stuttering of fourteen people who had stuttered for an average of twenty-four years. (Their stuttering continued to diminish toward zero over a four-month follow-up.) The techniques employed all involved breathing and speaking—clearly training in relevant skills. Who would argue that even major shifts in the organization of the stutterers' families would produce comparable results?

Perhaps the time has come to recognize that the question of whether or not our clients have skills deficits contains a false dichotomy. It seems more reasonable to suggest that some of them do and some of them don't. And among those with skills deficits, some may be able to overcome them on their own following system reorganization and some may require thera-peutic assistance.

The solution that I am proposing is a threefold one. Let us suppose that a strategic therapist is working with a family that contains an "identified client" who has a problem that might or might not involve a skills deficit. Following a number of inter-ventions that lead to systemic reorganization, which the thera-pist and all family members regard as real and important change, three outcomes are possible:

1. The client no longer has the problem. That is, competent, appropriate behavior replaces problem behavior. Such a result would suggest that the skills existed all along, but that hierarchical or other organizational problems in the family prevented their performance. For example, an adolescent starts to do well in school or a spouse's sexual problem disappears.

2. The client still has the problem but engages in self-training to acquire the needed skills. That is, he or she lacked the skills to overcome the problem, but previously was unwilling, fearful, or otherwise unable to do what was necessary to acquire them. The process of acquiring the skills may involve practice, exertion, and/or a willingness to endure embarrassment, anxiety, or failure. For example, an adolescent who had been doing poorly in school starts to study with good students and has conferences with teachers regarding material or methods that are too difficult to understand. Or one spouse with a sexual problem begins to talk about it, work on it with the other, and gradually overcome it as the result of an improved marital relationship. In this case, the client did have a skills deficit but also possessed the necessary resources to overcome the deficit. Organizational problems in the family, however, prevented the client from doing what was necessary to overcome it.

3. The client still has the problem but is responsive to skills training. That is, there really was a skills deficit all along, and one that could not be remedied without special help. One possibility that should not be ignored is that the client would have been responsive to skills training in the first place. The experience of behavior therapists suggests that such people really do exist. However, the more interesting case is that of a person who had a skills deficit, who was incapable of remedying it without professional assistance, but who was previously uncooperative or resistant. Following organizational changes in the family, however, the client now becomes cooperative and

improves in the expected manner with skills training. For example, a once resistant child cooperates with perceptual training for learning disabilities following changes in family organization, or a couple cooperates in the treatment of one spouse's sexual problem, where that spouse previously denied there was a problem or was unwilling to do anything about it.

The point of all this is that there is no need to view strategies of remediating skills deficits and of changing the organizational context of problems as inherently incompatible. In the first outcome, a skills training approach would have been inappropriate, while in some cases of the third outcome (where skills training alone would have been sufficient), an organizational change approach would have been ineffective. In other cases of the third outcome, both strategies—in appropriate sequence—would be necessary.

There is much that strategic and systemic therapists and behavior therapists can learn from each other. Coyne and Biglan's (1984) behavioral analysis of paradoxical family therapy techniques is one example of a contribution to this theoretical dialog. Perhaps reconsidering the issue of skills training in strategic and systemic therapies could be another.

Discontinuous Change

Discontinuous change is an idea whose time has come. A new way of looking at complexity, at continuity and change, has already established itself in the physical and biological sciences. Unfortunately, an understanding of this view of causality has not yet achieved prominence in the social and behavioral sciences, though a variety of new theoretical perspectives and practical applications has begun to emerge. Since an understanding of discontinuous change has implications for the way we view the world and ourselves, as well as for our values, this chapter is an attempt to focus attention on the issue.

Let us begin by exploring the concepts of continuity and change. In psychology, for example, the best predictor of future behavior is past behavior. Jennifer, a 24-year-old college graduate, who today feels trapped in a six-year relationship with an unstable man (James), unhappy in her work, and intimidated by her father, will very likely feel trapped in the same relationship, unhappy in her work, and intimidated by her father tomorrow. In two days, or a month, or a year, it is also likely that her behavior (i.e., her relationships with and feelings about men, co-workers, and family members) will be similar. But the further into the future we go, the lower the probability that her behavior will remain unchanged.

The way psychologists have interpreted this consistency (and there are parallels in other fields) is to view change as gradual. That is, over some initial period, there is no change at all; then little bits of change accumulate, like grains of sand, forming at first an ant hill and eventually—if one waits long enough—a mountain. While the mountain of change looks qualitatively different from the first few grains, the *process* of change has been gradual and quantitative throughout. Thus, qualitative differences are merely the result of allowing a gradual quantitative process to proceed for a sufficiently long time.

This implicit view of change as gradual informs the way people think of the world and influences the kinds of questions it is possible for them to ask. There are many different terms for describing such implicit views, each with a somewhat different definition and implications, and with varying usefulness in understanding differing circumstances or conditions. Some of these are *belief system*, *frame of reference*, *assumptive world*, *paradigm*, *epistemology*, *ideology*, *Zeitgeist*, and *Weltanschauung*. While a discussion of these viewpoints is not necessary to the focus of this chapter, those who are interested might consult Kuhn's *The Structure of Scientific Revolutions* (1962) regarding paradigms and Pepper's *World Hypotheses* (1942) regarding contextualism and mechanism. Hayes (1988) and Hayes and colleagues (1988) discuss behavioral implications of Pepper's work.

The view of change as gradual can be seen in the theory of evolution, in which natural selection operates on genetic variability over extended periods of time, eventually accumulating enough quantitative difference to be called qualitative (a new species). The history of science itself can be viewed as a process of gradual change: each experiment contributes to knowledge, until there is enough new knowledge to challenge old theories and suggest new ones. Gradual change is a pervasive way of organizing and understanding the world.

Before speaking further about change, it is worth pausing to consider what it means to stay the same. Whether or not some characteristic is viewed as staying the same depends in part on the size of the units in which it is measured, as well as on the length of time between measurements. Jennifer might be consistent in her attitude toward James from one day to the next on a two-point scale (like/dislike), or a three-point scale (like/uncertain/dislike), but not on a scale of seven or 100 points. Similarly, her attitude might be consistent if measured on ten successive days, but not on ten successive months. Another way of putting this is to say that—at every level from the subatomic to the cosmic—everything is constantly changing, so that to assert that something is the same means that its changes fluctuate within a certain range.

Finally, in order to say that something is unchanged, one must observe it at least twice. Since observing a phenomenon affects it (to differing degrees and in differing ways, depending on who is doing the observing and how it is being done), the possibility cannot be ruled out that it is the process of observation that makes it appear the same or changed. If someone asked Jennifer whether she were still going out with James, her response would depend in part on who that person was, on the relationship between them—male or female, close friend, acquaintance, or potential new manfriend—as well as on a variety of factors other than the requested information. In short, stability, or the belief that one can know that something is unchanged without all kinds of qualifiers attached to that knowledge, is an illusion.

Now let's consider continuity. There is an abstract mathematical concept of continuity (between any two points on a line, no matter how close together, there are lots of other points), but this idea is too exacting for our purposes. Discrete physical objects like grains of sand are not continuous in the mathematical sense. While much change may be gradual—each grain of sand is a very small part of the mountain—gradual change is not mathematically continuous, since it is possible to put two grains of sand so close together that no others can fit in between.

Instead of making this abstract distinction, I will be using the terms gradual change and continuous change synonymously to refer to the imperfect way in which physical reality resembles the mathematical ideal. If the phenomenon we are observing doesn't appear to change suddenly, we can regard its occurrence as continuous. We can observe in passing that, since gradual change takes place in small—but not infinitesimal—units, all change is discontinuous in the mathematical sense. This is merely a side issue, and not relevant to the main topic of discontinuous or sudden change as different from gradual change.

Considered in this nonmathematical sense, the concept of continuity has two main forms—apparent stability (e.g., homeostasis) and gradual change (e.g., Darwinian evolution). As we have seen, a phenomenon that appears stable actually varies over time, but within definable limits. Our body temperature appears to remain stable at 98.6° F. In fact, it varies by a degree or two over a twenty-four hour period. Studies of circadian rhythms have shown that not only body temperature but other physiological processes vary slightly, in predictable ways, over definable periods of time (Winfree 1987). Once again, it is the range of variation that is "stable." But thermal consistency is not a passive state—various active processes are at work to maintain it. The evaporation of our perspiration cools us, and we generate heat by shivering. We wear clothes. We heat our homes in winter, air condition them in summer, and have thermostats to control indoor temperature in a manner analogous to our bodies' own "homeostats." Even understood in this way, apparent stability is time bound. If we wait long enough, our body temperature will change significantly from 98.6° F, either temporarily, as when we get sick, or indefinitely, when we die.

The second type of continuity is gradual change. The idea of change as taking place little by little is one that applies not only to how things got to be the way they are (explanation), and where they are headed (prediction), but also to how to make something happen (control). A common view is that, since the world is complex and there are so many variables to take into account, change must be difficult to engineer.

For example, psychoanalysis has a view of causality, known as psychic determinism, that has its origin in nineteenth-century physics. Psychoanalysts believe that, just as a perfectly spherical billiard ball knocking into another stationary one on a frictionless plane completely determines the latter's motion, so all mental events are completely determined by events that preceded them. Thus, psychoanalytic therapy is slow because the problems that bring people to treatment emerge at the end of a whole lot of causes that must be addressed.

In contrast, behavior therapy, which developed much more recently, has a more contemporary and probabilistic view of causation. People at streetcorners cross more frequently when the light is green than when it is red, though the green light doesn't cause them to walk in the way that one billiard ball causes another to move. Rather, it increases the probability of walking, even though people sometimes stand when the light is green and walk when it is red. Behavior therapy's probabilistic view of causality could easily comport with the concept of discontinuous change described below. Nevertheless, while treatment is of much shorter duration than that of psychoanalytic therapies, behavior therapy as it is usually practiced relies on gradual processes of learning that require repeated trials.

In general, gradualists would say that the way to make change happen is to define where you are headed, set out for your goal one step at a time, and overcome the obstacles you encounter until you get there.

In addition to gradual change, some discontinuous change is predictable—for example, developmental stages. Since qualitative behavioral changes, such as the appearance of speech, or physical changes like puberty, occur regularly, they are easily assimilated to a gradualist worldview and are not the subject of this chapter.

Although many changes do occur gradually, or at least predictably, we are becoming aware that sudden, unpredictable, discontinuous change is surprisingly widespread. While a natural first reaction would be to ignore such phenomena and attempt to explain, predict, and control that which occurs regularly, it turns out that the opposite strategy is an extremely fruitful one. As a result, the common view of the world as manifesting gradual change is being challenged by a new view associated with the concept of discontinuous change. What is this view?

If continuous change is gradual, quantitative, and predictable, then discontinuous change is typically sudden, qualitative, and unpredictable. Looking through a kaleidoscope, one sees a complex pattern of reflected bits of colored glass. A slight turn of the cylinder leaves the pattern unaffected, as does a further slight rotation. Eventually, a threshold is reached, so that any additional rotation leads to a rearrangement of the shards and a new and unpredictable visual pattern.

While this pattern change is surely sudden and qualitative,

purists might want to argue that it is, in principle, predictable. That is, if we had all sorts of information, such as the exact size and shape of all the fragments of colored glass, their exact positions relative to one another, and the exact speed and amount of rotation of the cylinder, we would be able to predict the new pattern.

Perhaps. However, there is an important limitation to predictability, known as sensitivity to initial conditions (Gleick 1987), that reminds us that a very slight initial difference in the size, shape, or position of even one of the shards (or in some other variable) could lead to entirely different subsequent patterns. Sensitivity to initial conditions is sometimes referred to as the "butterfly effect." This metaphor points out that the additional turbulence from a butterfly's wings in one part of the world can be magnified by the swirling forces of nature to produce a hurricane—that otherwise would not have occurred—in another part of the world.

More to the point, the focus on predictability, while of possible usefulness in many instances, seems to be inconsistent with what the kaleidoscope is all about. One might call it an example of gradualist thinking. In situations where there are many determining elements that interact in complex ways, an observer can't measure everything. Rather than trying to make sense of what happens to every element, a reasonable strategy with complex systems is to accept unpredictability and see where we can go from there. (This is why, for the present discussion, it is unimportant whether we are talking about unpredictability and randomness in principle or merely for practical purposes.) We can count on the kaleidoscope producing one suddenly new and qualitatively different pattern after another; no pattern will gradually fade into its successor. The innovation is to spend some time studying the patterns.

To understand discontinuous change, we have to view phenomena as parts of ongoing, interactive, complex systems.

The science of ecology, for example, looks at the world in this way. It has grown dramatically in recent years and has studied discontinuous changes such as the sudden extinction of species when their environments change. Of special relevance to the present discussion, ecologists' influence has spread beyond their science to everyday life and has already had an impact on people's values. Technology, previously viewed as producing solutions to problems, is now seen by many as itself part of a large, ongoing complex system. The view that technological solutions can produce unexpected consequences—which may be worse than the problems they were developed to solve—is an example of the way thinking about discontinuous change is beginning to affect our outlook and lead us to rethink values such as progress.

Since discontinuous change usually refers to a change in pattern, and patterns are by definition relational, such change is not always self-evident. As opposed to continuous change, which is by definition only a bit different from what preceded it, a pattern change is something else. It may be obvious, as in the kaleidoscope example, but it may be subtle. The sequence 1, 4, 7625597484987, . . ., does not initially seem to manifest a pattern. The pattern, however, is there for the finding, and becomes evident once recognized $(1, 2^2, 3^{3^3}, \ldots ,)$.

One can infer that those looking for continuous change would value precise measurement, while those looking for discontinuous change would value pattern recognition. While these are not necessarily incompatible abilities, they are different, and they hint at ways in which the social valuation of abilities may be modified if the idea of discontinuous change becomes more widespread.

Another distinctive feature of discontinuous change is its emphasis on the key role played by random elements. Randomness is a problem for those with a gradualist worldview, something to be overcome in explaining causality or in moving one step at a time toward a designated goal. They recognize that the stranger one sits next to on an airplane may become one's spouse or employer, thus completely altering one's life—but ideally, they would like to be able to predict the encounter and say that its apparent unpredictability was an illusion based on inadequate information.

In contrast, those who think in terms of discontinuous change view randomness as a fact of life, something to be taken advantage of rather than overcome in promoting change. As an alternative to setting a goal and gradually working toward it, their strategy would be to expose people to new information, situations, and relationships, and see what happens. (A more limited goal would be to attempt to describe the conditions under which a chance encounter is more or less likely to lead to a new life path [Bandura 1982].)

In provoking—rather than planning—change, one begins by going beyond the phenomenon itself to see where it fits into a larger complex system. Since homeostatic or other continuity-maintaining processes are at work in the system, strategies for change involve provoking pattern disruption, such as by introducing new unexpected elements or interfering with event sequences. As the system reorganizes into a new pattern, it is understood that the nature of the new outcome is unpredictable. This is the case not only because of the presence of new elements, but more importantly because the complex interaction of multiple forces, each of which is to some degree unpredictable, makes the ultimate pattern that will emerge unforseeable.

Because discontinuous change is rapid, it is of great interest to therapists. A few clinically relevant examples may be useful in illustrating what it looks like.

Watzlawick and colleagues (1974), in developing their approach to brief therapy, sought out examples of spontaneous change that occurred without the intentional intervention of therapists or anyone else. Here is one of their examples:

> On her first day of kindergarten, a four-year-old girl became so upset as her mother prepared to leave that the mother was forced to stay with her until the end of the school day. The same thing happened every day thereafter. The situation soon grew into a considerable stress for all concerned, but all attempts at solving the problem failed. One morning the mother was unable to drive the child to school, and the father dropped her off on his way to work. The child cried a little, but soon calmed down. When the mother again took her to school on the following morning, there was no relapse; the child remained calm and the problem never recurred. [p. 79]

From the authors' perspective—and that of discontinuous change—the father's taking the daughter to school interrupted the interactional pattern that had developed among the mother, daughter, and those at school, allowing a new problem-free pattern to emerge.

Two condensed case studies can illustrate what discontinuous change looks like in brief therapy. The first is of my treatment of the woman mentioned at the outset of this article.

> When Jennifer, a couple of months after breaking up once again with her unstable manfriend James, began receiving 2:30 A.M. phone calls from him asking if he should commit himself to a mental hospital, she became desperate. She renewed contact with him and treated him compassionately, as she always had done; but she began to feel hopeless about ever escaping from him, her unsatisfying job, or her domineering father. She sought my assistance; and, fol-

lowing detailed questioning about her current situation and events leading up to it, I sent her home with a simple assignment: ask James to help her become more independent from her father.

The next session, Jennifer reported that James had reacted angrily to her request; and she was upset that, after all she had done for him, he wouldn't help her with a problem of her own. I suggested she call James at 2:30 A.M., so he would understand how important the request was to her.

Therapy lasted five sessions. During that period of time and in the months following termination, many changes took place. Jennifer broke up with James for good, applied to graduate school in a field different from her work (something her father had opposed), and was accepted by and entered a graduate program in a distant city (her father had opposed her moving away and she had felt too timid to do so). Prior to leaving, she invited her parents for dinner at her apartment—something she had never done—in a step toward a more egalitarian relationship among them.

From my point of view, Jennifer's asking James to help her interfered with the ongoing pattern of her taking care of him; and as that relationship reorganized it had ramifications in ever larger parts of her social field (and, presumably, of his).

The other case example is of the initial phase of my treatment of a family consisting of a father, a mother, and their 10½-year-old daughter Mary. They sought out family treatment because, according to the parents, they all had problems: Mary was picked on by her classmates (though she was doing well in school), had no friends, and was disobedient at home; the mother was depressed; all three had low self-esteem and were easily hurt; and the parents indicated that they had marital problems related to their daughter. They also indicated that

Mary's behavior was the most important problem and the primary reason they were seeking therapy, though I couldn't get a clear sense of why it was so important.

Given the parents' priorities, I spent much of the second session trying to get them to agree on something they wanted their daughter to do differently. With considerable difficulty I got them to agree (1) that she should make her bed every day before noon, (2) on a detailed definition of what constituted a made bed, and (3) on the consequences for making and for not making her bed.

In the third session, it turned out that the effects of the intervention had been mixed (e.g., some slovenly bed making), and that the parents disagreed over whether change was taking place. Had the result been more positive, I might have continued in the same vein. However, given the parental discord evident in the first two sessions, I switched to a paradoxical task (Papp 1983, Selvini Palazzoli et al. 1978) that I had prepared as a backup. I read the following explanation aloud and led them through a rehearsal of the ritual described below, which I asked them to do as indicated:

> Mary has low self-esteem and disobeys so that you (mom and dad—especially mom) can worry about her. By having low self-esteem, she shows that she is like her mom, and by disobeying she distracts her mom from worrying about herself—since she can worry about Mary instead. In addition, Mary gives her dad a chance to support her mom by getting him to yell at Mary when she acts up.
>
> For this reason, it might not be a good idea for Mary to change. Instead, the family can celebrate her helpfulness by performing the following ritual at least once a day—and extra times when she is particularly unhappy or disobedient:
>
> Mom lies down.

Mary stands at her side, holds her hand, and says, "It's all right, Mom. You don't have to worry. I'm unhappier than you."

Father pats Mary on the head, smiles at her, and says, "That's my girl!"

When the family came for the next session, it turned out that dramatic changes had taken place. Though they had performed the ritual only a few times, Mary's disobedience and low self-esteem had ceased to be problems. She had made her bed every day, and had even cleaned up her room without being asked. She had also slept over one night at the house of one of her friends—though the sudden appearance of those friends was unexplained. I dismissed Mary from therapy with the comment that her parents seemed not to need her help anymore. While she was in the waiting room, her parents revealed that they had had a big blowup about their sexual relationship during the same week, and the focus of therapy shifted to the marital relationship. In addition, the father, an ex-Marine, revealed the reason that he had considered Mary's problems to be so important. Her disobedience and talking back to him had made him so furious that he was afraid he might lose control and harm her.

From my point of view, the ritual interfered with the pattern of Mary's problem behavior deflecting the hostile interaction between her parents. Once her unhappiness and disobedience were redefined as helpful, they ceased to be useful in provoking parental concern and anger. Her withdrawal from the marital conflict led in turn to its escalation and the concomitant revelation of previously secret information. In addition, this example illustrates the difference between gradual change with the first intervention and discontinuous change with the second one.

In all three examples, it is the sudden and qualitative shift—

resulting from a change in the interactional pattern of which the problem behavior is a part—that makes it reasonable to regard the change as discontinuous.

While the idea of discontinuous change may itself appear discontinuous, we may point to intellectual antecedents that set the stage for it or provoke it. Probably the most important of these is a shift from viewing the universe as a harmonious and comprehensible Newtonian clockwork to recognizing it as operating probabilistically (quantum mechanics) and being, in principle, partially unknowable (Wolf 1989). In physics, the Heisenberg uncertainty principle set limits to what is knowable by pointing out the way in which making observations alters that which is being observed (Wolf 1989). Even more fundamentally, Gödel's proof demonstrated that mathematics, the logical language in which science expresses itself, is incomplete (Hofstadter 1980). That is, mathematical statements exist whose truth or falsity cannot be determined. Furthermore, given any unknown mathematical proposition, it is impossible to determine whether it is one of those undecidables.

Within the physical and biological sciences, discontinuous change has already achieved prominence in diverse areas. It can be found in the evolutionary theory of punctuated equilibrium, in which new species are thought to form rapidly and then remain stable over long periods of time (Eldredge 1985), in contrast to the theory of slower and more long-term gradual evolution. In addition, mass extinctions are thought to play an important role in evolution. For example, a random event—a comet striking the earth—may have been responsible for the extinction of the dinosaurs and most contemporaneous species (Eldredge 1985). Ecologists speak of the unpredictable effects of putting new substances into the biosphere; and global warming and depletion of the ozone layer are considered as (possibly) disastrous examples of unwanted discontinuous change (Fishman and Kalish 1990; Schneider 1989). Chaos theory has become prominent in many areas of science, as patterns of discontinuous change are found in the weather, population dynamics, heart and brain activity, and epidemiology (Gleick 1987, Pool 1989a,b,c). In mathematics, the area known as dynamical systems has experienced new excitement as an outgrowth of its applicability to the understanding of chaotic phenomena (Abraham et al. 1990; Devaney 1989, Ornstein 1989). (Since mathematics exists independently of the sciences, the attention to discontinuous change can be seen not as constituting new discoveries about the world but as reflecting an interest in such issues within mathematicians' social communities.) In fact, the history of science itself has come to be viewed as consisting of alternating periods of normal science and revolutionary paradigm change (Kuhn 1962)—an image of scientific evolution similar to the punctuated equilibrium theory of the evolution of life.

Outside of the physical and biological sciences, where discontinuous change has not yet become a prominent way of thinking, there are many signs of its growing importance. Within the arts, which are sometimes thought to be harbingers of new ways of thinking, chance elements have played an important role in recent work (Pool 1989d). There have been deliberate attempts to introduce randomness into the creation of contemporary music, dance, painting, sculpture, and literature.

Meanwhile, increasingly frequent examples can be found within the social and behavioral sciences of theoretical conceptualizations and practical applications involving discontinuous change. For example, in anthropology, rubbish theory (Thompson 1979) deals with the way artifacts such as cars, houses, or curios gradually lose value over time, then go through a period of worthlessness (rubbish), following which certain ones suddenly enter a phase of high and increasing value as antiques. Applications of chaos theory are being studied in economics, exploring whether the business cycle or the stock market behave chaotically, and in political science, applying chaos theory to the arms race (Gleick 1987, Pool 1989d). Social scientists are rethinking their views of child-rearing practices, as the emphasis shifts from the individual, with his or her own life cycle, to the family system and its organizational life cycle. Particular attention is now being paid to events at transition points in patterns of family interaction (Hoffman 1981), especially when new members enter or leave the system (e.g., the birth of a child, or an adolescent leaving home). We are now looking at how effectively the family as a whole reorganizes following such transitions, rather than just focusing on the members as individuals (e.g., no longer viewing parents' behavior as merely a collection of specific parenting skills or expressions of their personalities). Systems theory—with a concept of interference with state-maintaining processes leading to discontinuous change—is becoming an important force in psychotherapy; and many new brief therapies have been developed (e.g., Haley 1987, Minuchin 1974, Papp 1983, Watzlawick et al. 1974). As the case examples illustrated, problems are generally viewed as part of a complex pattern of repetitive interaction among people (rather than as existing within individuals); and therapeutic strategies are aimed at provoking change to qualitatively different problem-free patterns. Not surprisingly, therapists influenced by systems theory often work with a couple or family, rather than with an individual; and some professionals have begun consulting with businesses and other non-familial organizations to deal with interpersonal problems in those larger interactive contexts (Selvini Palazzoli et al., 1984).

As the concept of discontinuous change becomes more widely known, its usefulness is likely to be explored in increasingly diverse areas. It will be interesting to see what unexpected changes the future brings.

17

Uses of Paradox
in Supervision

Supervision, as an activity, falls somewhere in the area of overlap between teaching and therapy. Regardless of whether differences among these endeavors are more a matter of social labeling or reflections of distinct interactional patterns, their differing emphases are readily recognizable. Supervision is like teaching in that it involves the supervisor helping the supervisee to master knowledge and skills that are specifiable in at least a general way. And supervision—at least clinical supervision—is like therapy in that it involves a significant relationship in which the supervisor attempts to bring about changes in the supervisee's thoughts, feelings, and actions, especially self-directed ones.

People come to supervisors for help with problems different from those they bring to teachers or therapists. For this reason, both the nature of difficulties that arise in the course of supervision and ways of dealing with them tend to be somewhat different. When supervision is going smoothly, the role of the supervisor is more like that of a teacher. Issues of knowledge and skills predominate, and the supervisor (or at least this supervisor) attempts to be as clear as possible in order to facilitate learning. When problems arise, however, the supervisor may have to become more like a therapist. That is, rather than focusing solely on the content at hand, the supervisor may have to direct interventions toward the relationship in order to get the process moving again.

Paradoxical interventions have played an important role in therapy, particularly as ways of dealing with resistant clients and families (Fisch et al. 1982, Haley 1984, Madanes 1981, Palazzoli et al. 1978, Papp 1983, Watzlawick 1974). Such interventions, while at first appearing to be inconsistent with the goals of therapy, are actually designed to attain them. Given the wide range of problems with which they have been used, it seemed logical to try using them to resolve impasses in supervision, particularly when more direct approaches had already failed or seemed destined for failure.

The following examples from my supervisory experience are provided to illustrate the use of paradox in academic and clinical supervision with both individuals and groups of supervisees. My hope in choosing these examples is to illustrate the use of paradox in a range of supervisory relationships.

Example 1. A male graduate student who had done well in a couple of my courses asked to do an independent study with me, reviewing research in the area of paradox. While he was a bright and highly motivated student, whose seriousness, competence, and imagination I respected, I had noticed that a particular pattern of interaction had arisen with him in the past. In brief, he would ask intelligent questions, which I would do my best to answer. He would be appreciative of my answers, but would respond with more questions—indicating that perhaps he hadn't understood fully or that I had neglected to respond to some aspect of his question. Eventually, either in a sequence of questions, or over a period of time, he would become disappointed with me, communicating nonverbally either frustration at my not telling him The Answer that he knew I possessed or disappointment that I had not lived up to the high opinion of me that he believed I merited.

Since the independent study was in an area in which no one had all the answers, I felt reasonably sure that over the course of the semester the pattern would repeat itself. And since the independent study would involve just the two of us—without other students to turn to once the cycle got going—I felt that preventive measures were in order. I decided to predict the behavior, making its spontaneous occurrence less likely. Thus, in one of our early sessions, I said to him, "Since we're going to be working together all semester on this project, I thought I should mention to you a pattern that seems to have occurred between us in the past. Sometimes, when I've been unable to answer your questions, I've had the sense that you were frustrated with me or disappointed with me. I thought that I should mention it, so that we can recognize it if it occurs."

"You're doing it!" he said.

"I'm just pointing something out, so that we can both be alert to see if it happens."

He briefly insisted that I was using some kind of paradox with him, but when he saw that I responded only to the subject at hand and not to why I was doing what I was doing, he returned to the topic of the independent study. I am pleased to report that he didn't become frustrated or disappointed with me in the manner predicted. The course went quite well: I referred him to some readings he found helpful; he came up with some references that I had been unaware of; he wrote an excellent paper; and we both had some interesting insights that, however, fell short of divine revelation.

Example 2. A foreign-born female graduate student was working with me on a proposal for her doctoral dissertation. While she was competent in the research skills necessary for the task, her written English was quite weak. I had agreed to direct her research with the understanding that we would have two goals: that she would complete her dissertation and that she would learn to write English on a professionally acceptable level. Accordingly, she had made contact with a friend of hers who was an English teacher and who had agreed to go over all drafts of her work before they were submitted to me. The point of this exercise was not only to save me work but to use samples of her own technical writing as a basis for improving her skills.

As we worked on the project, she emphasized to me her desire to complete the dissertation rapidly. She indicated that she was a divorced working mother who had to provide for her adolescent son, and that she needed to complete her graduate training so that she could get a better-paying job. I expressed my willingness to do whatever was necessary to move her along as quickly as possible but emphasized that the key to rapid progress was the quality of her work. She, in turn, said that she would work hard and meet the terms of our agreement in order to finish rapidly.

I soon discovered that the quality of the writing in her drafts was quite poor, that they were extremely messy, and that changes that I requested often did not appear in subsequent drafts. In speaking with her, it seemed that part of the difficulty might have been due to her friend's lack of familiarity with psychological concepts and terminology, and part to a hesitation that some English teachers have to tinker with a person's unique style of expression. However, many of the errors were so egregious that it was inconceivable that her friend could have missed them. She then revealed that sometimes she went over drafts with her manfriend (an accountant) so as not to trouble the teacher too frequently. In addition, she began to criticize me as a nitpicker and refer pointedly to the way I was delaying her dissertation. I, in turn, became frustrated with her, told her that I refused to compromise on quality . . . and decided that something had to be done to put an end to the conflict that was escalating between us.

As I reviewed in my mind what had been going on, it seemed that the central issue was the one of her self-imposed deadline. She was cutting corners in order to meet it, and I was doing my best to help her to meet it, while becoming increasingly frustrated with her demands on me. Meanwhile, despite the extra time I was putting in going over unsatisfactory drafts, progress was actually slowing down—since it takes more time to submit a hasty draft and then revise it than to get it right the first time.

Accordingly, I implemented the following strategy. The next time she handed in a draft, I made corrections on the first page or two, and then stopped. At our meeting, I handed the entire document back to her (about forty pages) and indicated gently that while I had made corrections at the beginning, there really were too many errors for me to address. I told her that I had thought about the work, and that she really was being too hard on herself. There was no need to hurry in finishing the dissertation. I said that she should take her time with it and enjoy life. After all, she had gotten along without a Ph.D. for a long time, and there was no reason that another year or two—or even three—would make a difference. As long as she was working on it, I would stick by her. She reacted with vociferous amazement, protesting that she really did want to finish it as soon as possible. I responded in a calm·and supportive manner, reemphasizing that she was being too hard on herself and suggesting that she take it easy.

The interval before her next draft was longer than preceding ones, but its quality was significantly improved. In addition, she raised issues regarding the organization of the project that indicated inaccurate assumptions I never suspected she had. For example, she seemed to believe that the point of the literature review was to show that she had read voluminously on the topic (certainly a reasonable secondary goal) but wasn't aware that its primary purpose was to provide a logical and empirical rationale for the study she was proposing to undertake. Naturally, once these assumptions were brought out into the open, it was possible to correct them. In retrospect, it was easy to see that the conflict we had been locked in prevented her from revealing her inaccurate assumptions, since she felt herself under attack and would naturally hesitate to reveal areas of vulnerability.

In the weeks following my new approach, she finally developed an acceptable dissertation proposal. Whenever she began to press me to speed up, I would suggest that she slow down; and in this way the project was completed in an atmosphere of cooperation.

Example 3. I met once a week for three hours with a group of five advanced graduate students to supervise therapy cases that they were attending at placements in field settings. They were all beginning therapists, three women and two men; and one of the women is the subject of this example.

While she spoke in a quiet monotone, and with a carefully deferential manner, her overall style was passive aggressive. In particular, when I would comment on her work—and sometimes when I would discuss a theoretical or technical matter with the group—she would politely disagree with me with extraordinary persistence. Following a string of disclaimers regarding what an interesting, thought-provoking, or otherwise useful comment I had made, she would offer a well-intentioned *but*, followed by an explanation. This sequence of *yes-but*'s would go on without termination following any further explanations I might offer—or, for that matter, attempts on the part of other members of the group to intervene. The only ways to terminate the sequence were for me eventually to say something like "Well, you may have a point there," or otherwise agree with her or, alternatively, to infringe impolitely on her freedom of speech by insisting that we move on to discuss other matters. Either of these moves seemed to be followed by the faint trace of a smile on her face.

One day, as I finished commenting on a presentation of hers, I noticed her inhaling in preparation for her predictable reply. I held her off with the following request: "Could you phrase what you're about to say in such a way as to disagree with me?"

She responded with a protracted and uncharacteristic pause, following which she said that she wasn't sure that she agreed with my orientation and gave specific examples of areas of disagreement. I told her that all that was required from her was to understand the point of view I was presenting, that I recognized that her theoretical orientation was her own concern and I hoped it would continue to evolve throughout her career. I did expect her to try out my suggestions because I thought she might learn something from them, but if what she learned was that they were bad ideas, that was fine with me.

We had a rational discussion for a few more minutes, following which we returned to the clinical material. The unending series of *yes-but*'s no longer occurred during supervision.

Example 4. I met once a week for three hours with a group of eight advanced graduate students to supervise therapy cases that they were attending at placements in field settings. They were all beginning therapists, three women, and five men; and this example concerns three of the men.

The group of eight was a close-knit one—in part because of comments I had made during an orientation session two years previously. I had told them that a strategy of cooperation and working together would be more likely than competition to lead to success in the program. They had apparently taken this advice to heart and had developed an unusual degree of comradeship and closeness.

In my introduction to supervision I had emphasized that it required aspects of appropriate behavior that were more like therapy and other clinical interactions than like academic courses. Thus, all supervisees were expected to attend all sessions (barring illness or disaster, in which case they were to call to cancel in advance, if possible) and to be there on time. Since I was doing group supervision, I explained, it was best to start with everyone present.

Despite this introduction, three of the men in the group displayed a pattern of lateness and missing sessions. The first frequently arrived between a half hour and an hour late (though demonstrating the potential for becoming a talented therapist). The second—who still retained some of the flower child rebelliousness of the sixties—arrived equally late and sometimes missed sessions with poor excuses (though performing adequately in his clinical work). The third arrived equally late while missing numerous sessions. This last therapist was performing poorly: his personal problems were clearly interfering with his understanding of and interaction with a client. I should mention that he complained of his client being poorly motivated, coming late, and missing sessions. I approached this in part with indirect suggestions such as, "She'll have to learn that *you can't solve your problems by coming late"*—with indifferent results.

I first attempted to deal with the problem of lateness and

missed sessions by reemphasizing the rules of supervision—to no avail. Next, I attempted to get the group to arrive at a mutually acceptable solution. In the discussion that I led, no one suggested punitive consequences for unacceptable behavior. When I raised the possibility of fines paid by latecomers to those who were on time—or some similar solution—the group was unanimous in its negative reaction. Instead, their solution was for us all to meet a half hour earlier for coffee, and then to begin at the appointed hour.

I went along with this proposal for several weeks, during which time I met with the punctual therapists for coffee, while the other three continued their pattern of lateness and missed sessions unabated. Eventually, it became clear that stronger measures were called for.

I reasoned that the group's closeness—for which I was at least partially responsible—was preventing them from taking any action to discipline wayward members. It seemed, therefore, that an appropriate intervention would be one aimed at the entire group, in which the acceptance of lateness and missed sessions was defined as disruptive rather than supportive of group solidarity. Accordingly, once I had the entire group together, I made a little speech more or less as follows:

> I know that you're all starting out as therapists, and that you're self-conscious about your clinical work. For that reason I had hoped that I wouldn't have to say this; but I can't avoid it any longer. I just don't think it's fair that those of you who have been coming on time have set up the latecomers as scapegoats. We seem to be spending much of our time talking about lateness and missed sessions, so that all of you can avoid the anxiety involved in a close examination of your functioning as therapists.

The behavioral changes following this intervention were more dramatic than I had anticipated. The first of the late therapists began coming on time, and the second one stopped missing sessions and began arriving only five or ten minutes late—which I felt I could live with. The third therapist dropped out of the graduate program. He had been having a variety of personal, familial, and economic problems—the dimensions of which I had been only dimly aware of— that ultimately became too much for him. He obtained permission to finish out the semester in his practicum courses and limped through the remaining weeks more or less as before—but without the "symptomatic" collusion of his classmates.

In considering these four examples, I would like to make two brief points. First, 1 resorted to paradoxical interventions only when a more straightforward "teaching" approach either wasn't working or appeared likely to fail. Since the goals of supervision involve the mastery of knowledge and skills, indirect approaches run the risk of creating confusion where clarity is desired. (Naturally, a supervisee might be overly clear, and inaccurately so, about complex and subtle issues. If he or she resisted direct and varied attempts to deal with the matter, the supervisor might want to sow some confusion. But this is not an exception to the general principle of proceeding in a straightforward manner as long as it works.) In this way, paradoxical interventions can be seen as consistent with the goals of supervision, since they involve removing blocks to a task-oriented intellectual approach.

The other point, which follows from the above, is that once change took place I returned to a straightforward didactic approach. That is, when supervision is achieving its goals there is no need for elaborate indirect interventions. "If it ain't broke, don't fix it."

18

Relativity:
A Game for the
Nuclear Family

If the systems movement is ever to attain the significance of psychoanalysis or behaviorism, it will have to become a part of everyday life. Inspired by Liddle and Saba's (1981) "Systemic Chic," I first considered designing systemic apparel to further the noble cause. For several days I wore my belt buckled as a Möbius strip, but was distressed to find both the belt and my waist developing a crease. Alarmed by these linear manifestations, I abandoned my design for Calvin Kleinbottle jeans.

After going around in circles for a few days, the environment that I was unaware of organized me to conclude that I could make a greater contribution by inventing a family game. After all, if psychoanalysts and behaviorists could so powerfully influence family life, why shouldn't systemic therapists be equally disruptive? Hence, Relativity.

Relativity is a good, clean, wholesome game, fun for the entire family. Its name is based not so much on its explosive potential as on the expression "Where there's a will, there's relatives."

Since systems theory does not subscribe to linear causality, the consequences of playing the game are unknown. For this reason, it might be better only to imagine playing the game, rather than actually to play it.

GAME INSTRUCTIONS

Organizing the Game

Relativity is a family game and is to be played by the entire nuclear family when at home together. Since it is a verbal game, it might not be suitable for children who are too young to understand their part. (In one sense, this limitation is an open question, since it is arguable that all children understand their parts only too well. In any event, one could always try, and see what happens.)

Before actually playing, the parents have to get together privately to decide on the "names-of-the game." This is done by shared introspection. That is, the mother decides who in her family of origin each other member of the family reminds her of, and the father makes similar decisions for his family of origin. This should usually be obvious, but if a particular person presents a problem, previous slips of the tongue or similar behavior can offer helpful clues. For example, if father has several times in the past accidentally called his son "Joe" (his younger brother's name), that might suggest that "Joe" would be a good name-of-the-game for his son *relative to him*.

For each name-of-the-game, a reciprocal name or designation must be chosen for the other person to call the parent.

Thus, while father's name-of-the-game for son might be "Joe," son's name-of-the-game for father would be "big brother." (Calling father by his own name would be unacceptable, since it would be unclear that the name was being used in relation to father's younger brother, rather than to his son. Such substitutions are also useful when the same name appears more than once in a family.) If son reminds mother of her father, then she would call him "dad" or whatever she called her father, and he would call her "daughter." Note that the gender of family members can be disregarded in choosing names. Thus, if son reminds mother of her big sister Alice, she would call him "Alice" and he would call her "little sister."

Naturally, some families may have to adapt the rules to their special organization. Single-parent families, families with grandparents sharing their living quarters, families with more children than there are members in a parent's family of origin, and reconstituted (remarried) families are examples that come immediately to mind. In each instance, however, a solution can easily be found if the intent of the instructions is followed. That is, pairs of names should be substituted for each one-to-one relationship involving a parent, so that both the parent and other family member know whom they have been relabeled as in relation to each other. (Children retain their normal identities in relation to one another.)

Playing the Game

Once the parents have organized the game by arranging pairs of names-of-the-game for all relationships in which they are involved, the game can be played whenever the entire family is together. All that is necessary is to explain the pairs of names to the children and then continue life as usual—except that the new names are to be used in all communications.

One difficulty in explaining names is that everyone has to

learn that she or he has a different identity with each person spoken to. For example, an older sister would not only have to learn to call her mother "big sister" and her father "son," but would have to remember that she is "Amy" to her mother and "mom" to her father—while remaining unchanged in relation to her younger brother. Parents need to learn new identities for each other that go with each of their children.

Learning all these new identities takes time. For this reason, the game should be played for at least half an hour, so that at least ten minutes or so of interaction takes place with all participants comfortable in their new multiple roles.

Surprising though it may seem, it is possible that some family members might not like the game (or might not like certain roles in it). For this reason, the timing of its end—or for that matter, the decision of whether or not to play it again—is best left to the family's normal decision-making processes. It may fizzle out, end abruptly (e.g., when one or more players leave), or end by an explicit agreement to stop forthwith or after a specified period of time. Some families may even decide in advance how long they would like to play. Any of these alternatives is fine, as long as adequate time is allowed for all players to become comfortable with their multiple new roles.

As indicated, the game may be played whenever the entire family is together. Thus, if it were played at dinner by a family of four with a son and daughter, a brief interaction might sound like the following:

Father to son: Pass the salt, please, little brother.
Son to father: Here you are, big brother.
Daughter to father: May I have the salt when you're through, son?
Mother to father: Isn't the food salty enough, dad?
Father to mother: It's fine, little sister.
Father to daughter: Here you are, mom.

Aftermath

As you can see, this is a hell of a game! While the novelty may wear off after a while, a certain amount of laughter can be expected. Some people may find that it helps to try not to laugh—or at least not to laugh too much. Who knows? Some implicit family rules might even be made explicit or some family secrets hinted at.

A Modest Proposal: Prescription for the Family Therapy Movement

Family therapists have shown a laudable willingness to confront the big issues, to view therapy from a systems perspective, to understand and attempt to change behavior in the context of ever larger networks of human relationships. As family therapy has grown to the proportions of a true therapeutic movement, the time has come for us to grasp the reins of our destiny. If we truly have the instruments of change at our command, only a failure of courage or of faith can prevent us from using them on ourselves on a grand scale.

Where to begin? The answer lies with history. Let us look at the successful therapeutic movements of yesterday to find the key to their success; then we may unlock the future. As has been observed countless times, "Those who do not repeat the past are doomed to forget its lessons."

History teaches us that conflict is at the center of creative change. This is evident in a study of the growth of the psychoanalytic empire. Psychoanalysis was a movement of little significance until Freud, Jung, Adler, and others really began to have a go at one another. As a result of their battles, the analytic movement burgeoned and, before long, they actually had something worth fighting over.

In recent times, we have seen the same pattern with behavior therapy: the halcyon days of cooperative impotence have been succeeded by the era of creative fratricide. As the followers of Skinner, Lazarus, Wolpe, and others pummel one another into (temporary) submission, the movement reaches new peaks of influence.

And so, the path is clear for us. The prescription has written itself: conquest through self-annihilation!

Let us focus on our differences, not on what we have in common. Never discuss a substantive issue where an ad hominem attack will do. In our hospitals, clinics, and universities, let us strive for victories of principle and not be lured to ignominy by the sirens of live-and-let-live. And, in our professional organizations, let us heap scorn on those who deviate from the truth.

Only thus can we grasp our opportunity; only then will we fulfill our destiny.

Epilogue

I hadn't expected to write an epilogue; but even while writing this book, my orientation has continued to evolve. I've gotten quite interested in the solution focused therapy of Steve de Shazer and associates at the Brief Family Therapy Center (BFTC) of Milwaukee (de Shazer 1982, 1984, 1985, 1988, 1989, 1991, 1994, de Shazer et al. 1986, Walter and Peller 1992). This approach challenges the assumption that solutions are necessarily related to problems, and even questions the relevance of notions of causality to changing human behavior.

De Shazer's work is clearly described, open to research, sensitive to the social and cultural context of behavior, rejects the medical model of behavioral problems and their treatment, and is committed to brief treatment (thereby allowing people to live their daily lives without the interference of therapists and the mental health system). In short, solution focused therapy seems to share all of my relevant values except a commitment to integrating theoretical models of therapy with those of general psychology and thereby with the rest of science.

A thorough discussion of solution focused therapy is beyond the scope of this presentation; for those who are interested, the best place to start is with de Shazer's 1988 book *Clues: Investigating Solutions in Brief Therapy*, and Walter and Peller's 1992 how-to-do-it guide *Becoming Solution-Focused in Brief Therapy*. The following is my current thinking about five important elements in de Shazer's work.

1. *Define goals rather than problems*. Since the approaches I have been concerned with all emphasize clear goal definition, what is most distinctive here is the deemphasis on problem definition. "As long as you know where you're going and how to get there, it isn't important to know where you're coming from," BFTC therapists seem to assert. While other therapists would contend that a careful definition of the problem will indicate how to solve it (like producing a template for a key to open a lock), solution focused therapists argue that general principles of reaching solutions are sufficient; a skeleton key will do (de Shazer 1985).

2. *Emphasize "solution talk" rather than "problem talk."* Solution focused therapists argue that "problem talk" is self-perpetuating, while "solution talk" leads to change. It would appear that "solution talk" can be described in part as a process of changing clients' response expectancies to become more positive. In addition, the focus on what is going well ("solution talk") and deemphasis on what is going wrong ("problem talk") may also function as a distraction task. That is, if trying to solve a problem is sometimes like trying not to think of the word "hippopotamus," then "solution talk" can be seen

as analogous to listening to music or playing basketball—activities that have nothing whatsoever to do with hippopotamuses, or even words. On the other hand, there may be more to solution talk than the combined effects of changing clients' response expectancies and a distraction task.

3. *"Deconstruct" the problem*. Solution focused therapists attempt to demonstrate that because there are exceptions to the problem, the client's predicament isn't what it seems (e.g., uncontrollable or hopeless). Once again, I am interested in seeing whether the "deconstruction" process can adequately be understood as a persuasive process aimed at changing the client's negative expectancies.

4. *Find exceptions to the problem and encourage them to increase*. This is the main therapeutic strategy, though a wide variety of techniques and interventions has been developed to implement it. The question is whether this strategy can adequately be understood as one of increasing the frequency of competing responses (alternatives to problem behavior in the same situations) through a variety of means, including the modification of response expectancies.

5. *Encourage clients' expectation of change*. On the face of it, this seems to be the same as altering response expectancies (the placebo effect). Even so, a close examination of what solution focused therapists do—particularly as regards interventions based on implicitly systemic thinking—may indicate something distinctive that differs from or goes beyond the processes described by Jerome Frank (1961), Irving Kirsch (1990), and me (Fish 1973).

While there are differences between these five elements and the five principles discussed in Chapter 5, there is no basic inconsistency between them—except, perhaps, the assertion of solution focused therapists that it is unnecessary to define problems in order to solve them. Even here, focusing on solutions might be seen as a way of trying something different and seeing what happens.

As regards my considering ways of explaining solution focused therapy with concepts from general psychology (e.g., changing response expectancies, increasing competing responses, and using distraction), BFTC therapists would probably view such "explaining talk" as harmless, and fine with them if it makes me happy. In theoretical terms, however, they might prefer merely to describe behavior and what they do, and might question whether explanation is a useful or necessary concept in the therapy domain (and perhaps even for social behavior in general).

What is my reaction to this? I really don't know . . . yet.

So I have some thinking to do—and also some reading, some trying out of new ideas in therapy and supervision, and some discussing with colleagues. Perhaps I will even have to rethink some fundamental values (e.g., the importance of integrating theoretical models of therapy with those of general psychology). Then again, maybe I will be able to satisfy myself that solution focused therapy requires no new concepts—or no ascientific ones—to adequately explain it. In this case, both my understanding of the concepts that are adequate to explain solution focused therapy and my ability to apply them in practice will have been broadened and deepened.

I have no idea what I will think about solution focused therapy a year from now, or five years from now.

The process continues.

References

Abraham, F. D., Abraham, R. H., Shaw, C. D., and Garfinkel, A. (1990). *A Visual Introduction to Dynamical Systems Theory for Psychologists*. Santa Cruz, CA: Aerial.

Abramson, L. Y., Seligman, M. E. P., and Teasdale, J. D. (1978). Learned helplessness in humans: critique and reformulation. *Journal of Abnormal Psychology* 87: 49–74.

Ackerman, N. (1958). *The Psychodynamics of Family Life: Diagnosis and Treatment of Family Relationships*. New York: Basic Books.

Alland, A. (1971). *Human Diversity*. New York: Columbia University Press.

Azrin, N. H., and Nunn, R. G. (1974). A rapid method of eliminating stuttering by a regulated breathing approach. *Behavior Research and Therapy* 12: 279–286.

Bachrach, A. J., and Pattischal, E. G. (1960). An experiment in universal and personal validation. *Psychiatry* 23: 267–270.

Baer, L., Hurley, J. D., Minichiello, W. E., et al. (1992). EMDR workshop: Disturbing issues? *The Behavior Therapist* 15: 110–111.

Bandura, A. (1977a). Self-efficacy: toward a unifying theory of behavioral change. *Psychological Review* 84: 191–215.

_____ (1977b). *Social Learning Theory.* Englewood Cliffs, NJ: Prentice-Hall.

_____ (1982). The psychology of chance encounters and life paths. *American Psychologist* 37(7): 747–755.

Bateson, G. (1972). Culture contact and schismogenesis. In G. Bateson, *Steps to an Ecology of Mind*, pp. 61–72. New York: Ballantine. (First published in 1935.)

Bateson, G., Jackson, D. D., Haley, J., and Weakland, J. (1956). Toward a theory of schizophrenia. *Behavioral Science* 1: 251–264.

Belson, R. (1988). Introduction to special section on humor and strategic therapy. *Journal of Strategic and Systemic Therapies* 7(2): 1–2.

Bergin, A. E. (1962). The effect of dissonant persuasive communications upon changes in a self-referring attitude. *Journal of Personality* 30: 423–438.

_____ (1966). Some implications of psychotherapy research for therapeutic practice. *Journal of Abnormal Psychology* 71: 235–246.

_____ (1971). The evaluation of therapeutic outcomes. In *Handbook of Psychotherapy and Behavior Change: An Empirical Analysis*, ed. A. E. Bergin and S. L. Garfield, pp. 217–270. New York: Wiley.

Bergin, A. E., and Garfield, S. L., eds. (1971). *Handbook of Psychotherapy and Behavior Change: An Empirical Analysis*. New York: Wiley.

_____ (1994). *Handbook of Psychotherapy and Behavior*

Change: An Empirical Analysis, 4th ed. New York: Wiley.

Biaggio, A. M. B. (1980). The history of psychology in Brazil—with special emphasis on clinical psychology. In *Psychology in Latin America,* J. M. Fish, Chair. Symposium presented at the annual meeting of the American Psychological Association, Montreal, Quebec, Canada.

Bolton, H. C. (1888). *The Counting-out Rhymes of Children: Their Antiquity, Origin, and Wide Distribution.* New York-London. Reprinted 1972. New York: Gordon Press.

Breger, L., and McGaugh, J. L. (1965). Critique and reformulation of "learning theory" approaches to psychotherapy and neurosis. *Psychological Bulletin* 63: 338–358.

Brehm, J. W. (1966). *A Theory of Psychological Reactance.* New York: Academic.

Carroll, R. (1988). *Cultural Misunderstandings: The French-American Experience.* Chicago: University of Chicago Press.

Christie, R., and Geis, F. L. (1968). Some consequences of taking Machiavelli seriously. In *Handbook of Personality Theory and Research,* ed. E. F. Borgatta and W. W. Lambert, pp. 959–973. Chicago: Rand McNally.

_____ (1970). *Studies in Machiavellianism.* New York: Academic.

Cole, S. (1969). *The Unionization of Teachers: A Case Study of the UFT.* New York: Praeger.

Coyne, J. C. (1982). A brief introduction to epistobabble. *Family Therapy Networker* 6(4): 27–28.

Coyne, J. C., and Biglan, A. (1984). Paradoxical techniques in strategic family therapy: A behavioral analysis. *Journal of Behavior Therapy and Experimental Psychiatry* 15(3): 221–227.

Davison, G. C., and Valins, S. (1969). Maintenance of self-attributed and drug-attributed behavior change. *Journal of Personality and Social Psychology* 11: 25–33.

Degler, C. N. (1971). *Neither Black nor White: Slavery and Race*

Relations in Brazil and the United States. New York: Macmillan.

de Shazer, S. (1982). *Patterns of Brief Family Therapy.* New York: Guilford.

_____ (1984). The death of resistance. *Family Process* 23: 11–21.

_____ (1985). *Keys to Solution in Brief Therapy.* New York: Norton.

_____ (1988). *Clues: Investigating Solutions in Brief Therapy.* New York: Norton.

_____ (1989). Resistance revisited. *Contemporary Family Therapy* 11(4): 227–233.

_____ (1991). *Putting Difference to Work.* New York: Norton.

_____ (1994). *Words Were Originally Magic.* New York: Norton.

de Shazer, S., Berg, I. K., Lipchik, E., et al. (1986). Brief therapy: focused solution development. *Family Process* 25: 207–221.

Devaney, R. L. (1989). *An Introduction to Chaotic Dynamical Systems,* 2nd ed. Reading, MA: Addison-Wesley.

Dollard, J., and Miller, N. E. (1950). *Personality and Psychotherapy: An Analysis of Learning, Thinking, and Culture.* New York: McGraw.

Domhoff, G. W. (1974). *The Bohemian Grove and Other Retreats: A Study in Ruling-Class Cohesiveness.* New York: Harper & Row.

_____ (1983). *Who Rules America Now? A View for the 80's.* Englewood Cliffs, NJ: Prentice-Hall.

D'Zurilla, T. J., and Goldfried, M. R. (1971). Problem solving and behavior modification. *Journal of Abnormal Psychology* 78: 107–126.

Eldredge, N. (1985). *Time Frames: The Rethinking of Darwinian Evolution and the Theory of Punctuated Equilibria.* New York: Simon & Schuster.

Eysenck, H. J. (1952). The effects of psychotherapy: an evaluation. *Journal of Consulting Psychology* 16: 319–324.

Fisch, R., Weakland, J. H., and Segal, L. (1982). *The Tactics of Change*. San Francisco: Jossey-Bass.

Fish, J. M. (1970). Empathy and the reported emotional experiences of beginning psychotherapists. *Journal of Consulting and Clinical Psychology* 35: 64–69.

_____ (1973). *Placebo Therapy*. San Francisco: Jossey-Bass.

_____ (1992). EMDR workshop and openness. *The Behavior Therapist* 15: 180.

Fishman, J., and Kalish, R. (1990). *Global Alert: The Ozone Pollution Crisis*. New York: Plenum.

Forer, B. R. (1949). The fallacy of personal validation: a classroom demonstration of gullibility. *Journal of Abnormal and Social Psychology* 44: 118–123.

Frank, J. D. (1961). *Persuasion and Healing: A Comparative Study of Psychotherapy*. Baltimore: Johns Hopkins.

_____ (1973). *Persuasion and Healing: A Comparative Study of Psychotherapy*, 2nd ed. Baltimore: Johns Hopkins.

Frank, J. D., and Frank, J. B. (1991). *Persuasion and Healing: A Comparative Study of Psychotherapy*, 3rd ed. Baltimore: Johns Hopkins.

Franklin, B. (F.) (1969). Operant reinforcement of prayer. *Journal of Applied Behavior Analysis* 2: 247.

Freud, S. (1963a). Recommendations for physicians on the psychoanalytic method of treatment. In S. Freud, *Therapy and Technique*, pp. 117–126. New York: Collier. (First published in 1912.)

_____ (1963b). Analysis terminable and interminable. In S. Freud, *Therapy and Technique*, pp. 233–271. New York: Collier. (First published in 1937.)

Garfield, S. L., and Bergin, A. E., eds. (1978). *Handbook of Psychotherapy and Behavior Change: An Empirical Analysis*, 2nd ed. New York: Wiley.

_____ (1986). *Handbook of Psychotherapy and Behavior Change: An Empirical Analysis,* 3rd ed. New York: Wiley.

Gleick, J. (1987). *Chaos: Making a New Science.* New York: Viking Penguin.

Goldfried, M. R., and Merbaum, M. (1973). *Behavior Change Through Self-Control.* New York: Holt, Rinehart & Winston.

Gould, S. J. (1981). *The Mismeasure of Man.* New York: Norton.

_____ (1987). Freud's phylogenetic fantasy. *Natural History* 96(12): 10–19.

Haley, J. (1958). The art of psychoanalysis. *ETC* 15: 190–200.

_____ (1963). *Strategies of Psychotherapy.* New York: Grune & Stratton.

_____ (1973). *Uncommon Therapy: The Psychiatric Techniques of Milton H. Erickson, M. D.* New York: Norton.

_____ (1980). *Leaving Home.* New York: McGraw-Hill.

_____ (1984). *Ordeal Therapy: Unusual Ways to Change Behavior.* San Francisco: Jossey-Bass.

_____ (1987). *Problem Solving Therapy,* 2nd ed. San Francisco: Jossey-Bass.

Hall, E. T. (1959). *The Silent Language.* Garden City, NY: Doubleday.

_____ (1966). *The Hidden Dimension.* Garden City, NY: Doubleday.

Harris, M. (1964). *Patterns of Race in the Americas.* New York: Walker.

_____ (1968). *The Rise of Anthropological Theory: A History of Theories of Culture.* New York: Crowell.

_____ (1970). Referential ambiguity in the calculus of Brazilian racial identity. *Southwestern Journal of Anthropology* 26(1): 1–14.

_____ (1980). *Cultural Materialism: The Struggle for a Science of Culture.* New York: Vintage.

_____ (1981). *Why Nothing Works: The Anthropology of Daily*

Life. New York: Simon & Schuster.

———— (1989). *Our Kind: Who We Are, Where We Came From, Where We Are Going*. New York: Harper & Row.

Hayes, S. C. (1988). Contextualism and the next wave of behavioral psychology. *Behavior Analysis* 23: 7–22.

Hayes, S. C., Hayes, L. J., and Reese, H. W. (1988). Finding the philosophical core: a review of Stephen Pepper's *World Hypotheses*. *Journal of the Experimental Analysis of Behavior* 50: 97–111.

Heider, F. (1958). *The Psychology of Interpersonal Relations*. New York: Wiley.

Henry, W. E., Sims, J. H., and Spray, S. L. (1971). *The Fifth Profession*. San Francisco: Jossey-Bass.

Hoffman, L. (1981). *Foundations of Family Therapy*. New York: Basic.

Hofstadter, D. R. (1980). *Gödel, Escher, Bach: An Eternal Golden Braid*. New York: Basic.

Kelly, G. A. (1955). *The Psychology of Personal Constructs*. New York: Norton.

Kirsch, I. (1990). *Changing Expectations: A Key to Effective Psychotherapy*. Pacific Grove, CA: Brooks/Cole.

Koestler, A. (1972). Beyond atomism and holism: the concept of the holon. In *The Rules of the Game*, ed. T. Shanin. London: Tavistock.

Kohlberg, L. (1963). The development of children's orientations toward a moral order: I. Sequence in the development of moral thought. *Vita Humana* 6: 11–33.

Krasner, L. (1962). The therapist as a social reinforcement machine. In *Research in Psychotherapy*, vol. 2, ed. H. H. Strupp and L. Luborsky, pp. 61–94. Washington, DC: American Psychological Association.

———— (1976). On the death of behavior modification: some comments from a mourner. *American Psychologist* 31: 387–388.

_____, ed. (1980). *Environmental Design and Human Behavior: A Psychology of the Individual in Society.* New York: Pergamon.

Krasner, L., and Ullmann, L. P. (1973). *Behavior Influence and Personality: The Social Matrix of Human Action.* New York: Holt, Rinehart & Winston.

Kuhn, T. S. (1962). *The Structure of Scientific Revolutions.* Chicago: University of Chicago Press.

Lang, P. J., and Lazovik, A. D. (1963). Experimental desensitization of a phobia. *Journal of Abnormal and Social Psychology* 66: 519–525.

Lazarus, A. A. (1967). In support of technical eclecticism. *Psychological Reports* 21: 415–416.

_____ (1971). *Behavior Therapy and Beyond.* New York: McGraw-Hill.

_____ (1973). Multimodal behavior therapy: treating the "BASIC ID." *Journal of Nervous and Mental Disease* 156: 404–411.

_____ (1974). Multimodal therapy: BASIC ID. *Psychology Today* 7: 59–63.

Lazarus, A. A., and Abramovitz, A. (1962). The use of "emotive imagery" in the treatment of children's phobias. *Journal of Mental Science* 108: 191–195.

Lenski, G. (1966). *Power and Privilege.* New York: McGraw-Hill.

Lenski, G., and Lenski, J. (1974). *Human Societies: An Introduction to Macrosociology,* 2nd ed. New York: McGraw-Hill.

Leopold, W. F. (1952). *Bibliography of Child Language.* Evanston, IL: Northwestern University Press.

Levine, F. M., and Tilker, H. A. (1974). A behavior modification approach to supervision of psychotherapy. *Psychotherapy: Theory, Research, and Practice* 11: 182–188.

Liddle, H., and Saba, G. (1981). Systemic chic: family therapy's new wave. *Journal of Strategic and Systemic Therapies* 1(2): 36–39.

Lorion, R. P. (1978). Research on psychotherapy and behavior change with the disadvantaged: past, present, and future directions. In *Handbook of Psychotherapy and Behavior Change: An Empirical Analysis,* 2nd ed., ed. S. L. Garfield and A. E. Bergin, pp. 903–938. New York: Wiley.

Madanes, C. (1981). *Strategic Family Therapy*. San Francisco: Jossey-Bass.

———— (1984). *Behind the One-Way Mirror: Advances in the Practice of Strategic Therapy*. San Francisco: Jossey-Bass.

Manning, E. J. (1968). Personal validation: replication of Forer's study. *Psychological Reports* 23: 181–182.

Masters, W. H., and Johnson, V. E. (1970). *Human Sexual Inadequacy*. Boston: Little, Brown.

Mills, D., and Bishop, M. (1937). Onward and upward with the arts: songs of innocence. *New Yorker*, November 13, pp. 32–42.

Minuchin, S. (1974). *Families and Family Therapy*. Cambridge, MA: Harvard University Press.

Minuchin, S., and Fishman, H. C. (1981). *Family Therapy Techniques*. Cambridge, MA: Harvard University Press.

Minuchin, S., Montalvo, B., Guerney, B. G., et al. (1967). *Families of the Slums*. New York: Basic.

Mischel, W. (1968). *Personality and Assessment*. New York: Wiley.

Murdock, G. P. (1972). Anthropology's mythology: the Huxley memorial lecture, 1971. *Proceedings of the Royal Anthropological Institute of Great Britain and Ireland for 1971*.

Newton, E. (1979). *Mother Camp: Female Impersonators in America*. Chicago: University of Chicago Press.

Ornstein, D. S. (1989). Ergodic theory, randomness, and "chaos." *Science* 243: 182–186.

Orwell, G. (1954). Politics and the English language. In G.

Orwell, *A Collection of Essays,* pp. 162–177. Garden City, NY: Doubleday. (First published in 1946.)

Ostrander, S. A. (1984). *Women of the Upper Class*. Philadelphia, PA: Temple University Press.

Papp, P. (1983). *The Process of Change*. New York: Guilford.

Parloff, M. B., Goldstein, N., and Iflund, B. (1960). Communication of values and therapeutic change. *Archives of General Psychiatry* 2: 300–304.

Parloff, M. B., Waskow, I. E., and Wolfe, B. E. (1978). Research on therapist variables in relation to process and outcome. In *Handbook of Psychotherapy and Behavior Change: An Empirical Analysis,* 2nd ed., ed. S. L. Garfield and A. E. Bergin, pp. 233–282. New York: Wiley.

Parsons, T. (1951). Illness and the role of the physician: a sociological perspective. *American Journal of Orthopsychiatry* 21: 452–460.

Pentony, P. (1966). Value change in psychotherapy. *Human Relations* 19: 39–45.

_____ (1981). *Models of Influence in Psychotherapy*. New York: Macmillan.

Pepper, S. C. (1942). *World Hypotheses: A Study in Evidence*. Berkeley, CA: University of California Press.

Pike, K. (1954). *Language in Relation to a Unified Theory of the Structure of Human Behavior, vol. 1*. Dallas, TX: Summer Institute of Linguistics.

Pool, R. (1989a). Is it chaos or is it just noise? *Science* 243: 25–28.

_____ (1989b). Is it healthy to be chaotic? *Science* 243: 604–607.

_____ (1989c). Is something strange about the weather? *Science* 243: 1290–1293.

_____ (1989d). Chaos theory: how big an advance? *Science* 245: 26–28.

Reik, T. (1949). *Listening with the Third Ear*. New York: Farrar, Straus.

Reviewer, A. (1974). Comments. *Journal of Applied Behavior Analysis* 7: 497.

Rogers, C. R. (1951). *Client-Centered Therapy: Its Current Practice, Implications, and Theory.* Boston: Houghton Mifflin.

Rogers, C. R., Gendlin, G. T., Kiesler, D. V., and Truax, C. B. (1967). *The Therapeutic Relationship and Its Impact: A Study of Psychotherapy with Schizophrenics.* Madison: University of Wisconsin Press.

Rohrbaugh, M., Tennen, J., Press, S., et al. (1977). *Paradoxical Strategies in Psychotherapy.* Symposium presented at the annual meeting of the American Psychological Association, San Francisco.

Rosenthal, D. (1955). Changes in some moral values following psychotherapy. *Journal of Consulting Psychology* 19: 431–436.

Rotter, J. B. (1954). *Social Learning and Clinical Psychology.* Englewood Cliffs, NJ: Prentice-Hall.

Schachter, S. (1971). Some extraordinary facts about obese humans and rats. *American Psychologist* 26(2): 129–144.

Schneider, S. H. (1989). *Global Warming.* San Francisco: Sierra Club Books.

Scott, T. R. (1991). A personal view of the future of psychology departments. *American Psychologist* 46(9): 975–976.

Selvini Palazzoli, M., Anolli, L., Di Blasio, P., et al. (1984). *Dans les Coulisses de l'Organisation* [Behind the scenes of the organization]. Paris, France: Les Éditions ESF.

Selvini Palazzoli, M., Boscolo, L., Cecchin, G., and Prata, G. (1978). *Paradox and Counterparadox.* New York: Jason Aronson.

———— (1980). Hypothesizing—circularity—neutrality: three guidelines for the conductor of family interviews. *Family Process* 19: 3–12.

Shapiro, F. (1992). Dr. Francine Shapiro responds. *The Behavior Therapist* 15: 111, 114.

Skinner, B. F. (1971). *Beyond Freedom and Dignity*. New York: Knopf.

—— (1974). *About Behaviorism*. New York: Knopf.

Spradley, J. P. (1979). *The Ethnographic Interview*. New York: Holt, Rinehart & Winston.

—— (1980). *Participant Observation*. New York: Holt, Rinehart & Winston.

Stewart, E. C. (1972). *American Cultural Patterns: A Cross-Cultural Perspective*. Yarmouth, ME: Intercultural Press.

Stewart, E. C., and Bennett, M. J. (1991). *American Cultural Patterns: A Cross-Cultural Perspective*, 2nd ed. Yarmouth, ME: Intercultural Press.

Stone, L. J., and Church, J. (1957). *Childhood and Adolescence: A Psychology of the Growing Person*. New York: Random House.

Szasz, T. S. (1961). *The Myth of Mental Illness: Foundations of a Theory of Personal Conduct*. New York: Hoeber-Harper.

The new epistemology: What's it all about, Gregory? (1982). *Family Therapy Networker* 6(4): 26–27.

Thompson, M. (1979). *Rubbish Theory: The Creation and Destruction of Value*. New York: Oxford University Press.

Toffler, A. (1970). *Future Shock*. New York: Random House.

Ullmann, L. P., and Krasner, L. (1965). *Case Studies in Behavior Modification*. New York: Holt, Rinehart & Winston.

—— (1969). *A Psychological Approach to Abnormal Behavior*. Englewood Cliffs, NJ: Prentice-Hall.

Ulrich, R. E., Stachnick, T. J., and Stainton, S. R. (1963). Student acceptance of generalized personality interpretations. *Psychological Reports* 13: 831–834.

Upper, D. (1974). The unsuccessful self-treatment of a case of "writer's block." *Journal of Applied Behavior Analysis* 7: 497.

Walter, J. L., and Peller, J. E. (1992). *Becoming Solution-Focused in Brief Therapy*. New York: Brunner/Mazel.

Watzlawick, P., Beavin, J. H., and Jackson, D. D. (1967). *Pragmatics of Human Communication: A Study of Interactional Patterns, Pathologies, and Paradoxes.* New York: Norton.

Watzlawick, P., Weakland, J. H., and Fisch, R. (1974). *Change: Principles of Problem Formation and Problem Resolution.* New York: Norton.

Welkowitz, J., Cohen, J., and Ortmeyer, D. (1967). Value system similarity: investigation of patient–therapist dyads. *Journal of Consulting Psychology* 31: 48–55.

Winfree, A. T. (1987). *The Timing of Biological Clocks.* New York: Scientific American.

Wolf, F. (1989). *Taking the Quantum Leap: The New Physics for Nonscientists.* New York: Harper & Row.

Wolpe, J. (1958). *Psychotherapy by Reciprocal Inhibition.* Stanford, CA: Stanford University Press.

Wolpe, J., and Lazarus, A. A. (1966). *Behavior Therapy Techniques: A Guide to the Treatment of Neuroses.* New York: Pergamon.

Yablonsky, L. (1967). *Synanon: The Tunnel Back.* Baltimore, MD: Penguin.

Credits

I appreciate the permission to include the following brief works, all of which have been slightly changed from their original form:

Chapter 10 is based on my presentation at the 1980 conference of the Rocky Mountain Council on Latin American Studies. The procedings of the meeting were subsequently published and I am grateful to Dr. J. J. Brasch of the University of Nebraska, who edited the volume along with S. R. Rouch, for permission to use it here.

Chapter 11 was presented at the first Latin American regional meeting of the International Council of Psychologists in Campinas, São Paulo, Brazil, in 1978. I am grateful to the Pontifícia Universidade Católica de Campinas, which published the annals of that meeting, for permission to use it here.

Index